Media-Ready Feminism
and Everyday Sexism

SUNY series in Feminist Criticism and Theory
―――――――
Michelle A. Massé, editor

Media-Ready Feminism and Everyday Sexism

*How US Audiences
Create Meaning across Platforms*

**Andrea L. Press and
Francesca Tripodi**

Cover art by Gregory Dalton

Published by State University of New York Press, Albany

© 2021 State University of New York

All rights reserved

Printed in the United States of America

No part of this book may be used or reproduced in any manner whatsoever without written permission. No part of this book may be stored in a retrieval system or transmitted in any form or by any means including electronic, electrostatic, magnetic tape, mechanical, photocopying, recording, or otherwise without the prior permission in writing of the publisher.

For information, contact State University of New York Press, Albany, NY www.sunypress.edu

Library of Congress Cataloging-in-Publication Data

Names: Press, Andrea L., author | Tripodi, Francesca, author.
Title: Media-ready feminism and everyday sexism : how US audiences create meaning across platforms / Andrea L. Press and Francesca Tripodi.
Description: Albany : State University of New York Press, [2021] | Series: SUNY series in Feminist Criticism and Theory | Includes bibliographical references and index.
Identifiers: ISBN 9781438481951 (hardcover : alk. paper) | ISBN 9781438481975 (ebook) | ISBN 9781438481968 (pbk. : alk. paper)
Further information is available at the Library of Congress.

10 9 8 7 6 5 4 3 2 1

Andrea:
To my children, Jessica Beth Press-Williams and Joshua Michael Press-Williams, who have brought immeasurable joy to my life and will help create a nonsexist future.

Francesca:
To all the women in this world fighting for equality. May this book help expose the everyday sexism that keeps us from achieving our goals.

Contents

Acknowledgments	ix
Introduction	1
1 Considering the Limits of Extreme Misogyny: *Game of Thrones* as Feminist? (with Sarah Johnson-Palomaki)	21
2 Prudes, Sluts, and Sex: The Classing of Female Sexuality in the Era of Media-Ready Feminism	45
3 Balancing Work and Family: What "Choice" Conceals	67
4 Swipe Right for Consent: Hookup Culture, Tinder, and Structural Sexism	101
5 Wikipedia: Sign(s) Say Keep Out	127
Conclusion: A World Beyond Media-Ready Feminism	153
Notes	163
Bibliography	169
Index	201

Acknowledgments

We have been working on this book for a long time and owe a great debt to many fellow scholars, administrators, and mentors. We'd like to thank the University of Virginia Office of the Vice-Provost for Faculty, the College of Arts and Sciences, and the Power, Violence, and Inequality Collective for providing funding for the class that gathered the data we drew from in chapter 4. The Departments of Media Studies and Sociology contributed to this class as well, and we offer them thanks. Many of our common colleagues in both departments offered kind advice and support as we sought to bring this project to a close. In particular we are grateful to Allison Pugh for her incisive intellectual companionship and razor-sharp criticism of earlier proposal drafts. A great debt is also owed to our fabulous editor, Rebecca Colesworthy of State University of New York Press, who has been excited by this project since she learned of it. We have benefited much from her brilliant editorial eye and skillful stewardship through the review and revision process. We would also like to thank Michelle A. Massé, editor of the SUNY series in Feminist Criticism and Theory, for her constructive comments and support as she embraced this project. We are grateful as well to two anonymous reviewers whose comments and criticisms made this a much stronger book. In addition to our collective thanks we'd also like to take a moment to provide some individual acknowledgments.

Andrea Press: I'd first like to thank my fabulous colleagues in the Department of Media Studies for providing a generative, supportive, and inspiring intellectual home that nurtured and helped advance our ideas. In particular I'm grateful for Christopher Ali, Hector Amaya, Aniko Bodroghkozy, Andre Cavalcante, Shilpa Dave, Camilla Fojas, William Little, Jennifer Petersen, Siva Vaidhyanathan, Bruce Williams, and a whole new generation of colleagues including Meredith Clark, Kevin Driscoll, Jack Hamilton, Elizabeth Ellcessor, Aynne Kokas, David Nemer, and Lana Swartz, who will help with the next book. All have helped build one of the most exciting intellectual and collegial environments in my—or any—field. Thanks also to our Sociology colleagues, in particular Allison Pugh, Jennifer Bair, Sarah Corse, Fiona Greenland, and Josipa Roksa, who make going to work a joy. My advisees in Sociology, including Anna Cameron, Fan Mai, Bailey Troia, Mike Wayne, and Shayne Zaslow, and coauthors Francesca Tripodi and Sarah Johnson-Palomaki have made my work at the University of Virginia memorable and meaningful. Julia Adams, Laura Grindstaff, Sonia Livingstone, Peter Lunt, and Sherry Ortner—all close colleagues though living far afield—generously offered advice on earlier proposal drafts and gave extended critiques of our ideas as they germinated; we cannot imagine this effort without them. Thanks also to Julia Adams, June Deery, Tamar Katriel, Tamar Liebes, Sonia Livingstone, Angela McRobbie, Sherry Ortner, Jessica Ringrose, and Helen Wood for your invitations and your feedback on my presentations.

I have presented earlier drafts drawn from research conducted for this project to audiences in the Department of Communication and Media Studies at the London School of Economics, the Department of Cultural Studies at Beijing Culture and Language University, the Institute of Education at University College London, the Department of Communication and Journalism at Hebrew University, the Department of Communication at the University of Haifa, the Department of Anthropology at UCLA, the Department of Communication and Media Studies at Fordham University, the Department of Media and Communication at the University of Leicester, the Department of Sociology at Goldsmith's University, the Department of Communication and Media at Rensselaer Polytechnic Institute, the Department of Media and Communication at De Montfort University, the International Gender Studies Institute at Oxford University, and the University of Chicago. Together with Francesca we presented aspects of the book in the Department of Sociology and Calhoun College, Yale University. Many thanks to the colleagues who gave generous feedback and critique at these presentations.

I am particularly grateful for the support of my former colleague Tamar Liebes, who is no longer with us but whose legacy and camaraderie continue to inspire. She embodied the essence of the feminist spirit with her truly untiring and comprehensive support of women's intellectual work, and I and so many others miss her terribly. She is an enduring role model. I would like to also give a special thanks to the incomparable Sonia Livingstone for her valuable intellectual and personal friendship over the last several decades. She has been a consistent source of intellectual nurturance and I owe her an immense debt. She deserves all the awards she has garnered in her exceptional career and is a nurturant, generative presence that transcends description. I am also grateful for support from the International Gender Studies Institute, Oxford University; the Virginia Institute for the Humanities; the Yale Center for Comparative Research; and the University of Virginia for awarding me the William R. Kenan Jr. Endowed Professorship, which afforded additional research time for the writing of this book. Most of all, I am grateful to my coauthor, Francesca Tripodi, who exemplifies a collaborative academic spirit alongside a stunning commitment to do the highest quality work possible in the interests of those in society who stand to benefit most from truly feminist academic work. It has been a privilege to coauthor with her. We are both grateful to Sarah Johnson-Palomaki for her excellent research on *Game of Thrones* and for agreeing to collaborate with us on chapter 1.

I am very indebted to my children, Jessica Beth Press-Williams and Joshua Michael Press-Williams, for their continuing interest in my work and their attempts to clue me in to the experiences of newer generations of media consumers. They have grown up with this book and have shared their time with me with the writing of it. They have been unfailingly supportive and generous and are great role models for their mom. I am very proud of the kind, concerned, and committed adults they have become. Finally, I am profoundly grateful to my husband, Bruce A. Williams, to whom I owe a great intellectual and personal debt. I cannot imagine writing without hearing his voice in the background urging me to go smarter, deeper, and better, all the while railing at me about politics. Thanks for your patience, Bruce, I'll have more time to read the paper now!

Francesca Tripodi: I'd like to first acknowledge Andrea Press. Thank you for being the perfect graduate school advisor and making the experience a chance to "learn and grow." You have been a wonderful mentor, helping me navigate the streets of academic life. It has been an honor to work alongside someone of your intellect, humor, and kindness. I am also thankful to my other mentors at the University of Virginia—Allison Pugh, Siva Vaidhyanathan, and Sarah Corse were the dream team of a dissertation committee. When I was pregnant with both my children, Allison provided an immeasurable amount of support, for which I will always be grateful. I could have never made it through graduate school without those in the Media Studies Department at the University of Virginia who saw in me a level of intellect I did not see in myself. Siva, thank you for your unwavering support and being such a champion for my academic success. I'd like to acknowledge my former colleagues at James Madison University and my new colleagues at the School of Information and Library Science at UNC-Chapel Hill.

Given the nature of this book, I would also like to thank my mom and her close friends "The Broads." Growing up, this dynamic group of strong, clever, warm, and hilarious women made a real impact on my life. These women grew up together and saw one another through all of life's cycles. They taught me the importance of real friendship and helped shape me into the woman I am today. I learned from The Broads the importance of "sisterhood," but I am so lucky to have a real sister. She is brilliant and supportive and the only person with whom I can have entire conversations without actually speaking words. Both of my parents are so important to me. My mom and dad offered nothing but support growing up. It wasn't until raising my own children that I realized how much work they put into raising us. I can only hope I end up doing half as good as the job they did. Both my parents and my lovely in-laws provide a tremendous amount of support. In particular, your involvement in helping me raise my own kids allows me to do things like write books.

Speaking of parenting, I would like to thank my children and my life partner. It's funny to think that as Andrea and I started this project I was pregnant with my daughter, who is now three. To my children—you are a joy and I can't imagine my life without you. I love being your mom. To my husband—your support, kindness, and love do not go unnoticed. Thank you for taking this journey with me. I love you.

Introduction

In October of 2017, our social media accounts began spilling over with people in our networks posting the same message—from Twitter to Instagram, two words flooded our consciousness: Me Too. The #MeToo movement was powerful, featuring a distinguished and growing list of sexual harassers—politicians, actors, directors, doctors, academics, businessmen, and philanthropists whose time was up. The movement seemed to open a watershed of silence—almost every day a new name was added to the list, demonstrating the pervasiveness of sexual harassment and assault. At the same time, media coverage treated the issue as though sexual harassment and assault were novelties, failing to recognize the deep roots of the subject or the fact that Lin Farley coined the phrase "sexual harassment" back in 1975. To be sure, #MeToo is a significant call to action, but it is also an opportunity to understand how the political culture embedded in media's use of #MeToo is rooted in a context of widespread, everyday sexism that transcends the terms of this newer movement. And while awareness created by the hashtag has helped reveal the widespread normativity of sexual harassment, it has also focused primarily on white,* upper-class women, rendering the original framing by Tarana Burke less visible to the public eye.

In many respects, #MeToo is part of a wider dynamic that many academics have researched in depth. These studies argue that mass media reflect both popular and neoliberal feminism, essentially depoliticized ideologies

---

*The authors have intentionally used "white" vs. "White" when speaking about the racial identity of those who participated in our studies. We did this because of the historical use of the phrase White by White supremacists. Given that many institutions, including the Associate Press, are grappling with this very issue at time of publication we decided to go with the existing standard. Nonetheless, we want to acknowledge that Whiteness is a racial identity and that by not capitalizing whiteness we are working within a standard that can normalize racism.

that focus on individual empowerment versus structural change (Banet-Weiser 2018; Rottenberg 2018). #MeToo has helped both men and women admit knowledge of the ongoing existence of harassment and assault in a variety of workplaces, including but not exclusively those associated with Harvey Weinstein. However, we also see examples of pushback—pundits, opinion writers, or viral posts wondering why accusers did not speak up earlier? Such contradictions posit a necessary analysis not only of mass production but also of its *reception*. While #MeToo might be thought of as reifying popular feminist logics, engaging with audiences' reception of the hashtag also unveils the complexity of our cultural moment, which contains popular feminism certainly but also a trajectory toward a shift in how feminism is incorporated and accepted more widely.

In this book, we argue that part of our culture's ambivalent response to #MeToo can be explained by fact that sexist interactions are so frequent they have become an expected pattern of action (Nelson 2018; Lithwick 2018). Consider how this everyday sexism unfolds in coverage of the #MeToo movement. First, the popular media accusations against Weinstein discounted the earlier cases in which people did speak up (e.g., Ambra Battilana Gutierrez, the Filipina Italian model who did file assault charges against Weinstein with the New York City Police Department, although they declined to prosecute). The widely publicized #MeToo movement initially overshadowed Tarana Burke's earlier contribution. While she was mentioned inside *Time* magazine's 2017 "The Silence Breakers" as the person of the year, she was not selected for the cover (in her place were Ashley Judd, Adama Iwu, Susan Fowler, Taylor Swift, Isabel Pascual, and the bent arm of another women representing the millions of women still silenced). *Time*'s discussion of silence breaking also made the current moment seem like an anomaly, glossing over the history of sexual harassment activism more generally. After all, Anita Hill had openly discussed the sexual harassment charges against Supreme Court nominee Clarence Thomas in her 1991 televised testimony. And, predating Anita Hill, there had been a substantial grassroots movement to document and address sexual harassment—a term coined decades earlier in 1975 by feminist labor activist Lin Farley and taken up by grassroots activist groups such as Women Organized Against Sexual Harassment (WOASH).[1]

While #MeToo was an important catalyst on social media, the campaign fails to comprehensively engage with the pervasiveness of everyday sexism—to be fair, a big task. This explains why Matt Damon can say, "There's a difference between patting someone on the butt and rape or child molestation. Both of those behaviors need to be confronted and eradicated without question, but they shouldn't be conflated" (Eppolito 2017). While Damon faced public critique for his comments, which try to differentiate between everyday sexism and outright assault, in some ways we agree with him that these two phenomena ought to be differentiated—yet we assert that they are related as well. In some ways, everyday sexism is integrally connected to the epidemic of sexual assault, and these connections should be unpacked in everyday cultural understandings of sexism. Popular feminism, though "having a moment" (Gill and Toms 2019, 97), is embroiled in an ongoing struggle for the visibility of feminist sentiments and often fails to unpack the complexities of the issues, which include the pervasiveness of sexism in everyday life.

The sensationalized sexism discussed in the #MeToo movement also tends, in popular journalistic coverage and in much of its social media presence, to gloss over important feminist issues such as work-life balance, body positivity, gendered income inequality, and the underrepresentation of prominent female figures in leadership positions, all of which are persistent areas of gendered inequality, having been addressed only incompletely by feminist action for social change. The structural sexism that supports and accepts these inequalities is so ingrained that we argue it has become what Goffman (1959) would refer to as part of our "unthinking routine." Not unlike Aristotle's notion of a "habit" or *hexis*, our data demonstrate that sexism has become, in the words of sociologists Ritzer and Ryan, an "acquired yet entrenched state of moral character that orients our feelings and desires in a situation, and thence our action" (2017, 317).

Normative sexism persists alongside the overwhelming turn of media culture toward popular feminism. While popular feminism is bound to the elite definitions of reality that legitimize social inequality and thwart participatory democracy (Fenton 2016), the media nevertheless have a history of operating as a true fourth estate that at times clashes with their increasingly neoliberal, corporate sensibility. This manifests in our concept of media-ready feminism, which we argue occurs *at the moment of reception* in the cases where media break through the strictures of popular feminism and address structural sexism. #MeToo incorporates a dimension of media-ready feminism alongside its popular feminism. For example, the truly breakthrough feminist dimension of #MeToo is important for shedding light on the pervasiveness of sexual assault, though by focusing on the sensational cases and their glamorous victims, coverage frames assault as unusual, as a break in our unthinking routine, and not emblematic of everyday sexism. What is needed instead is in-depth media coverage leading toward a fundamental understanding of intersectional inequality and the role sexual assault and harassment play in the perpetuation of unequal power dynamics in the United States. Yet the coverage of #MeToo resonates sufficiently with women's experiences of both misogyny and everyday sexism to effectively constitute a moment of "break" in a popular feminist hegemony, a break that opens the possibility of a more in-depth understanding of feminist issues. There is a magic to the #MeToo moment, which was a true media *break*, in spite of its well-analyzed limitations.

In the words of Alyssa Milano as she tweeted back to Damon when he insisted that not all men are bad: "It's the micro that makes the macro." Indeed, we agree: without understanding the micro—which includes not only media representations, but also how *audiences interact with and engage in media representations*—we lack a deeper understanding of why the same situations women have been facing in the workplace have continued at the macro level for decades. We need to better define the terms we are using in this struggle, such as the difference between assault and harassment; but we need also to acknowledge and recognize the pervasive persistence—alongside outright misogyny—of macro-level and micro-level "everyday sexism": the pervasive problem of sexism as an everyday experiential occurrence for most women that penetrates the conventions of everyday life and structures the macro-sociological foundation of gendered inequality. Not only do "the media" rarely engage with this boundary-making process, but we find that when they do, audiences are hesitant to embrace the messaging. This is the media-ready feminist moment of reception: a rejection of the possibilities of breakthrough feminist media representation and media coverage. Throughout this book we will both identify the spaces in which media aim to push the boundaries of hegemonic feminism (conceptualized most recently as "popular feminism" in Banet-Weiser [2018] and as "neoliberal feminism" in Rottenberg [2018]) and also shed light on how audiences engage with the meaning making attendant upon this production. We conceptualize this interactive process at moments of media breakthrough as *media-ready feminism*. Our study focuses on the ways in which audiences at times either reject media-ready feminism—but also at times receive and elaborate its meanings as transgressive.

Media-ready feminism is similar in some important respects to three recently articulated versions of feminism: Banet-Weiser's "popular feminism" (2018), Favaro and Gill's "glossy feminism" (2018), and Rottenberg's "neoliberal feminism" (2018). It also incorporates postfeminist ideas and sensibilities as articulated by Gill (2007) and Tasker and Negra (2007). Yet media-ready feminism differs from each of these concepts in important ways as well. It is an active, sociologically based conceptualization of audience reception that encompasses *both* media's attempt to transcend these crucially limited versions of feminism *and* the processes of domestication through which media audiences and users revert to more limited cultural schemas despite the widespread awareness of their limitations, which results from the reach of everyday sexism. Similar to the "enlightened sexism" articulated by Douglas (2010)—that sexism is acceptable given the newly widespread belief in feminism—and to feminism's "double entanglement" intricately described by McRobbie (2009a, 2013)—that feminism coexists with more conservative ideologies in neoliberal society—feminist representation nevertheless showcases "empowerment" in many forms (from the twenty-something singleton, to the newly married pregnant woman, to the working mother trying to balance life's demands). Yet it often does so through simultaneously showcasing consumption as the mechanism by which empowerment is achieved and perpetuating archetypal heterosexual, cis-gendered attractiveness and heteronormative life stages through a racially homogeneous lens. In media-ready feminism, the idea that women are white, middle-class, and heterosexual, criticisms made of second-wave feminism's mode of address, is too often normalized. And in contrast to the postfeminist assertions that individuals are rejecting the term "feminism," media-ready feminism encourages women (and men) to embrace a feminist label, while at the same time stripping this label of its political content by implying that feminism is a movement long over and accomplished (Banet-Weiser, Gill, Rottenberg 2010).[2]

In these features, media-ready feminism is similar to the popular and neoliberal feminism that has already been widely discussed in feminist literature (Banet-Weiser, Gill, and Rottenberg 2018). Yet we argue that media—even widely consumed popular media—often contain the seeds of a more fundamental feminist critique, providing an opportunity for the public to engage in discussions of the structural gendered inequality that ensures the persistence and reproduction of everyday sexism. However, even as media images push the boundaries, examining the process by which audiences engage and react to these stories provides the opportunity to augment earlier scholarship by confronting reactions to the disconnect between experience and media culture that characterizes the lives of everyday women in the #MeToo era. Media-ready feminism reinforces a culture that negates and downplays women's experiences of everyday sexism while simultaneously pushing the boundaries of what Rottenberg terms "actual feminism," a feminism concerned with equality and gender justice.[3] Media-ready feminism focuses on these "magnified moments" (Hochschild 2003, 16), analyzing how audiences make sense of narratives that advance feminist goals in a cultural milieu that restricts feminist discourse. Our concept contains a fundamental insight into the limits of media's feminist influences and its ability to facilitate and enable feminist social change.

While recent discussions (Banet-Weiser 2018, x) have highlighted feminist scholars' ambivalence at their own reception of popular feminism given that such narratives do contain elements of a feminism we all resonate with, our study delves further both into precisely these contradictions within many media representations and into the contradiction between lived experience and media culture experienced by a wide swath of media audiences and users. Unlike popular and neoliberal feminism, media-ready feminism can push the boundaries of the limited white, liberal, heterosexist, middle-class feminism that predominates in mainstream media; but because of this, it also encounters pushback from audiences unable to translate their media consumption according to the transformative dimensions of feminist social movements. This reception study attempts to unpack the slow way in which media work to facilitate social change. Yet transcending the boundaries of a more regressive popular feminism is quite difficult for the audience members we sampled, and in this book we probe and describe the actual *process* through which feminism that is media-ready is tamed and accommodated during reception in order to fit, explain, and make sense of the lived experiences of those we studied.

Drawing on a series of case studies, we probe audiences' difficulties in confronting radical media content, tracing the operation of media-ready feminism across a variety of media platforms and documenting the work audiences do to resist, recuperate, and revert representations and platforms that push the boundaries of popular feminism. We describe what we feel is the true import of a media feminism that contains critical and transcendent elements. This is the almost Gramscian hegemonic process through which audiences end up acceding to these dominant cultural ideas of feminism, ideas that are contradicted—in the case of women—by their experience of a constant, reliable barrage of sexist treatment in many realms of life, the "everyday sexism" of our title.[4]

What is it like, we ask, for women and men who have come of age in the era of popular and neoliberal feminism to experience everyday sexism and even at times popular misogyny? How do they make sense of such a contradictory cultural environment and experience, where the common culture is dominated by feminisms in their varied incarnations, feminisms that frequently focus on an individualism inconstant with the tension of collective sexism in our everyday? How do audiences—media viewers, users, in some of our examples, creators—reconcile such dramatic contradictions in the course of their everyday lives and at different life stages? And how do they capitalize—or fail to capitalize—on media's transcendent moments, in which transformation is imagined and envisioned?

To introduce our framework, we use the rest of this introduction to present an example illustrating the operation of media-ready feminism. We then discuss how each chapter in the book draws from reception and/or use of a different media *platform* to further elaborate this thesis.

"I Don't Regret My Abortion": Media-Ready Feminist Reception

To observe media-ready feminism in action, we draw from a message posted to the now-defunct forum Yik Yak. This social media app was widely popular on college campuses in the United States from 2013 to 2014 and often involved the collective though anonymous discussion of popular and political issues. Using geolocative technology, Yik Yak restricted access to a limited area of users but allowed them to "peek in" on other places. While not exclusive to college campuses, Yik Yak organized the communities on the app around college locations (e.g., University of Southern California or Virginia Tech). The example we use below is drawn from an interaction captured by Tripodi (2017). In the Yik Yak screenshot in figure I.1, a user posts about her personal experience with abortion. As you can see from the text, this user is directly engaging in a debate about a woman's right to choose but is also pushing back on what we would argue is the newly popular idea that makes abortion decisions palatable for popular feminism—that women will inevitably regret their decisions.

Not only is the content of this Yak unusual, but the large number of supporters of this message (757) is equally surprising. As Tripodi's research demonstrates, typically Yik Yak succumbs to a form of algorithmic

Figure I.1. Screenshot of the Yik Yak thread in which the original poster writes about not regretting her abortion.

censorship (e.g., deletion, which we will discuss later), whereby only sentiments agreed upon by the majority of users are allowed to persist. Moreover, the high number of upvotes (at the time of this screenshot there were upward of 750) means this message was visible for a longer period of time than other Yaks because it ultimately transferred from the new list to Yik Yak's "hotlist" of ultra-popular Yaks. Getting on the hotlist is significant in itself because it increases a post's visibility—depending on the traffic, hotlist posts typically last about an hour, in contrast to "new" content, which often disappears as rapidly as ten minutes after posting, especially in cases where there are a large number of users on the app. As we can see at the bottom left corner of this post and in subsequent comments, the post remained on the "hotlist" for at least four hours. Such a large number of upvotes indicates its popularity. However, a closer analysis of the comments following this post reveals a powerful demonstration of the typical domesticating reception by which media-ready feminism is often received. The initial post, a somewhat radically prochoice sentiment, is modified to offer a limited set of situations in which a lack of regret concerning abortion can be deemed "appropriate."

One instance of this is immediately visible in the second commenter's text that no one is "excited," evoking ideas of harm and danger present in the "abortionist as evil" trope common to anti-abortion rhetoric (Condit 1989). The comment following this indicates that women do regret their abortions—but that they "probably regret unwanted children more." A few comments later, the discussion turns to rape—an extreme argument often invoked in favor of abortion by those who support reproductive rights only very conditionally.

In the screenshot in figure I.2, one commenter writes sarcastically, "Yeah, I totally regret my rapist's fetus." This comment is followed by a debate among users as to whether the commenter was raped, or whether she is speaking on behalf of rape victims who decide to have abortions—a perspective on abortion that has long been widely accepted—even though the right is currently contesting the right to reproductive choice as a series of states pass laws restricting access to abortion even in rape and incest cases (Reints 2019). Interestingly enough, however, and central to our argument about how media-ready feminism is created and received, rape is not discussed at all in the initial post.

The modification of the initial sentiment calls on sociologist Karen Cerulo's (2000) theory of "story elaboration." Much like the headline or story lead of a news article, fellow Yik Yak users are only processing the

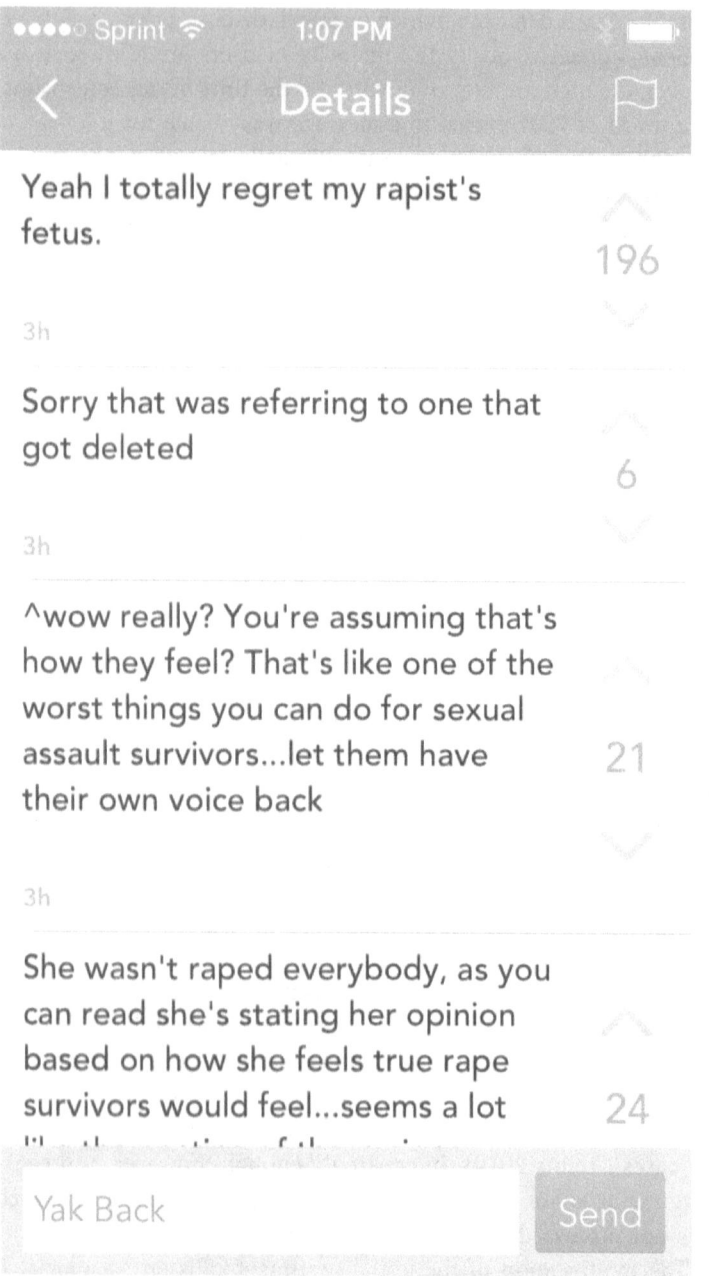

Figure I.2. Comments to the original post on Yik Yak debating whether the original poster was pregnant due to rape.

initial soundbite briefly, but then they proceed to fill in the blanks guided by the rules and scripts dictated by their sociocultural context. Similar to a newspaper headline, the original Yak professing "no regret" over an abortion is then "filled in" by remaining users, creating a dialogue that is compatible with broader sociocultural opinions limiting choice. As a result of this modification, the original sentiment of the user is ultimately changed—deradicalized—to fit the cultural context of abortion opinion within the southern university at which this Yak was observed. Modifying and changing the content to fit this narrative effectively silenced the original feminist expression that someone had an abortion and did not regret it. As one commenter notes, it was only after the poster seemed to acknowledge that she was speaking on behalf of women who were raped that "her yak started getting upvotes like crazy"—perhaps from a popular feminist public who were influenced by the ideology of popular feminism to ignore the collective experience of American women, in which (depending on the source) 30 to 40 percent have at one time or another considered abortion.[5]

We've noted a similar modification process applied to other Yaks, tweets, and online expressions initially expressing other radical political sentiments on topics other than feminism. So, for example, following the events of Ferguson, Missouri, while some Black student activists tweeted the increasingly influential #BlackLivesMatter, many in the broader populace began modifying this epithet to the more universal and less racially pointed #AllLivesMatter. At the University of Virginia, a Twitter campaign began in the wake of a recent article in *Rolling Stone* detailing (erroneously, as it later turned out) the brutal campus rape of a student named "Jackie" under the handle #IStandwithJackie. Following criticisms of the article, this was modified on campus feeds to #IStandwithSantaClaus and other belittling variations, as the Twitter campaign #BlackLivesMatter was immediately mocked with #AllLivesMatter. These processes underscore what we argue in this book characterizes the domesticating reception of media-ready feminist breakthrough moments.

Media-Ready Feminism and Its Reception across Platforms: The Case Studies

In sum, media-ready feminism 1) shares the following features of "popular feminism" (Banet-Weiser 2018) in that it embraces the name feminism—while depoliticizing the movement, focuses on women who already dominate media representations (white, heterosexual, young, cisgender, upper middle class), and fails to engage with the broader structural issues that maintain and reproduce everyday sexism; 2) shares with the new "neoliberal feminism" (Rottenberg 2018) the focus on the individual as a unit rather than collective action and as a result views the ideal of "work-family balance" as something to be worked on at the individual level only; 3) however, what media-ready feminism adds to this conversation is an understanding of how media can at times be transgressive, pushing the boundaries of what is popularly considered acceptable by offering an authentic reaction that collectively acknowledges pervasive everyday sexism.

Audience ethnography reveals that when true breakthrough feminism emerges it is often met with resignation, reversion, or resistance—audiences fight back, because the common culture embodies everyday sexism as well as popular feminism. By only looking at examples of popular or liberal feminism in the media, a feminism that is limited, scholarship can miss media's genuinely "critical" moments. Media have often been important progressive social forces in struggles for gender equity (Dow 1996; Haralovich and Press 2018). Unfortunately, these moments of media transgression do not always lead to meaningful social change, because popular and neoliberal feminism do not encourage audiences to develop a language accordant with transgressive feminism and social change. By recognizing these moments of critique, this book also aims to capture audiences' ambivalence when dealing with these tensions as they respond to both a popular feminist media hegemony and media moments that pierce through it. A recent proliferation of feminist media scholarship captures today's feminist climate but nevertheless misses the opportunity to consider how audiences engage with popular feminism, neoliberal feminism, and feminism that falls outside these boundaries. By focusing on moments of reception, this book sheds light on how women and men grapple with these tensions and problematize, at times embrace, and often fail to challenge the prevalence of everyday sexism.

Our case studies illuminate the process by which both popular feminism and neoliberal feminism are reproduced, repackaged, and reaffirmed by audiences struggling with the everyday sexism they experience. Based on our findings, we argue that when media push boundaries, existing feminist pushback is not strong enough to combat the larger structural issues necessary for achieving equality. Media-ready feminism is regularly transformed into a more acceptable form of debate that engages with the inequalities of those who already hold a position of power in society, ensuring that the struggles of women of color, transgender individuals, sexual minorities, and lower socioeconomic populations too often fall on deaf ears. This is what we classify as feminism that is "not media ready."

In the chapters that follow we pursue a sociologically based inquiry of media reception, following media audience members, creators, and users as they navigate a contradictory media landscape containing extreme instances of feminism counterbalanced by both everyday sexism and extreme misogyny. That so many women from so many walks of life have retained their optimism, sanity, and commitment to feminism in this environment is a testament to the strength and persistence of our feminist heritage. This book is dedicated to the women who have generously shared their life stories and reactions to popular media with us. We hope the media environment can make increasing headway against the everyday sexism and the popular misogyny it currently supports.

The book is organized around five cases—centered on reception "moments." Each of these moments demonstrates how audiences negotiate the complex relationship between media-ready feminism and everyday sexism. The distinct cases focus on the feminist issues of sexual violence, work-family balance, the sexual double standard, dating apps, and online sexism inside a widely used knowledge platform. In each example, media grapple with issues central to the feminist movement in its current media incarnation. Through these cases, we build the theory of media-ready feminism employing the methodological traditions of audience ethnography and media reception. Drawing in part on feminist methodology as we employ these methods of reception analysis, we rely heavily on the words, perspectives, and worldviews of many people whose social positioning often renders them less "audible, less visible, and thus less able to shape the structures influencing their lives" (Avishai, Gerber, and Randles 2012).

While individual analyses of these cases yield important understandings of the connections between media creation and reception, theorizing across the data sets allows us to begin to generalize and elaborate these patterns. Such comparisons between seemingly incompatible types of media reception nevertheless shed light on an analytical pattern whereby respondents confront media-ready feminist moments of transgression but use a series of strategies to revert these moments back to the disempowered, analytically inert popular versions of feminism most often encountered in our media and culture. Given the breadth of the media environments we study in this project, such a repeated pattern was somewhat surprising, but it enabled us to flesh out a new and timely model for reception research in the current media environment. The way this hegemony of popular feminism works is clearly demonstrable through reception research, which helps illustrate the process through which transgressive ideas are domesticated in the process of reception. Each case study combines interpretive analysis of media representation with the investigation of reaction to or engagement with these issues, using focus groups, individual interviews, and ethnographic observations of both physical and virtual environments. What we find is a complex interplay between the articulation of actual feminism in the context of women's experiences of everyday sexism and their responses to it.

One assumption of popular feminism is the element of the postfeminist sensibility (Gill 2007) that we live in a sexually empowered world where both women and men can be sexually aggressive and active. In chapter 1, we confront one of the most remarkable media phenomena, the text of the remarkably popular television series *Game of Thrones*, adapted from the equally popular series of novels by George R. R. Martin. Reception of this text allows us to examine the way audiences actually push back on a paired representation of popular feminism and "popular misogyny" (Banet-Weiser 2018). Yet the popular feminism of *Game of Thrones* is often *so* extreme that it becomes transgressive. Powerful women rulers are *so* powerful they rule "dragons" and large kingdoms, and regularly outsmart the men in their world. Powerful female warriors are *so* powerful they triumph over all other forceful warriors, exhibiting an almost invincible female masculinity (Halberstam 1998). Yet sexual violence against women is regularized in the narrative and visual text of this show, a sexism shown to be an accepted and normal part of everyday life. This text presented a rare opportunity to peek at an extreme example of the way an almost shockingly transgressive feminism is paired with what might be termed its opposite—regressive misogynist images that shock even audiences used, in the Trump era, to a background of popular misogyny. Responses to this show on the whole fail to note and challenge that extreme feminism and misogyny are so often paired in its imagery.

In chapter 2, we consider a text that moves from explicit misogyny to sexism of a more common, everyday sort, the kind of "background" sexism that constitutes the everyday sexism of our title, alongside a more muted feminism that is nevertheless at times media ready. We hone in on a particularly transgressive media moment contained within an episode of the popular television show *Jersey Shore*, an episode entitled "Dirty Pad" (S2, E9). As we collectively viewed and discussed this episode with a series of the show's fans, we shed light on how, in this instance, media-ready feminism fought back against the double sexual standard that persists in our culture and the ways in which audience members confront and accommodate to the contradictions of a culture characterized by a popular feminism existing alongside the everyday, assumed sexism supporting a continuing double standard of sexual conduct for men and women. In the episode, one of the characters is labeled a "slut" based on her sexual behavior (she's too active, in too many different contexts). Though the labeled cast member objects to this with a feminist argument about parity of gendered sexual activity, no one else in the cast backs up her perspective or defends her behavior. Instead, they undermine it and criticize her resoundingly for her behavior, criticisms seemingly motivated by a nonfeminist, judgmental double standard for women's sexual behavior.

When we spoke with respondents viewing the episode, they said that the episode really seems to hit home for them, and that the double standard is a genuine dilemma that they continually face. There remains an "economy of sexual capital" for women, who face dual pressures to be both sexually liberated but to avoid the traditional pitfalls of this: being labeled a "slut." By drawing on language used in the episode and by our respondents, we demonstrate how the show's media-ready feminism paints a picture of the "empowered" woman who enacts sexual freedom; yet in the moment of reception, both in the words of characters on the show and by those in our audience study, that moment is quickly shut down. Both the show's cast and viewers in our study are unable to address the fact that women who engage in casual sex continue to be labeled "sluts" in everyday experience. Viewers recount this fear *and* the text illustrates it as it proceeds beyond its breakthrough feminist moment.

Popular and neoliberal feminism assumes that work-family balance is a woman's individual problem to solve—that despite the structural gender imbalances that persist, "each woman must choose" a path for herself. Chapter 3 draws on the once exceedingly popular television show *Desperate Housewives* to document the travails of individual women trying to solve the work-family balance issue, illustrating how the show's media-ready feminism begins to challenge the notion that this dilemma is inherently an individual problem to solve, presenting this problem to a population that ultimately lacks the structural language to push forward on this insight. Women's experiences as mined in our focus groups reveal that they understand at some level that the impossibility of work-family balance is a structural problem that many women face in different ways (e.g., following the impact of divorce; returning to the labor force after a break for childrearing; being overlooked for promotions at work, in part because of child care responsibilities). Yet, for the most part, women lack the analytic vocabulary to describe the problem in social structural terms. In addition, women who work often possess the feminist insight that they are not being judged according to the same standards as are men, who easily and regularly pass them by in the labor force, and this engenders conflicting attitudes toward combining work with career for affluent women who, unlike most women, have a choice to withdraw from the paid labor force. Working women are also hyper- and critically aware of continuing sexual attention from superiors to themselves and to other, often younger, women. This further supports a negative and often cynical attitude toward women's potential in the workplace and a particularly suspicious attitude toward women who succeed, a cultural trope reflected in the episode. The chapter well illustrates the power of popular feminist representations to influence women's interpretations of their own experiences, particularly for affluent women who find themselves reflected in the representation. Yet it also illustrates the failure of media-ready feminism's transgressive moment to spark an authentically feminist response to this problem, even in the white, relatively affluent women who connect more with this representation. This holds true despite the widespread insights women's experiences of everyday sexism give them into the inadequacy of a simplistic popular feminist formula to successfully resolve their conflicts.

The particular version of media-ready feminism in this episode fails to speak to the experiences of less affluent women, who do not find their situation reflected because they do not grapple with issues of choice yet face tremendous obstacles as they attempt to support their families. African American women and a Latina immigrant woman in our sample also find the episode unrepresentative of their experiences both culturally and economically. For the former, family experiences most often include strong working women role models; for the latter, a strict father has restricted her participation in cultural life in the United States in ways this media-ready feminism does not capture.

The white, affluent bias of media coverage of working mothers is nowhere more evident than in the college admissions scandal of 2019. As we write this, *Desperate Housewives* star Felicity Huffman, playing the lead woman "Lynette" of our episode, is serving jail time for her participation in the scandal. Falling prey to the pressures of affluent moms, Huffman hired an illegal college placement service to falsify the credential of her daughters as they applied for admission to elite colleges, thus ensuring them a place in a prestigious private university that they apparently could not otherwise earn. Huffman, a glamorous, white, wealthy star of television and film, embodies the unspeakably affluent working mom—her net worth has been estimated at upward of $20 million (Shannon-Karasik 2019)—whose experience overshadows cultural discussion of work-family balance. Sociologist Annette Lareau (2003) discusses the process of "concerted cultivation" undertaken by (primarily) mothers in higher socioeconomic status families to ensure the reproduction of class status for their children. The college admissions scandal illustrates that this pressure is experienced by mothers at the highest rungs of the socioeconomic ladder, and there has been no shortage of media attention to their wrongdoing (Shannon-Karasik 2019; Jackson 2019). Yet these particular activities are confined to the highest percentage of earners in our society, who are almost entirely white (96.1 percent by some estimates; see Moore 2017). Descriptions of these particular pressures touch very little on the experience of the vast majority of working mothers who earn only a fraction of this group's annual income, and who face a series of other pressures left out of the general cultural conversation.

Twenty-first-century dating brings with it a seemingly limitless number of potential partners. In chapter 4, we explore how apps like Tinder perpetuate popular feminism by framing dating as a source of sexual agency. The ability to swipe right (indicating an interest in continuing the relationship) or to swipe left (abruptly halting contact) amplifies the narrative that the app enables women to assert control over their sexual conquests. Unfortunately, merely empowering women to make initial connections fails to account for the normative "situational" sexual expectations we observed on the college campus we studied—the persistence of an everyday sexism that supports a climate of sexual violence against women. As recent data on the epidemic of sexual assault on college campuses and elsewhere indicate (Wade 2017), our study also finds that a boundary exists whereby women no longer feel comfortable saying "no" to sex yet continue to define engaging in casual sexual activity as an example of feminist agency, whether they enjoy these encounters or not (relevant to this, recent research documents the paucity of female orgasms in the casual sexual encounters Tinder often fosters [Armstrong, England, and Fogarty 2010]). This is the intrusion of media-ready feminism into the popular feminist appearance of Tinder. Exploring the relationships between the popular feminist appearance of Tinder and the everyday sexism involved in the "tacit consent" implicit in the sexual activity Tinder facilitates, this chapter examines how many straight women on college campuses again lack the transgressive language they need to confront the pressure to consent. We then contextualize this case in relation to the reaction to "Grace's" much-publicized accusation of sexual assault against Aziz Ansari in order to reiterate why #MeToo is a clear example of a transgressive media-ready feminist "moment" that stands out from the popular feminism more often dominating mainstream media discourse.

In chapter 5, we use ethnographic observations of "edit-a-thons," Wikipedia's "Articles for Deletion" pages, and in-depth interviews to argue that the culture of Wikipedia remains entrenched in patriarchal systems of inequality. Not only is it difficult for new editors (typically women) to feel comfortable adding to Wikipedia, but the standards for what constitutes "notability" for a biography page, such as the number of exhibits in well-known art museums or periodical coverage of events, are linked to systemic biases against women's inclusion. We find that while Wikipedia's motto of the "free encyclopedia that anyone can edit" and the nature of its edit-a-thons themselves constitute the promise of a media-ready feminist redress to this system, its structural environment explicitly ignores the persistence and strength of the everyday sexism that curtails the ability of edit-a-thons to follow through on this promise. Drawing on examples of how women modify their actions in edit-a-thons (from username selection to avoiding editing certain spaces), this chapter demonstrates how avid Wikipedia editors practice what they term "stealth feminism" in order to avoid harassment. This chapter illuminates how in doing so users wishing to combat the "gender gap" on Wikipedia (Adams and Brückner 2015) work only in what they describe as its "quiet corners," and documents how this perpetuates the problem of gender asymmetry on the world's largest encyclopedia.

In conclusion, the coexistence of media-ready feminism and everyday sexism is not without consequence. As was made evident in the 2016 presidential election, media-ready feminism played a significant role in framing Clinton's campaign. Throughout the election period, the press hailed her *Lean In* mentality, embraced her hard-hitting demeanor, hailed her performance in the presidential debates, and emphasized at times the truly radical dimension of potentially placing a female executive in the White House. The polls reaffirmed her imminent success, convincing those of us who followed the media coverage of the election that she would become the first female president of the United States. At the same time, the media failed to account for Trump's almost constant use of everyday sexist language—his dismissive remarks about Hillary's appearance, his comment that she was a "nasty woman," his constant discussion of whether women were attractive, his seemingly innocuous "locker room talk," and his criticism of a beauty contestant's weight gain, all would resonate with many voters embroiled in the unquestioned culture of everyday sexism. The sheer fact that media criticism of his rhetoric was framed as "surprising" is evidence that sexist, patriarchal attitudes are commonplace and underreported—part of our everyday, accepted reality. Further, as Banet-Weiser argues (2018), with the Trump campaign popular culture crossed the line from accepting everyday sexism to accepting popular misogyny. In addition, the much-discussed phenomenon that younger women failed to identify Clinton's candidacy as a feminist triumph illustrates how popular feminism frames feminist social change as an already-accomplished victory, thereby disempowering the much-needed feminist activism that remains. Yet though media show evidence of a new "traffic in feminism" as documented by scholars such as Banet-Weiser and Portwood-Stacer (2017), a discussion focused simply on media representation is unprepared to confront the type of hegemonic sexism exhibited in the Trump campaign, which for many viewers remained intact despite feminist criticism and analysis (Ortner 2016). In this book, we use reception study in conjunction with media analysis to try to make sense of this explicit coexistence of such contradictions. As the findings from our cases demonstrate, the problem of patriarchal barriers will persist (Rubin 1997 [1971]; Lerner 1986; Ortner 2014) if citizens are left with no penetrative, transgressive ideologies that actively challenge them.

But that is not to say that all hope is lost. We believe that by writing this book, we can shed light on why the idea of "feminism" as a popular concept can potentially disrupt instead of simply sensationalize. We think that expanding the purview of what constitutes feminism in our media to include those who fail to identify with the movement is a good first step. We also believe that by exposing the ubiquity of media-ready feminism and exploring its impact, we can begin to embrace a kind of equality that has up to this point been media "unready."

1

Considering the Limits of Extreme Misogyny

Game of Thrones as Feminist?

Introduction

The phenomenal popularity of HBO's series *Game of Thrones* offers an ideal place to illustrate the notion of media-ready feminism.[1] *Game of Thrones* is an eight-season serialization of George R. R. Martin's best-selling five-volume set of novels. The series has drawn attention in the feminist and mainstream press for both its explicit, extreme misogyny as well as its unusually strong women characters. This has sparked online debate about the nature of *Game of Thrones*' feminism, best represented by a discussion on *Bitch Media*'s website: "With every season of *Game of Thrones*, one question has become more insistent among those in the blogosphere: 'Is *Game of Thrones* feminist?'" This debate is so salient that even misogynist websites like *Return of Kings* have featured articles like the one entitled "How Feminism Is Ruining *Game of Thrones*," a defensive response to the strength of the show's female characters. These debates highlight that feminism is currently a contested concept (Johnson, forthcoming) open to a variety of definitions and approaches. The debate over *Game of Thrones*' feminist qualities functions as a kind of litmus test among critics and the public regarding what feminism is and whether it's currently palatable.

This chapter is cowritten with Sarah Johnson-Palomaki. We are very grateful for her participation in this research and for generously giving us access to her master's thesis data on the reception of *Game of Thrones*.

The heated nature of these discussions and debates is indicative of media-ready feminism in action. For the most part, *Game of Thrones* mirrors popular feminism, offering a plethora of individually highly empowered women characters who utilize their sexual prowess as part of their power. Yet the show also pushes the boundaries of popular feminism in characters like Brienne of Tarth and others, while presenting its representations alongside images of extreme misogyny. This unique set of representations offers an unparalleled set of coexisting extremes. In particular, characters like Daenerys Targaryen, Arya Stark, the evil Queen Cersei, and Sansa Stark have sparked conversation about the meaning of "feminist" representation itself. However, the ambivalence regarding how audiences respond to these characters and the pushback the show has received via feminist media provide the perfect opportunity to showcase media-ready feminism in action.

The extreme misogyny featured in the series alongside its strong women characters is also fodder for reflection in this chapter. The show includes multiple instances of sexual violence and other types of violent acts committed against women, including the strong female characters mentioned earlier. The show is also characterized by a notable hypersexuality featuring female nudity. Since this show predated the #MeToo era, it is of interest to this study to consider how the misogynistic violence, hypersexualization, and female nudity included in the show have sparked both criticism and enjoyment and, of course, are perhaps central to the show's broad appeal and popularity in a patriarchal culture. Also of interest are the many broader public discussions of why extreme and ubiquitous sexual violence is and should be acceptable as presented in this series. *Game of Thrones*' texts, and critics' and viewers' responses to them, exemplify media-ready feminism in that these commentaries are constantly invoking its feminism while often justifying misogyny. In addition, one characteristic of *Game of Thrones*' *feminist brand* is that immediate pushback against its most powerful incarnations is *already embedded* in the text in the form of its extreme misogyny.

Game of Thrones' feminism is invoked, critiqued, and celebrated in a variety of ways by different media outlets. Popular press and feminist media have shown interest in many of the characters, and for different reasons. In the following section we discuss a series of variations in the way these press outlets have commented on the show and the issues concerning feminism the show has raised. Following this, we contrast the comments of audience members gleaned both from online forums and drawn from our interview data, again focusing on their response to the show's extreme brand of popular feminism. We conclude with a discussion of how media-ready feminism describes the unique nature of the show's contradictory text and makes sense of both the online and media reception of the show, and much of the audience response to it found in our interviews. While in the chapters that follow we focus on the coexistence of everyday sexism and media-ready feminism in response to representations rooted less in the genre of fantasy, in this chapter on *Game of Thrones*, our focus is on examining media-ready feminist reception of the combination of moments of breakthrough feminism with the extreme misogyny in the text.

Methods

The reception data on which this chapter is based was collected by Sarah Johnson-Palomaki between seasons 5 and 6 of the show. Johnson-Palomaki investigated both online reception and interviewed actual viewers. To sample the show's online analyses, she adopted a strategy of nonrandom purposive sampling of internet articles engaged in this conversation, finding these sources in the top two hundred links in a Google search for "*Game of Thrones* feminist." After eliminating duplicates, shorter articles, forum pages, and so on, she composed a final sample of forty-two articles published or distributed through a wide variety of websites, including from explicitly feminist sites (*Jezebel*), to broader popular culture–related sites (*Buzzfeed*), to more traditional venues for media critique (*Vanity Fair*).

In addition to the textual data, Johnson-Palomaki conducted in-depth interviews with forty viewers. She initialized data collection with a series of nonrandom purposive outreach techniques (e.g., listserv emails through the local university, posting flyers around town) and used snowball sampling to find additional interviewees. Her final sample was sixty percent female and seventy-two percent white, and interviewees ranged from eighteen to seventy-three years old (with a median age of twenty-eight). In-depth interviews varied in length, ranging from forty-five minutes to just under three hours. Johnson-Palomaki conducted interviews with both individuals and groups (comprised of two to five interviewees), with group interviews drawing from those who had a regular "viewing group" and often watched and discussed *Game of Thrones* with fellow interviewees.

The interview schedule had an hourglass structure, first discussing the show broadly, then moving to discuss the specific gender politics respondents see as relating to the show, before finally broadening out again to a discussion on feminism in the media, culture, and society. Using Sarah Johnson-Palomaki's analysis of the show and responses from her focus groups, Press and Tripodi then analyzed the data according to the "media-ready feminism" theoretical framework they had developed in conducting the research and analyses that comprise the rest of this book.

Reception of *Game of Thrones* in the Press: A Focus on the Characters

Game of Thrones' breakthrough feminist moments hinge on the way it quite originally presents a spate of exceptionally powerful female characters who take leadership in the extremely misogynistic society pictured. In addition, several of the most important of these characters are queered in interesting ways. Both popular and feminist media tend to focus on these powerful and queered characters, noting the ways they defy traditional representations of feminine sexuality and feminine power. We take some time to introduce the most-discussed characters before analyzing media and audience responses to them.

Daenerys (Dany to fans) is a central, much-discussed figure on *Game of Thrones*. Much of the feminist excitement about this show in the media has hinged on discussion of her character. At the time of the interviews[2] Dany was the most salient feminist character in the show, and the most obvious place to start as we examine the show's feminism is with her. Daenerys was initially presented as a young victimized girl, sold by her brother and raped by her new husband, notably in an incident absent from the books but inserted into the show as a particularly egregious example of its extreme sexual violence. Despite the rape, Daenerys grows to love her husband and comes into her own as a powerful woman and ultimately even a contender for the throne. When her husband dies, she walks into his funeral pyre with one of their wedding gifts, three long-fossilized dragon eggs. From this fire she then emerges, naked and unharmed, with three small live dragons. Daenerys rules over her followers with the help of her three dragons, to whom she is a "mother" figure. She is also committed to justice for the needy and defenseless. With her dragons and now undyingly loyal followers, she goes on a series of campaigns to free slaves and the disempowered from their unjust rulers. While her desire to lead the world as a just ruler is honorable, she ultimately is not able to escape her bloodthirsty family past, which leads to her undoing in the final season. In this way, despite her immense strength and commitment to justice, Daenerys's story is ultimately a tragic one, warning viewers of the threats associated with female power as the truly mega-powerful Daenerys succumbs to the influence of her power-hungry family. Though she reaches a height of power over the course of the show, she meets with a tragic end that, given the extent of her prior success and power, is quite unexpected and hits viewers by surprise. Such a stereotypical punishment meted out to a powerful woman undercuts the breakthrough feminist quality of Daenerys's political and military power.

However, throughout the series, media and viewers were drawn to Dany as a powerful woman figure for a variety of reasons, pointing to her intelligence, integrity, and femininity as indicators of the show's inherent feminism. In doing so, reviewers and viewers often discuss the extreme misogyny Dany has faced, remarking on her strength and growth. A writer for the prize-winning group blog *BoingBoing*, overtly grappling with *Game of Thrones*' feminism, points to Daenerys as evidence of the ways in which the show offers an unusual and noteworthy advocacy for women, saying that "by exploring the ways women push back against the limitations of a male-dominated society, *Game of Thrones* has created some of the most compelling female protagonists on TV. . . . Daenerys Targaryen—the woman who stands the best chance of actually ruling Westeros—combines her inherent intelligence and morality with the physical power of her dragons." While the article also uses a feminist perspective to criticize the nudity and sexual violence of the show, the discussion about Daenerys exemplifies the ways in which *Game of Thrones* provides images which, in their definition, fulfill our criteria for what counts as a media-ready "breakthrough feminist moment" in its portrayal of women characters. However, in this fantasy world, everyday sexism has been replaced by a graphic representation of rapes and lethal violence against women. Yet, interestingly, media accounts of the show find the power of Daenerys's representation to be such that it overcomes such misogyny and holds their interest. We therefore argue that the series contains a feminist quality that eclipses other popular fantasy book-to-screen series such as *Lord of the Rings* on this dimension, given that neither of these feature a series of powerful women characters rivaling Daenerys and other leading *Game of Thrones* females.

In discussing Daenerys as a feature central to the show, viewers consistently note her unusual power and success. In one reception pattern, viewers identify the extreme and structural misogyny facing women in this fantasy world, and then praise the unique and creative ways Daenerys in particular is able to face this oppression. This is best seen in the following passage from the *HBO Watch* fan site in their official description of the show:

> A young woman in a world created and run by men, Daenerys is denied her humanity, physically and verbally abused, and traded as a piece of property. Then she starts to take over the world. She's a more adult, more complicated (and arguably more flawed) character than Hermione [the main female character in the *Harry Potter* series], and I can't get enough! . . . Daenerys is playing the war game, and to do so she needs to fight to kill, but otherwise her leadership is marked by a love for humankind and a moral fight to right wrongs and fight oppression. . . . Why do I love her so much? Dany breaks the mold, both in terms of the roles assigned to gender, and the definition of leadership. She leads with compassion and love, and earns respect, instead of instilling fear in her followers to force their allegiance. She also has great instincts, the courage to follow her gut, and the moral obligation to fight oppression. As long as she can marry her intellect with her compassion, she has the capacity to be the most fearsome contender for the throne, one that would bring balance and harmony to the seven kingdoms, as she is the type of leader people would gladly and proudly join ranks to fight alongside her. (Keyham 2013)

We see in the first section of the passage an identification of structural misogynistic oppression faced by women as a collective, followed by the praise for a complex, agentic representation of female leadership. This passage perhaps surprisingly critiques gender roles and gendered notions of power without devaluing the often-feminized values of "compassion and love." Instead, these traditionally feminine values are incorporated into a new vision of powerful leadership that we see embodied in this character, at least until the show's conclusion.

This pattern of acknowledging Daenerys's intelligence, integrity, and, interestingly, her femininity was also seen throughout discussions of *Game of Thrones*' feminism in the popular press, as in this passage from *Huffington Post*:

> Let's not forget about Daenerys, who despite being initially controlled by the men in her life, has risen to the top pretty much by herself—her dragons don't count as men because well, they're not—and she has no qualms about killing people who get in her way, handing out mercy where it's needed and she entertains the opinions of the girl from Hollyoaks even though she was once a slave and doesn't deem herself worthy. Again, a woman with more balls than a lot of the men in the program. (Hopper 2015)

Perhaps not surprisingly, in the explicitly feminist press, Daenerys's image in particular has inspired a lot of debate and even confusion because of what is perceived as its extreme feminist qualities. There is often an acknowledgment of Daenerys's power, as in an article in *Feminspire*, which remarks on how Dany is "an example of how a character and a person can be strong without being physically capable and a testament to the power that everyone has within them" (Payne and Henderson n.d.). Daenerys is presented visually as a very "femme" woman who is not particularly physically strong but embodies stereotypical notions of female beauty with her long blond hair and voluptuous figure. Some might say this tempers her power, but *Feminspire* finds a way in this passage to note that, in fact, this representation can be seen to expand notions of how female power is embodied.

Media often focus on other *Game of Thrones* characters as well, as they articulate the way feminism is referenced within *Game of Thrones*' representations. Two of these characters, both warriors so often discussed in tandem, are Arya Stark and Brienne of Tarth. Arya is a young girl born to royalty who, after the criminalization and execution of her father in season 1, must live life on the run in an attempt to stay alive. Brienne, while a smaller character, takes up considerably more space on the small screen as "an androgynous, loyal, ridiculously tall" knight-like woman who fights on behalf of various protagonists throughout the series (as discussed in Hopper 2015). Like Daenerys, these women characters are often discussed in the popular press as women fighting extreme misogyny in feminist ways. Unlike Daenerys they embody a type of "female masculinity" (Halberstam 1998) in their muscular physiques and their demonstrable prowess as warriors. For example, *WhatCulture*, in an article entitled "5 Characters That Prove *Game of Thrones* is a Feminist Show," argues that Arya "will push the boundaries of what is expected of young girls" (Meadows 2013), and *Buzzfeed* calls Brienne "a gender-bending, fierce knight who has to fight 10 times as hard as her male counterparts, which she welcomes" (Arthur 2013). Both of these pieces allude to the boundary-breaking feminist qualities of these characters.

Influenced by the calls for an intersectional and queer feminism, feminist media have remarked explicitly on the female masculinity of Arya and Brienne as further evidence of *Game of Thrones*' feminism. *Feminspire* argues that "Arya is immediately set up as a character who rejects the social constructs of femininity and gender roles and is very much her own person, despite her young age." They go on to discuss Brienne as "deep and complex," stating that she "chose to be a knight, chose to defy the norms, and chose who[m] to ally herself with. She was not pushed into it, nor used, nor played with. Everything she does is her own choice, and it's bizarrely rare to see a female character have such agency." Blogger *The Feminist Femline* argues in a list of "10 Reasons Why Arya Stark Is the Baddest Bitch in Westeros" that "she ain't no lady" (Falotico 2014). *Livingly*, a progressive women's lifestyle site, states that "we can't talk about feminism and awesome girl power moments in *Game of Thrones* without discussing Brienne, the lady knight who has battled her way valiantly into what is perhaps one of the strongest female roles on the show" (Madani 2015). As a part of the article, *Livingly* draws on a meme where Brienne is giving a sideways glance to another female character with a caption that reads, "Hey girl, you don't have to adhere to the conventions of a patriarchal society."

As with popular media discussions of Daenerys, feminist outlets also discuss the portrayal of structural oppression of women characters. *Bitch Media* describes Brienne as "the knight who swings her sword fearlessly but knows she's just as vulnerable to rape as a lady without armor" (Zeisler 2013), even though in the show she is saved from rape several times and at other times fights back effectively against assault. Brienne's femininity, like Daenerys's, combines a stereotypical feminine vulnerability with strength. However, feminist media offer a more nuanced discussion of feminism that both allows for and demands more diverse representations of women, and often invokes details of the structural oppression women face and the kinds of changes that would be necessary to rectify this. *Game of Thrones*' characters provide a diversity of feminist representations but pair these with representations of extreme sexual violence and misogyny that both undercut its feminism and, at the same time, foreground the problems of patriarchal oppression. Rather than offering yet another example of popular feminism, *Game of Thrones* features a more complex approach to feminist representation.

The most nuanced and pointed examples of *Game of Thrones*' feminism takes place in discussions around the character of Sansa Stark. The center of much debate in feminist media, Sansa is a character that has been humiliated, beaten, and raped, all by multiple men to whom she is married off for political gain and manipulation. Two husbands, the cruel Joffrey Baratheon and the arguably crueler Ramsey Bolton, abuse Sansa mercilessly, seeing her victimized over multiple occasions throughout the show's run. Sansa becomes an undeniably stronger character as the series goes on, using her "sexual wiles" (Docketerman 2014) and "political and social cunning" (Siede 2015), as the mainstream media often point out, to advance her personal and familial goals. The feminist media, however, have used the character of Sansa to raise a complex conversation about popular feminism.

A good illustration of this can be found in the feminist fan website *The Mary Sue*'s discussions about Sansa. Sansa's abuse was much discussed in feminist media as illustrating the popular charge that *Game of Thrones* is not feminist, a prominent line of argument coexisting alongside arguments that the show is the most sophisticated and extreme feminist text on television. After the brutal rape of Sansa by Ramsey, *The Mary Sue* announced, "We Will No Longer Be Promoting HBO's *Game of Thrones*." Despite its editor being a personal fan of the books, the magazine argued that they will stop covering the show, asserting that "rape (should) not be a necessary plot device" in Sansa's story arc. Other feminist media outlets agreed, taking issue with the show's overall levels of sexual violence in general and the treatment of Sansa in particular.

However, some in the feminist media point to the narrative of Sansa Stark as, paradoxically, evidence of *Game of Thrones*' progressive feminist stance, as in this article in the feminist media organ *Balancing Jane*, which references real-world sexism as the justification for Sansa's rapes:

> Yes, Sansa's treatment was horrendous. Yes, it was terrible to watch a character who had just recently escaped so much trauma and who appeared to be recovering spirit and strength to be so brutalized. Yes, rape is an abhorrent act. But real women

are raped in real life. Often repeatedly. Often after regaining strength from previous abuse. Often at the hands of people who[m] they depend on. Often. Too often. To suggest that Sansa as a character is somehow now deficient or that her reaction . . . is somehow insufficient is troubling to me.

. . .

I know that Sansa is not a real person, but if critics can use a feminist argument to turn away from the show on her behalf, surely I can use a feminist argument to say that she deserves me to stick around and be on her side.

In this piece, the author argues that the show's representation of Sansa's rape is an empathetic one that asks viewers to be intensely critical of the extreme misogyny of the show and, in doing so, to be critical of the misogyny in the real world. From this perspective, the piece argues, *Game of Thrones*' text is a truly feminist portrayal. Sansa's growth as she moves forward from this too-common trauma of sexual violence is one, they argue, that should be recognized and supported by fans. Yet often, as we have seen, both feminist and mainstream media, in media-feminist fashion, simply criticize the show for being too violent or misogynist, rather than recognizing the truth dimension of its portrayals as pertinent to actual and current societies, or alternately recognizing that these portrayals might be central to the show's popularity in a patriarchal culture.

From one perspective, then, *Game of Thrones* takes a genuinely feminist approach in portraying the very real though extreme misogyny faced by many women. The highly "feminized" strength Sansa uses to overcome her challenges is an integral part of how her strength is portrayed, as was true in the case of Daenerys. The following, which underscores this perspective, is seen in a post on *Everyday Feminism*:

Because Sansa doesn't have stereotypically "masculine" traits (like physical bravery and leadership skills), people consider her weak. . . . But Sansa is far from a weak character. Let's put her story in perspective: she witnesses her father being executed, and suffers physical, verbal, and emotional abuse from her fiancé. At the end of it all, though, she takes a chance and is able to escape. . . . I know it's because she doesn't solve her problems by fighting back physically or by standing up for herself directly. Instead, she uses her "feminine" traits to her advantage. She becomes adept at reading other people's feelings, which helps her navigate the often murky waters of court politics. And she uses her good manners as a shield to hide her own intentions, so that she can appear the obedient fiancé and therefore survive. But she's never praised for any of these things, because none of these things are what we think of as heroic. Which begs the question: why shouldn't they be?

Again, as seen in *Bustle*:

> While Daenerys has been most fans' feminist role model throughout *Game of Thrones*, Sansa is quickly ascending up the ladder and becoming another feminist hero to root for in this show. We can all learn a lot from her and her struggles, and it's her life experiences that make her such a formidable force.

Sansa's narrative is a strongly popular feminist narrative in that it portrays the structural, if extreme, misogyny women face quite explicitly, and highlights in an empowering way how women like Sansa can survive and overcome this misogyny. Her strategies for doing this, however, are often highly "feminized," and this is a source of continuing conflict in reception of the show. The extreme femininity of Sansa and Sansa's narrative has been at the center of debates about the actual breakthrough quality of the feminism in *Game of Thrones* as demonstrated by the interview data discussed later in this chapter.

Out of all of the *Thrones* women, the story of Cersei Lannister is perhaps the most stereotypically foreboding. A villain from the beginning, she is the power-hungry queen, then queen mother of the seven kingdoms, father to future king Joffrey and his younger, gentler brother Tommen, and the incestuous lover of her twin brother Jamie. This affair leads to the seeming death but ultimate crippling of Bran Stark, one of Sansa's young brothers. Cersei ruthlessly calls for the death of Sansa's innocent pet dire wolf and aggressively takes power after the death of her husband, King Robert. She is blamed for (or, at least, blamed for not stopping) much of the mistreatment of Sansa Stark while she is in King's Landing, and, like the iconic Evil Queen in the tale of "Snow White," is generally suspicious of all women younger and more beautiful than she. *Bitch Media* calls her "the steely, uncompromising dowager with plans."

However Cersei is not presented entirely according to the tropes of the evil queen: her saving grace is her love for her children and family (including her twin brother Jamie). A near-violently protective mother figure, her love for Joffrey and Tommen overrule her hunger for power (at least until later seasons and the suicide of Tommen). This is evidenced by another much-discussed and controversial scene in which Cersei is raped by Jamie while she is in mourning over Joffrey's death. Despite her love for Jamie, she audibly and physically rebuffs his advances as her heart longs for her dead child. *Buzzfeed* discusses her sympathetically, noting that "Cersei's grievances feel real and poignant. She was forced by her father to marry Robert, who didn't love her, and has been denied real, direct power because she's a woman." Cersei gives them a platform on which to discuss women's general lack of power. And the feminist *Feminspire* goes even further:

> Although Cersei is an incredibly flawed and often amoral character, she is a compelling example of a woman who fights tooth and nail to gain power in a world run by men. (SW) She is also one of the women on this list who "breaks the rules" so to speak when it comes to expressing her sexuality, shamelessly enjoying sex and seducing men into her bed. She owns her sexuality, sometimes even using it to help her gain or maintain her power.

Like *Buzzfeed*, *Feminspire* finds the somewhat stereotyped Cersei nevertheless to be an ideal character to tout for her feminism.

Regardless, by the end of season 6, Cersei's thirst for power overcomes even her love for her children, and her violent actions lead to the suicide of her youngest son, Tommen, leaving her with ultimate power, though childless. Cersei's narrative suggests that women, at least evil women, are motived by two things: children and selfish power, with the latter eventually overcoming the former. The depiction of her thirst for power is a stereotype given that the powerful adult men on the show are not similarly labeled as "selfish" but instead are seen as powerful, ambitious, and fit for war and competition. Again, despite her strength and agency, the feminist potential of Cersei Lannister is restrained by common misogynist media tropes.

Media-Feminist Reception

Viewers interviewed picked up on the often sophisticated representations of feminism in Game of Thrones. Though viewers often used the label "feminist" to describe this show, they grappled with depictions of sexual violence coexisting alongside the text's representation of powerful women, violence that often involved these characters. While they enjoyed following strong female leads, they also expressed disgust for the extreme sexism of the most violent kind that was an integral part of the representation of women. Viewers' comments on both its notable feminism and also on what was read as its notable sexism formed an integral part of their responses to Game of Thrones and were central as we assessed a media-ready feminist "accommodation" pattern whereby the breakthrough feminism of the show, embodied in both its strong women characters *and* from some perspectives in its relentless depiction of sexual violence and misogyny, was downplayed in its reception. To an unusual degree the contradictions within the show's representations were indicative of our culture's melding of an accepted popular feminism with an accepted everyday sexism. In the case of this show, viewers tended to read its misogyny more as gratuitous, titillating violence and sexuality aimed at heterosexual male viewers than as an expose of patriarchal structures—and indeed, from one perspective, its sexual violence was precisely the former. One heterosexual white woman in her late twenties notes this explicitly:

> I still don't get that. What bothers me almost more than portraying violence against women and in a context where that happens is the things that I feel like are very much calculated for the male viewer to like be turned on and want to watch the show more, so just like beautiful women being naked for no particular reason.

Contradictions between the text's feminist aspects and this gratuitous violence were apparent to viewers. So for example when discussing Game of Thrones and its treatment of male and female characters in a focus group, Blaze, a straight, white, twenty-one-year-old college student, and Katie, a straight, white, twenty-year-old college student, alluded to its complicated and contradictory set of representations, yet they note that the show's women were as powerful as its men, and that this constituted an unusual level of feminism that stood out to them. Yet they comment explicitly that the addition of gratuitous violence to this undercuts the show's feminism:

BLAZE: The show portrays people of both genders as real people.

KATIE: Yeah, I'd say it treats like females and male characters pretty equally. Like, I feel like, they don't necessarily like discriminate. But I also think they add a lot of stuff that's just kinda extra unnecessary. Like, I'm pretty sure, I mean, obviously I didn't read the books but I've heard the whole, like in the first season, throughout they added a lot of violence onto Daenerys from the books.... They've added a lot of rapes, I've heard. As compared to the books, where it's kinda like, why would you do that?

Another viewer underscored this, again questioning as "baffling" (and disturbing?) the difference between the portrayal of Daenerys in the books versus the TV show: "It's baffling to me because, essentially, Daenerys was raped on her wedding night [in the TV show] but that didn't happen in the books, like, I don't understand, why you would add that on, like, why?"

Viewers strained to understand the show through the framework of popular feminism. Nevertheless viewers notice the increased sexual violence of the television show text as compared with the books, and they questioned the necessity of its level of violent representations, using a critical feminist perspective to do so. They note the presence of gratuitous sexual violence and cannot come up with an explanation for it beyond appealing to salacious heterosexual male viewers. Viewers wonder why increased violence was deemed necessary as the show was written, a question that became a particular trope for viewers who had read the books and noticed the increased sexual and misogynistic violence in the show. Some even use a postfeminist critique to rationalize that the violence was "ok": though the extreme misogyny was gratuitous and unnecessary, it need not be seen as a serious affront to the show's feminism—and this rationalization process allowed audiences to continue watching the show. In this way many viewers were able to downplay the show's violence, accommodating it to their popular feminist framework.

In a separate interview, Heather, a straight, white, twenty-five-year-old illustrator, commented on this as well, but at the same time noted that the misogyny of the show *blunts* its actual feminism:

I don't think it's inherently a feminist show. I think it might just be advantageous to make it, I don't know, seem like it is? I

mean, there are a lot of strong female characters, but it seems a little bit like an off note sometimes.
(Heather stops and thinks here for a minute, then seems to change her mind.)
I feel like it is an inherently feminist show in that there are all these strong female characters but I also feel like there are points that feel very insensitive and aren't very well written.

Heather recognizes *both* the misogyny of the show and its strong female characters.

In most focus groups and interviews, however, viewers remarked on the strong female characters first: this is why they watch the show, what they like about the show, and what makes the show unique. For them these characters make the show genuinely feminist, despite the ubiquity of its violence against women. This is a premier example of media-ready feminism, in that viewers don't seem to have a language to make a *connection*—either feminist or otherwise—between the show's portrayal of misogyny, sexual violence, and pure unadulterated violence itself, and its rather straightforwardly popular feminist portrayal of unusually strong female characters. The two are simply compartmentalized and received differently, with some expressed incomprehension of their coexistence in this text.

Viewers recognizing the popular feminist qualities of characters and, in doing so, and in calling it feminist, at times appear to go out of their way to simply justify or write off as "historical" (rather than relevant to the present) the show's extreme sexual violence and what they see as its outright misogyny. This is often done by remarking on the generic traits of the show. For example the straight, white Karlyn, despite her praise for its feminist characters, justifies *Game of Thrones*' misogynistic elements in discussing the pseudo-historical tone of the show: "Well, um. I think that the genders are definitely stuck in a certain role, because of maybe the time period that the story kind of takes place in, like middle ages."

However, a few viewers do note the contemporary relevance of the show's misogyny. For example Liz, a straight, white, thirty-five-year-old academic tutor, states:

> I think it's, it's honest and real with misogyny throughout history. And I get upset when people get offended, like oh, that was a rape scene, and it's like you do realize that that's

occurring in real life right now all the time? And, and rape has always been, um, a source of power in wars and in battles.

Although Karlyn attributes the show's depiction of sexual violence mainly to its historical setting, Liz discerns more current truths in the show, taking it as an illustration of the sexual violence that remains a strong part of our culture. For her, despite its historical setting, *Game of Thrones* functions as an actual feminist illustration of gendered social dangers. In this way she thwarts what we argue is the tendency to downplay and domesticate extreme feminism when audiences see it in the media. While the media form pushes the boundaries, audiences are often hesitant to identify and embrace the expressions of feminism they see, pushing back in a way that tempers the feminist flames. Liz sees the continuing need for feminism and mentions it in the context of the show's representations. In this way they also were able to rationalize rape as entertainment via their feminist critique. The thinking goes "of course, women are getting raped today and this has been a part of history," and some see this as justifying—however uneasily—the entertainment value of including rape in the show's representations, in addition to the value inherent in the alleged historical accuracy of including the representation of rape.

Marc, an eighteen-year-old, white, feminist-identified male, attempts this even more overtly by explicitly claiming that the show's violence and misogyny—it's "bad" qualities, in his words—are only there to highlight that "this isn't the way things should go down." Like Liz, he reads *Game of Thrones*' violence as a feminist cautionary tale. For this reason, Marc says, "I think there are definitely a lot of problems like that where women are either abused or victimized in different circumstances. I don't think it makes it necessarily less feminist because they're portraying it as, like, this is a problem." He attributes a critical feminist perspective to the show's misogynistic violence. Marc is claiming here that the show's extreme violence and even its misogyny actually magnifies its feminism, and that the show successfully promotes a critical perspective on misogyny and violence and is an example of feminist television at its best.

Liz and Marc's reception of this component remain in the minority, however, with most viewers distancing the present from this type of violence because it is deemed historical, fictional, or both, and thereby justifying its presence in a text that is feminist in other ways. For example Randy, a straight, white, twenty-seven-year-old graduate student, excuses the misogyny in the show by claiming that it is just indicative of the fantasy genre: "But, so I think the, you know, all the, you know, rape and sexuality with women, you have to remember that this is a fantasy world." In the fantasy genre, so much of the text is simply fabricated, out of the imagination; for most viewers, this extends to the show's depiction of gendered, sexual violence as well. None remarks that this is a particularly *patriarchal* imagination that deems this type of gendered sexual violence entertaining; as none mentions that the sexual violence might be central to the show's appeal and profitability, in a world that values the spectacle of gendered sexual violence and deems this the ultimate entertainment.

Game of Thrones exemplifies what we feel is, from a feminist perspective, almost a new genre: moments that push the boundaries of popular feminism, while combining with an exaggerated, hyperviolent misogyny that is offered alongside its strong female representations. *Walking Dead*, an extremely popular series still running on AMC, is another example of a similarly violent show in the fantasy genre, though on this show the violence is less gendered and less sexual. Many viewers react critically quite explicitly to this extreme misogyny. But the theory of media-ready feminism accounts for the fact that viewers uniformly lack a language that truly grapples with these textual contradictions, and with an unusually blunt portrayal of patriarchy. Though this media text itself in some ways pushes at the boundaries of popular feminism and, from one perspective, raises questions about ubiquitous, extreme misogyny, hypersexualization, and sexual violence, viewers are stuck: as media-ready feminism might predict, they lack the language to push past the categories of popular feminism and acknowledge these truly critical media moments.

For example, one viewer, Marie, an eighteen-year-old, Hispanic college student from a working-class background, spoke strikingly of *Game of Thrones* as both "inherently bad" due to its extreme sexual violence and misogyny, yet also good in that it promoted critical insight into feminist issues. To illustrate this opinion Marie spoke first of the powerful female characters, mentioning their standout qualities. She noted that Daenerys and Sansa (alongside other strong women characters like Cersei) were strong female characters that are "developing" their "female power and authority and respect in a male dominated world." Because of this, she deems the show feminist, and others echoed her arguments.

Viewers speak of this power even in the cases when characters exhibit hyperfeminine qualities as well. For example, Katie isolates Daenerys's popular feminist qualities, discussing how much she likes Daenerys because of how "powerful" she's become. As in the show's press reception, viewers often discuss Daenerys as their favorite character not only because of her strength but also because of her strong, powerful, but somewhat extreme *femininity*, which jumps out from the text for many viewers. Karlyn, a straight, white, twenty-seven-year-old office manager, praised Daenerys as an extreme character and focused at first on her strength and independence: "I mean, there are women on there that are strong, and they have their own personalities, and they have their own lives that don't revolve around a man or anything. These are women that don't answer to anyone, like Daenerys." Yet characters' hyperfemininity might open the way for the show's plethora of sexual violence.

Viewers do not make these connections, however. They strive instead to justify the show's violence and misogyny to retain their championing of its strong women. For example, Marie, quoted earlier, notes that she appreciates the show's strong women characters and that this underscores its feminism for her, even though the hypersexualization and violence on *Game of Thrones* makes her "uncomfortable." When asked what she thought about this peculiar pairing of feminism with misogyny, Marie, like Liz but more hesitantly, attempted to assert what she saw as the show's pathbreaking feminism by working hard to justify the violence as itself helping viewers to assimilate and understand the show's extreme feminism:

> MARIE: I guess what I'm trying to say is, like, the show's more so feminist in that manner because it's, like, shedding light on real life issues.
>
> INTERVIEWER: So earlier you said that the sexualization kind of made you uncomfortable . . . how does that. . . . Because now it sounds like you're saying its feminist in a way to be showing that . . .
>
> MARIE: Yeah . . . I guess, just, like, the graphic nature of it is uncomfortable, but I guess the message behind is even more strong. Like, the amount of time they spend on these scenes and the way they portray them . . . it just objectifies them so much that it becomes disgusting in a way . . . it reinforces the commentary behind it. . . . It's bad, like, inherently, but it's good because of the awareness it raises and what it draws attention to.

Marie has a nuanced interpretation of the text that accommodates both its breakthrough feminism and its gratuitous sexual violence. From a feminist perspective she explained the extreme misogyny by suggesting that the narratives in *Game of Thrones* urge the viewer to be critical of the extreme misogyny in the show, thereby encouraging a feminist critical consciousness even vis-à-vis misogyny more broadly. Justifying these conflicting representations required an enormous amount of work, however, and was not entirely successful. She wasn't prepared to push this perspective. She was hesitant. It went against the grain of a more conventional reception of the show.

Importantly, as discussed earlier in relation to Liz's excusing of rape in the show, *Game of Thrones*' media-ready feminism provides the viewer with breakthrough feminist characters in an explicitly misogynist world, but in its reception, most viewers flounder for the tools needed to understand its sexism and misogyny as their discussions move subtly from the existence of these qualities in the television text to considering their own lives. And as we've mentioned, the misogyny and sexual violence of *Game of Thrones*' representations, and its historical setting, makes it easy for viewers to distance these factors within its representations from the everyday sexism of their own world. Many viewers attempt to simply dismiss the violence in the text as unimportant to its feminism.

For some viewers, when they compared leading female characters to leading male characters, the women's strength came up short: this was a new perspective on the limits of *Game of Thrones*' feminism. As might be expected of the fantasy genre, the show's women were constantly in "survival" mode, where their extreme strength could emerge and become visible. However the male characters, though also existing in a fantasy world, had strength preexisting their extreme challenges, and this led to some discomfort. Consider for example the comments of this focus group:

> VERONICA: Thinking about, like, *The Hunger Games* and *Divergent* and *Game of Thrones* it makes me think, like, do women have to be in a survival role to be a strong lead? Like, it goes back to them doing what they have to do to survive and being this, like, strong person, but, like, they have to be in that role. But is that what the media and people are more comfortable with? 'Cause anyone in that role would have to be a strong character.

RUSSEL: Yeah, that makes me kind of uncomfortable. Because then they're being put in a position where they have to prove their worth if that makes any sense. Like, they're only getting this far because they've proven themselves. But you should have a baseline of respect and equality without having to prove yourself.

SJ: Yeah, that's interesting. Because I guess if we think of Jon Snow . . .

RUSSEL: He never had to do anything. You always just liked him because he was just there. They make you hate Sansa. They make you hate Cersei. They make you get frustrated with Arya because she makes rash decisions from the beginning.

These viewers note gender differences in the *Games of Thrones* universe of characters but seem to note similar gender differences in other fantasy shows as well, which makes them wonder about the underlying feminism even of shows featuring unusually strong female leads like this one. And as we've mentioned earlier, viewers also note the extreme femininity of some of *Game of Thrones*' most powerful women, like Dany.

Media-ready feminism emerges as the characters most universally touted as "feminist" repeatedly get some critical pushback in viewers' responses to them. For example, more often than might be expected given her positive portrayal in media discussions of the character, viewers respond to Daenerys in surprisingly negative ways indicative of an audience steeped in everyday sexism. One viewer, for example, Arlyn, a straight, white, female-identified college student, is disturbed by what she sees as the disjuncture between Daenerys's power and what she sees as her incompetence to rule:

"I want to like Daenerys more than I do—I don't think she's bad but I think she goes where the wind pushes her—a dangerous thing for somebody who has that much power . . .

She takes control [but] she has no idea what she's doing. [It's like,] "Look at me I have so much power" but she has no idea what to do with it. I imagine she's going to die, I can't imagine it going another way for her [a prescient remark made two years before her demise in the last season].

This is some notable pushback on the almost uniformly positive portrayal of this extremely powerful woman. What's notable about this comment is its reliance on stereotypes about women in power, particularly evident with the phrase "she has no idea what to do with it [her power]," which invokes the incompetent woman in a powerful position. The research shows that women in such positions of power and authority are constantly called upon to prove they *do* know what they are doing (Press 2012b, 2012c). This sentiment does not characterize the majority of the comments made about her, but Daenerys does inspire some pushback on her unusually powerful image.

Sansa is perhaps an even more controversial character, and viewer reception of her characterization corroborates this. As media-ready feminist reception might dictate, both her "feminine" and her "feminist"-power qualities inspire a decidedly mixed response. Viewers find her distinctly "unlikeable," as the literature shows is a more general problem for strong women in our culture (Bordo 2017). For example Jane, an Asian, straight, female student, finds Sansa "annoying": "I want to like her but she's just so annoying. . . . I want to like her so much but she's just such a little, I don't know, a priss almost." Others, like Wylis, a white, straight, male college student in his early twenties, finds her too passive to like:

> Like, I think the one I like least is probably Sansa, cause she seems to be more passive than she does active. Like, all of her actions are based on what other people want rather than be proactive for what she wants. . . . And you can't really blame her for everything, but you can still kind of get annoyed . . .

In an online forum, Melissa, a white woman in her thirties working in graphic design, responded to the question asking who her least favorite character was with the following: "SANSA! Entitled, spoiled little bitch, no backbone, a user of anyone to get what she wants."

Time and again, audiences who describe themselves as "feminist" fall back on misogynistic tropes often used to discuss the power of women in the most negative terms. While *Game of Thrones* is arguably trying to advance feminist character development, the audiences are more inclined to reject her sacrifices as "weak." This is a crack in the argument that a popular feminist perspective is generally accepted: while at one level we may tolerate the presence of strong women, and accept their presence in media representations, we don't like them, and much reception of them seeks to undermine their power with critical comments and negative responses to their actions. We saw this playing out in media coverage of Hillary Clinton's run for the presidency and repeatedly witness this phenomenon in the evaluation of women's leadership in a variety of forums (Bordo 2017; Press 2012b).

Perhaps a more progressive counterexample to the media-ready feminist viewer responses we have noted are viewer responses to the more "masculinist" female characters on the show. As with feminist press coverage, many viewers were drawn to the female masculinity—some might say, the queerness—of Arya and Brienne, further evidence of their breakthrough feminist potential in that these characters are freed from the extreme femininity we see in other strong women characters. Alex and Jon, straight, white, twenty-one and twenty-two, discussed this:

> ALEX: Yeah! Arya kicks butt. Um . . . there's a lot of, like, themes about femininity in Arya's story about how, like, when she loses her hair at the end of season 1 when the night's watchman protects her and says, "Okay, you're pretending to be a boy now," you, like, "I have to protect you from this society where . . . you know . . . it's like medieval, so I'm going to make you look like a boy." There's this whole story with Arya Stark about her losing her identity . . . which includes losing her femininity. . . . she's specifically going against what femininity is like in her culture. She was the closest thing to a tomboy that could be in that culture. She likes fighting, she likes adventured . . .
>
> JON: And her father tells her . . . she's like, "Do you think I could be a great swordsman" and he, like, crouches down and puts his arm around his daughter and you're like, "Yes, he's gonna empower her!" and he's like, "You'll meet a great husband someday," and you're like, "You suck Ned Stark, I like you but that's wrong!"

Viewers make similar remarks about Brienne. Jon remarks on her queerness:

> Yeah. . . . So she's possibly agender, possibly gender fluid. . . . Brienne is one of the most wholesomely good characters in this hell of a universe. She absolutely struggles with the fact

that society tells her she's supposed to be feminine and she specifically doesn't look feminine.

Amanda, a straight, Mexican American, thirty-year-old graduate student, discusses Arya and Brienne in strongly feminist terms, focusing on the unusually strong masculine tropes in their representation. She praises their lack of sexualization relative to many other representations of women in the media:

> (Laughing) And, I don't know, characters like Brienne and Arya, like I feel like, there are so many shows that would like to claim they're feminist because they have a strong female lead, who's a bad ass and kicks ass and stuff, but she's always sexualized. So the fact that they have these characters that fit that description and really are not at all sexualized and also not like, made into like, monsters. They're just people.

Even in a show criticized for its nudity and hypersexualization, the characters of Arya and Brienne transcend traditional representations of women in such a way that makes *Game of Thrones* a notably feminist show for many viewers.

Viewers seem to have an easier time accepting the female masculinity of Arya and Brienne than they do the complicated combination of feminine sexual power and political strength represented by the characters of Sansa, Dany, and Cersei. For some reason seeing the masculinist women as powerful is less disconcerting for the viewers in our study. It is only when the show violates the boundaries of traditional femininity by portraying the ultrafeminine Sansa as gaining strength through violence, or the ultrafeminine Dany as a strong female political and military leader that audiences are ambivalent in that reception.

We find this interesting and noteworthy for a variety of reasons. Perhaps Arya and Brienne carry less stereotypical baggage as they break the bounds of traditional representations: maybe viewers are simply ready for the type of feminist-inspired change they represent. Moreover, despite the plethora of sexual violence it features, the show fails to engage with Arya and Brienne in overtly sexual ways. Brienne of Tarth is never raped on the show and rarely appears nude on camera. Arya's loss of her virginity is also framed as powerful: when determined not to die a virgin, she chooses her longtime best friend to help her satisfy this wish. While this portrayal made some uncomfortable because Arya was first portrayed in the show as a child, in fact one of the strongest female characters on the show is never raped. Yet none of the audiences seemed to note this contradiction—that the two most masculine female characters, often perceived as the strongest women on the show, were also rarely sexualized or filmed without clothing.

Conclusion

Since the time of data collection, *Game of Thrones* has come to an end. Ultimately, Daenerys and Cersei died. While Arya and Brienne survived to the end, gaining some power, it was Sansa who rose to the most powerful female role. Unexpected perhaps, or a cautionary tale that the most powerful women sow the seeds of their own destruction? *Bitch Media* sums up the debate about *Game of Thrones*' feminism as follows: "So does it matter if *Game of Thrones* is feminist? Maybe not. But what does matter is that it's one of the few shows to give us a reason to even argue the case—and if it yields a richer array of characters in the TV shows that will inevitably try to rip it off, all the better."

We agree with this assessment that *Game of Thrones* offers us a richer array of characters than do most current media products. Yet we also think it's important that in media-ready feminist fashion, these characters are not received without criticism and suspicion, particularly when viewers consider their more extreme feminist qualities. The combination of extreme femininity, heterosexual power, and extreme political power that we see with the characters of Cersei, Sansa, and Daenerys particularly seems to upset a wide swath of the viewers in our study. More masculinist figures of power such as Arya and Brienne were received with less ambivalence and seemed to pave the way for viewers to move beyond media-ready feminism to a genuinely feminist moment. In chapters to come we fill in the contours of media-ready feminism and discuss further the ways media, and viewers, can deepen into genuinely feminist positions.

2

Prudes, Sluts, and Sex

The Classing of Female Sexuality in Media-Ready Feminism

Introduction

The kind of paradoxical attitudes toward feminist sentiments that we have been discussing in this book help perpetuate the contradictory cultural climate for women in which in the sexual restrictions of a misogynistic culture are operative alongside ostensibly accepted and realized feminist ideals of equality and opportunity. This silencing of feminism, particularly with regard to sexual issues, is part of a broader cultural trend in which, according to Frank Bruni in a *New York Times* op-ed piece, US culture applies sexual epithets differently to the genders in a phenomenon he calls "one-way wantonness" (Bruni 2012). Newer hookup culture solidifies society's contradictory attitudes toward women's sexual expression. Even newer coverage of the #MeToo movement often reinvokes tropes of the way sexual violence has been covered over the past several decades. While sexual violence "makes good copy" (Kitzinger 2004, quoted in Orgad 2019), stories of sexual harassment and assault are often highly sensationalized by a prurient focus on victims rather than perpetrators, as Orgad (2019) argues is continuing to characterize coverage of the #MeToo movement.

The result of this coverage is that images of women in news media as well as entertainment media continue to be inappropriately sexualized. Women are aware of the cultural risks to which a highly sexual image exposes them. Even in the current age, they continue to be cautious in displaying their sexuality, while necessarily heeding newer pressures to engage in sexual activity rather than being labeled prudish. Bruni's "one-way wantonness" is a perfect description of the cultural situation in which a woman can still be criticized for acting sexually and challenging traditional sexual mores; as *Jersey Shore* character Angelina put it, "A guy can do it but girls can't."

Even in the wake of second-wave feminism these cautions hold true. The range of epithets traditionally applied to women for wanton sexual activity—*hussy, harlot, hooker, slut*—continue in our post-second-wave popular feminist world. Some sexual insults explicitly connect to bigoted racial and social-class insults. Words such as *floozy* or *whore*, for example, implicitly connect women's sexual misbehavior to specially classed and raced derogatory epithets (Bobo 1995; Bogle 2001). For women, the slope between sex-based and class- and race-based insults is slippery indeed. Not surprisingly, women of color and working-class women are particularly sensitive to these labels, as they are more at risk of insults and other harms than are those insulated by race and class privilege.

Women's constrained relationship to sexual pleasure has always been a focus of concern for feminist activism and theory. Barbara Ehrenreich discussed in great detail the historical privileging of male sexual pleasure in patriarchal societies. Within this framework, cisgender heterosexual women's rights are limited to "bargaining" with their sexuality, using it to obtain male protection by focusing on male pleasure (Ehrenreich 1983). Second-wave feminist writing widely discussed topics like the "myth of the vaginal orgasm," pushing back on the idea that women's sexual pleasure was inherently tied to an orgasm achieved only through heterosexual vaginal intercourse (Koedt 1970; Vance 1984).

Since such second-wave critiques, cultural perspectives ensuring the right of heterosexual women to enjoy sex have grown but "pleasure gaps" persist, as demonstrated by research that documents the gendered "orgasm gap" existing within popular hookup culture, whose sexual practices prioritize male sexual pleasure over female (Armstrong, Hamilton, and England 2010).

Hookup culture as well explicitly does not prioritize and even discourages emotional relationships between sexual partners (Wade 2017). In fact, new research indicates that those who insist that an emotional connection is necessary before they can feel sexual attraction constitute a growing sexual minority. Termed "demisexuality," this category of intimacy is already an optional identity category on Facebook and has been widely written about in popular discussions of sexuality.[1] While this newish identity category is not specifically linked to heterosexual women, it speaks to a growth in the hyperpersonalization of the sexual experience, and to the desire of some youth to maintain a *personal connection* as prerequisite to sexual intimacy, a position that ironically hearkens back to the gendered cultural norms about sexual behavior predating second-wave feminism. Overall, the growth of demisexuality speaks to important gaps or lacks in the current, still-patriarchal sexual culture.

Within a rapidly changing sexual world, this chapter aims to address how, and to what extent, female pleasure in heterosexual encounters is prioritized or diminished in the current cultural moment. Are the sexual and emotional needs of cisgender heterosexual women met in different ways now that the sexual climate embraces a wider spectrum of gender identities and sexual expression? Does a freer and more inclusive sexual environment provide an opportunity for women's sexual and emotional gratification as well as men's? How are newer sexual practices resisting or supporting patriarchy? How and in what ways are one's classed and raced positions wrapped up in sexual satisfaction?

Armstrong and Hamilton (2015) describe how the college experience for heterosexual women remains static—how women get caught in a tightrope act between enacting sexiness but not trashiness, between seeming available but not too interested in sex. Those who fail the "intimacy test" are blocked from serious relationships—labeled as not suitable girlfriend material. They describe how working-class women in college often break the rules unknowingly, subjecting themselves to demeaning and even violent treatment from the male hosts of fraternity parties and other gatherings they attend (2015, 55) more often than those who know the classed rules of these interactions. This research suggests that the experience of hookup culture is highly classed and still bound by overtly patriarchal norms.

Women's sexual images have a history of being highly raced and classed in our media culture, and these two categories are often intertwined in representations. Scholars of racial stereotyping note that the "jezebel" stereotype, defined as referring to a presumably "oversexed," young Black female, is an enduring trope in cultural representations of African American women (Bogle 2001). Such racial stereotyping has a persistent, concrete life in current dating and sexual cultures. For example, research shows that women of color are often judged as undesirable when it comes to the status-marking process of hookup culture—excluding Asian women, who are also racially judged, in this case paradoxically as the most "desirable" racial status in hookups (Wade 2017). Likewise, Wade (2017) finds that men of color are also racially stereotyped, ranking "lower" on the heterosexual desirability ladder in hookup culture, with Asian men in this case being seen as too feminine and therefore holding the lowest hookup-culture status.

These findings indicate that race and class combine with gender to play central roles in establishing norms of sexual desirability in today's sexual marketplace. In ongoing work, Press has argued that as Hollywood film developed a series of highly sexualized images of women, images of great significance in our cultural imagination for several decades, these images were all intricately classed and raced (Press and Rosen 2017; Press 2021). Examples of such class-based stereotyping pertain to both "lower-class" and "upper-class" categories. The term "white trash" is still widely recognized to connote a lower-class woman of loose sexual morals. In general "trashy" as an adjective applied to women can mean a highly sexual woman, a woman with lower-class origins, or both (Press and Rosen 2017). The extremely popular Marilyn Monroe's star image exhibited a level of overt "trashy" sexuality in many of her most iconic film roles, which portrayed her as a poor woman seeking to better her condition through bargaining with her sexuality. Monroe's enduring popularity indicates that many were attracted to her specifically lower-class incarnation of sexuality.[2]

"Upper-class" women have also been identified with a type of sexual stereotyping. A primary example of this can also be drawn from the history of Hollywood film in the form of the notorious "Hitchcock blondes." The Hitchcock blondes were a series of star images created by famed film director Alfred Hitchcock and placed in roles central to his immensely popular Hollywood films of the 1940s, 1950s, and 1960s. Hitchcock blondes were women who dressed tastefully and expensively, often in nonrevealing, buttoned-up clothes. The director described them as women who didn't allow their sexuality to become too visible. In this way, he believed they projected a "classy" sexy persona. Grace Kelly, who later became a real-life princess when she married a prince she met while filming a Hitchcock film, is often spoken of as the quintessential Hitchcock blonde in that she represented the ultimate embodiment of this high-class sexuality.[3] Hitchcock never featured women of color in his films and preferred blondes with light complexions, in this way emphasizing their "whiteness" (Spoto 2009). Hitchcock explicitly contrasted his blondes to the trashier Marilyn Monroe star persona of the 1950s. Interestingly, Monroe was also known for the extreme "whiteness" of her image (Banner 2008). Both these "white" stereotypes contrast markedly with the kinds of sexual stereotypes most often applied culturally to women of color (Bogle 2001). Many famous women of color recount wrestling with the "jezebel" stereotypes to which they were expected to conform (Bogle and Singleton 2019).

While for decades film was the most popular mass medium in the United States, starting in the mid-1950s, television began to usurp this status. For the latter half of the twentieth century and continuing into the twenty-first, television remains the most-watched mass medium (Laghate 2018). Over the past several decades, television studies have proliferated, and television scholars richly discuss the conventions of a plethora of television genres, including the significant rise of "quality" television in the 1990s and beyond that has become a repository of high status and widely viewed media imagery (Newman and Levine 2011). While social class and race have become increasingly visible in a number of high-quality television products, such as HBO's extremely popular production *The Wire* (2002–2008), famous for its portrayal of the African American underclass, reality television as a genre has become widely known for picturing a non-middle-class, white population.

Many scholars have noted that the reality television genre has often been a locus for portraying class and racial distinctions (Wood and Skeggs 2011, Grindstaff 2002, 2011; Ouellette and Hay 2008; Couldry 2011; Walkerdine 2011; Wood 2011; Coleman et al. 2019). It is on reality television that we find some of the most explicitly lower-class images in the televisual world, and some of the most stereotyped characters of color as well. The massive hit show *Jersey Shore*—originally aired from 2009 to 2012 but back on the air as *Jersey Shore Family Vacation* in 2018–2019, with continued episodes being planned as we write this—is a prime example of reality television's classed world of images. The cast constitutes its identity in ethnic terms: they call themselves "guidos," which in American English is generally a slang term for urban Italian Americans. Nevertheless, of the original cast members, only one is actually from an Italian American family. The others are only half Italian, adopted by an Italian family, or simply not Italian at all. In the context of this show, it seems that "guido" is more of an umbrella term for lower-class whites of different backgrounds as it is used on this show (Grindstaff 2011).

Discussions of women, women and sexuality, and feminism were relatively plentiful in the course of the *Jersey Shore* text—but this chapter focuses on a moment in which the show chose to *challenge* the double standard. The cast members' discussions openly acknowledge that women are not able to hook up in the same way as men, with some overtly labeling this as discriminatory. We examined how viewers reacted to a cast discussion of the issue in which one woman defended sexual freedom for women but then was criticized by the rest of the cast, who maintained that it was *not* acceptable for women to have multiple partners—openly asserting gender inequality in sexual relationships. For us this was an explicitly media-ready feminist moment, worthy of reception study.

Methods

The reception analysis in this chapter is drawn from focus groups with women and men of varying class statuses and racial identities, who discussed sexual attitudes and then viewed a clip from the *Jersey Shore* episode entitled "Dirty Pad" (S2, E9), further discussing these issues in light of the clip following its viewing. Four of these focus groups were conducted with students at a flagship state university with a majority of students occupying high socioeconomic positions (measured by the educational attainment and salary of their parents). Of these groups, two were racially homogeneous (white) members of a sorority on the campus and two were recruited through the university's multicultural council in an effort to provide a more diverse set of opinions on the series.

A separate focus group consisted of women who attended a less competitive state university and were first-generation college students. This group was representative of the ethnic diversity of the university in which white students are a minority. Two other focus groups were conducted with high-achieving, rural high school students who had been selected for a summer program at a prestigious urban university designed to encourage first-generation students to attend college. Altogether, we spoke with sixty-five respondents about this episode. All the interviews were transcribed and coded for references to issues of social class, feminism, gender, sexuality, and the sexual double standard. The names of all quoted participants are pseudonyms.

The "Dirty Pad" episode of *Jersey Shore* was selected because in this episode, cast members address normative ideas about women's sexual behavior, what it means to be a "slut," and the differences between the ideal sexual behaviors that "should" be practiced by heterosexual men versus heterosexual women. The episode features a moment in which cast member Angelina espouses feminist objections to the "double standard," saying that it is not acceptable for general criticism to be leveled only at women with multiple partners and not at men, and noting that this level of gendered inequality was unfair. This moment stood out to us as an example of television's new relative capacity to express explicitly politically progressive feminist sentiments. Focusing on this moment allowed us to better understand and theorize the notion of media-ready feminism. Was this opinion truly revolutionary? How did audiences react to this moment? Were they supportive of the character who embraced sexual equality or did they also frame her behavior as unacceptable? Given the socioeconomic differences among those studied, we were also able to determine the extent to which their social class position might impact the ability of audiences to be "ready" to sympathetically receive what seemed to us the feminist set of opinions expressed on the show.

Our discussion focuses also on the ways in which class and race make a difference as respondents interpret and discuss the double standard. We discuss that some people of color and working-class respondents accept and support the double standard. We felt this was particularly notable given the explicitness with which second-wave feminism criticized this cultural attitude head-on (Vance 1984). By demonstrating how *Jersey Shore* simultaneously embraces and depoliticizes feminism; privileges the experiences of white, heterosexual, young, upper-class women as actions to aspire toward; and fails to acknowledge the underlying structural inequalities of everyday sexism, we use this case to articulate how even when a television show features a media-ready feminist moment, the radical sentiments expressed do not inspire widespread support, particularly when the raced and classed nature of sexuality call some feminist discourses into question.

Why *Jersey Shore*?

Despite the fact that the show has been off air for many years, *Jersey Shore* was cable television's top-rated show among viewers twelve to thirty-four years old during the six seasons it aired on MTV. Rather than focus on a narrative whereby people had to "shed" their lower-class "markers" to achieve success, *Jersey Shore* embraced and celebrated the way its cast embodied a classed, ethnic identity, without making explicit reference to social class. As the popularity of the show increased over several seasons, cast members began to also "perform" this identity in live appearances and through commercial endorsements, further complicating the authenticity of their characterizations.[4] In this way, the show's use of the term "guido" is embedded with class markers not unlike shows like *Here Comes Honey Boo Boo* that use phrases like "white trash" or words like "hillbilly" to connote the class position of the people on the show while simultaneously avoiding the explicit language of social class, as is the cultural norm in the United States.

In distinct contrast to reality television shows that present middle-class status as something to aspire to (and often prescribe the makeovers or alterations necessary to achieve it), *Jersey Shore* was not about self-improvement. On the contrary, the show's conspicuous absence of discussion about how these resolutely non-middle-class characters might get their act together and achieve more middle-class jobs, clothing habits, bodies, and goal-directed everyday lives created an aura of escapism rather than reformation. This theme, hated by critics but seemingly loved by young audiences, goes against the grain of much of the terrain of television programming in general in its celebration of a non-middle-class lifestyle.

While at times it appeared that *Jersey Shore* was simply an exploitive portrayal of working-class people and their divergent lifestyles (Wood and Skeggs 2011, 17), it also at times pushed the boundaries for feminist expression. The show's female characters were portrayed as strong, with the ability to take care of themselves, and embodied a level of sexual empowerment in many forms (e.g., some opted for monogamous relationships while others celebrated and participated unabashedly in hookup culture). The sexual activity of the show's cast members was always very public and a central narrative thread. Because the cast lived together in a group house with shared bedrooms and little privacy, would-be partners usually went into a special room—referred to by the cast as the "smush" room—when they were planning to have sex. The consequently public nature of house-based sexual activity was cemented by the collective custom of recording each house member's sexual exploits on a white board visible in the house living room. The white board allowed the cast to publicly list their sexual conquests, opening these to the comments of the entire group.

Nonetheless, the show's focus on recreational sexuality played out differently for men and women, which interjected a conservative note into the show's radical support for working-class versus middle-class mores. The show's men were frequently shown heading toward the gym to perfect their bodies (coining the phrase "GTL"—gym, tan, laundry), creating the bodies that in their minds served as their primary means of attracting women. Although the women on the show are similarly present-oriented and pleasure-seeking and therefore ostensibly presented as the men's sexual equals, the pursuit of sexual pleasure did expose them to a set of judgments that the men seemed to escape. By analyzing the discourse around the gendered double sexual standard as it appears in the episode "Dirty Pad" (S2, E9) and then analyzing the responses of focus group participants to this particular vignette, this chapter unpacks responses to *Jersey Shore*'s brief media-ready feminist moment.

The Episode

"Dirty Pad" originally aired on MTV on September 23, 2010. The episode featured an in-depth discussion of the sexual behavior of one of the women in the cast, Angelina. In this episode, Angelina was beginning to date a man named Jose, but one night she decided to have sex with another cast member living in the house, Vinny, with whom she had been indulging in an on-again, off-again flirtation. The following night, she brought Jose home to the house and slept in a separate room with him—which other cast members interpreted to mean she had had sex with him; although behind closed doors, hidden from the other members of the cast but in full view of the audience, she in fact rejected his advances despite remaining in the smush room.

Therefore, in the episode, Angelina appears to the cast members to have had two different sexual partners over two nights (she furthers this speculation by drawing a second "line" under her name on the white board after going with Jose to the "smush" room). However, the camera tells viewers—but not the other cast members—that she had not in fact had sexual relations with her second partner. Yet Angelina does not contradict the cast members' assumptions when the incident is addressed, critically, in the house's collective discussion. She keeps silent, it is revealed later, to avoid making herself vulnerable to the alternate criticism that she "led Jose on" with the expectation of sex, which would have led to her being called a "cock-tease" or some worse epithet. Her dilemma indicates how female sexuality is policed from both ends: Angelina faces potential criticism not only for having too many sex partners, but also for *not* engaging in sexual activity when she enters the smush room with a potential partner. Angelina chooses to face criticism for the former, rather than admit that she has in fact *not* engaged in sexual activity with two different partners two nights in a row.

Angelina is prepared with a defense for the slut charges that she knows she will face. When the name is applied, she fights back, claiming that the "slut" slur is unfairly gendered, and that men would not face criticism even for exactly the same behavior. She is prepared to speak back to the house's criticism on the basis of this feminist-based criticism.

The morning after Angelina emerges from the smush room with Jose to the collective view of house members, many of the cast members are filmed critically commenting on the context of what they see as Angelina's "excessive" sexual activity. This discussion begins when a couple of the men—Mike "The Situation" and Vinny—glance at the "sex board" and observe in tones partly envious, partly accusatory, that Angelina has two "marks" in a row. During his "confessional,"[5] "The Situation" provides the critique that Angelina, unlike men who act similarly, is a "whore" for sleeping with two men. He explicitly embraces the gendered double standard by referring to an implied general public opinion that recognizes and supports it: "It's not sad there's a double standard, everybody knows there's a double standard. . . . Everyone loves the guy that gets girls. He's the man, he's the pimp. And then, everybody doesn't like the girl who is a 'whore,' and that's Angelina." Although Angelina immediately chimes in with her critical response—asserting, "I'm a single girl, like, what do you want me to do?"—this position is not given much air time. Her attempted feminist statement is glossed over as the show progresses, cutting from Angelina's objection, "I hate that whole thing that a guy can do it but girls can't," to several of the other cast members contradicting Angelina's position.

"Snooki," who became perhaps the best-known celebrity from the show, comments in her characteristically colorful fashion, in a way that deflects attention from her own behavior and asserts her superiority in this regard to Angelina: "Angelina got it in with Vinny because she's a 'loosey-goose.' And then, she had sex with Jose, the next day. Whore [finger flicks in accusatory fashion]. Just sayin'." Snooki's comments are followed by Jenni "JWoww" who similarly criticizes Angelina's apparent behavior and distances her own behavior from it: "I know there's a double standard, but you're bringing home guys left and right, you're fucking guys left and right who live in this house, who don't live in this house. You're giving them a reason to humiliate you." Jenni's statement is the final comment in the discussion, and it recognizes the sexual double standard. But like Mike's comment, Jenni's simply accepts the double standard and accepts the assumption that it is widely recognized and generally accepted, which is signaled as she goes on to talk about how many aspects of Angelina's behavior can come in for criticism here (the fact that she picked house residents as well as the "fact" of her multiple partners). Jenni predicts the inevitable social humiliation that will result from Angelina's actions, an outcome apparently so obvious it needs no further explanation. In the guise of trying to be helpful as a friend to Angelina, and to help her deflect criticism, she invokes the double standard to condemn her sexual activity.

This discussion therefore presents the feminist paradox of this cultural moment: the gains of the feminist movement are taken for granted while the critical feminist sentiments that are still necessary are simultaneously repudiated. The "Dirty Pad" episode offers a complex and nuanced portrait of media-ready feminism. Angelina's sexual behavior is premised on a strong feminist ideal of gender equity, which asserts that women should have the same privileges as men. She says as much, appealing to women's right to equality to justify her actions.

Yet the group debate in which the cast members have an uncritical discussion and acceptance of the double standard lacks any of the feminist political critique of gender inequality, heterosexuality, and traditional monogamy, the structural perspective underlying these sentiments. JWoww's comments, for example, caution Angelina to respect the current political climate in which overly sexual behavior by a woman, even in the era of hookup culture, persists in exposing her reputation to serious damage, giving people "a reason to humiliate [her]." Moreover, the show fails to engage with the second-level double entanglement whereby Angelina felt trapped into claiming that she slept with Jose to begin with. She did not want to be labeled a cock-tease,[6] or some version of a "prude," but at the same time her desire to avoid one label simply earned her another—she effectively had to choose between being called a slut or a prude. Her plight dramatizes the continuing cultural ambivalence around women and sexuality in which our culture simply cannot come to terms with women exhibiting an unregulated sexuality.[7]

Our engagement with audiences reveals that this episode's discussion of the double standard resonates with real issues that many viewers are grappling with in their lives. Indeed, considerable evidence indicates that sexual behavior and attitudes among young people have changed dramatically in recent years and that women are engaging in "hookups"— sex supposedly without ties—in record numbers (Wade 2017). Although hookup culture seems to challenge conservative sexual attitudes, evidence indicates that many heterosexual women who participate in hookup sex often do so with conflicted emotions and ambivalence about the experience and its impact.[8] While an active and overt sex life is certainly more acceptable for women in the era of hookup culture than it was in prior eras, studies show that women remain ambivalent about the meaning and desirability of the multiple sexual partners customary for those who hookup, and that they can incur the label of "slut" for engaging with multiple partners (Farvid, Braun, and Rowney 2017; Farvid and Braun 2016; Beres and Farvid 2010).

Findings

Members of our focus groups were conscious of the conflicting pressure women face generally to seem "feminist"—independent in their life choices, including their sexual activity—as well as to seem simultaneously more traditionally gendered and therefore constrained or dependent. Marcy, for example, a member of a middle-class sorority group, sums up these pressures as follows:

> Even if you act like you're not a feminist, say you're like a tomboy, you still get stereotyped for being a tomboy because you're not girly enough, but you also get stereotyped for being too girly-girly. Like I wear skirts. My boyfriend is like why are you wearing a skirt, that's very girly. I'm like I should be able to wear what I want and not have you think I'm more or less of a woman because I'm doing what I want.
>
> I feel like new feminism is more like women should be allowed to do what they want and it shouldn't be like you're not raising a family or oh you're not in the nine-to-five workforce. If someone wants to be a homemaker, they have the complete right if they want to do that, to be a homemaker and raise kids. I don't want to do that, and I shouldn't be judged because I don't want to do it.
>
> I find that most of the guys I end up dating are behind that when you say it without the feminism label. They're like, oh, yeah, you want to go to grad school, good job, I want to see you succeed, I want to see you do well, or you want to

raise kids that would be fine, I want you to do that, I want you to do what you want.

These responses reveal the conflicting pressures that some young women feel to look and plan their lives as both traditional women and feminist women—and the way they are criticized for whichever path they follow.

Just as importantly, however, the responses to the question of women's sexual freedom among participants in the focus groups revealed a notable divide between comments made by groups of middle-class women and those of working-class women. The attitudes of the middle-class respondents were more reflective of the assumed feminism that previous scholars such as Banet-Weiser (2018) and Favaro and Gill (2018) have found in current popular media perspectives—what Banet-Weiser and others now term "popular feminism"—which in this case would cause women to assert women's right to become sexually active to a degree, though perhaps not to the degree advocated by Angelina in this vignette.

The working-class women and women of color, however, reflected other attitudes, closer to the critiques of Angelina expressed by JWoww and Snooki. Feminist scholarship has often detailed the complex meaning of sexual freedom for women of color, who have long had to contend with the "jezebel" stereotype stigmatizing them for too much sexual activity (Bogle 2001). Working-class white women have a long tradition of using their sexuality to increase their own, and their partner's, respectability by restricting sexual activity (Phipps 2009). Working-class women of color face dual pressures—based on both sets of stereotypes—to limit their sexual activities. Our data indicate that popular feminism operates as less of an unchallenged force for these women, who still feel pressured to restrict their sexual activity in the interests of avoiding stereotypical labels and increasing their hold on respectability. For members of each of these groups, the double standard is much more of a force than are popular feminist pressures to enact free sexual expression (Scharff 2012).[9]

Perhaps in consequence, in the *Jersey Shore* episode we viewed, which portrayed an almost militantly working-class-identified cast of characters, Angelina's plea for equality is quickly glossed over and the reality of the double standard reasserted in very traditional terms, invoking the word "slut" and other labels commonly applied to sexually active women. In addition, any sentiment to the contrary was as quickly overrun and silenced in working-class focus groups as in the show, apparently dismissed as a discourse not to be entertained or considered seriously—at least in public.

As the theory of popular feminism might predict, the middle-class respondents were more conflicted in their responses to the *Jersey Shore* cast's seeming acceptance of the double standard. Their explicit investment in a popular form of feminism—in this case, the idea that the double standard is wrong—coexisted with their reluctance to reject certain seemingly non-feminist values, as reflected in their ambivalence toward and partial acceptance of the double standard in judgments of sexual behavior. This explains how JWoww could both acknowledge the double standard as troubling, yet also note that a woman's sexual activity with multiple partners—"excessive" sexual freedom for women—was troubling as well. Although both the working-class and the middle-class respondents accepted this silencing of more explicitly feminist views, only the middle-class respondents combined this with expressing a sensibility acknowledging both traditional and feminist pressures. Middle-class participants were cognizant of the *contradictions* within a culture that both takes a certain amount of feminism for granted but also accepts a double standard that promotes evaluating women negatively for their sexual activity.

Their increased openness to the idea that limiting women's sexual freedom might be troubling was perhaps related to their ability to avoid the jezebel stereotypes that plagued women of color and to their increased access to class respectability when compared with working-class women. They risked less, even when choosing to participate in hookup culture. When directly addressing the issue of the double standard, therefore, middle-class women declared it wrong but accepted that it exists, going further than JWoww in expressing discomfort with its inequities. We found middle-class respondents' extended discussion of the double standard to express the conflict they experience between feminist notions regarding women's freedom—even their imperative—to express their sexuality, and the concurrent possibility that they will be stereotyped and severely criticized for exercising these freedoms.

The middle-class women in our study appeared to have developed a set of strategies to help themselves cope with these complex dual pressures. Prominent among them was a tendency to cultivate a studied silence about the issue of their own sexual activity, as demonstrated in their repeated comments about the way they discuss (or rather, don't discuss) their sexual hookups with multiple or casual partners. Silence was their dominant strategy:

Don't ask about it.

You don't talk about it.

Don't say you're a girl and you've slept with this many people.

It's no one's business.

These findings parallel our discussions in chapter 4 where we find a corresponding silence around the assumptions implicit when participants "swipe right" for connection on Tinder, essentially giving tacit consent to sexual activity without actually actively consenting. They are also corroborated by the more extensive study of sexual behavior on campuses from which our data on Tinder was culled.[10]

So, for the middle-class women, the primary issue regarding their sexual behavior during the focus groups was how to negotiate the embedded popular feminism that has afforded them freedom of sexual activity in the face of a remaining implicit everyday sexism that condones a differential set of standards and judgments for women's and for men's sexual behavior. This is an ongoing problem despite the fact that embedded popular feminism is strong and has affected their judgments of men as well: in a move toward increased equality, the "stud" is very clearly no longer a uniformly popular symbol, if in fact this behavior was ever widely endorsed (though Ehrenreich [1983] would argue it was). In women-only groups, middle-class women often explicitly noted that they are not impressed with men who are too promiscuous and are fully as critical of this behavior in men as they are in women. One gender-mixed group of middle-class male and female college students had this exchange:

JOSHUA: I'm trying to gripe with it because, yeah, like a guy who sleeps with a lot of girls is cool, and a girl that sleeps around, yeah, anyone would look at her and be like, "Oh yeah, she's kind of a 'ho' [slang for 'whore']."

ALICIA: So there is a—(inaudible).

SARAH: But I mean I would do it for a guy that slept around. I would be like—

ALICIA: I won't say that it's cool for a guy to do it. It's just more acceptable.

JOSHUA: Yeah, that's very true. For one it's acceptable, and for one it's not.

And another woman in the group goes on to say: "If a guy sleeps around I'm going to have that stigma on him also. I'm going to be like I'm going to stay away from him. He sleeps around," though she goes on to say that men themselves will not think badly of someone for this.

This shift in women's attitudes toward men's sexual activity seems to be one of the enduring legacies of the feminist movement and might go along with a new media-ready, critical feminist sensibility. We noted that this critical attitude toward men's "excessive" sexual activity extended across class groups in our study. Interestingly, some of the men in our mixed groups (all of whom were middle class) were quick to acknowledge—and to criticize—the existence of a double standard of sexual behavior among their peer group. And surprisingly, they were less reluctant than middle-class women to invoke feminism in critiquing it, perhaps an effect of the mixed-gender setting and a desire to seem overtly feminist.

Among the working-class respondents in this study, the articulation of the relationship between an assumed popular feminism and the implicit sexism of the double standard worked differently, with the embedded popular feminism appearing less salient with respect to this issue. These respondents were less concerned about gender inequality vis-à-vis sexual behavior and instead perceived and remarked critically on the cast members' departure from more traditional norms of gendered behavior, in line with their own desire for respectability and concern to avoid negative stereotyping. Some, in fact, even called the cast and their actions "not normal," language they applied in particular to the female cast members' sexual behavior. This language invokes an assumed "middle-class" normality of gendered respectability, but it also implies acceptance of the sexual double standard. They found Angelina's performance of sexual freedom humiliating and disturbing, and they worked hard to distance themselves from it.

Consider, for example, this exchange among a mixed-race group of working-class women, which contains a brief reference to fighting the double standard while at the same time seems rather unquestioningly accepting of it:

PRESS: So what do you make of it? So you're telling me in a way that the women [on *Jersey Shore*] don't act normally but the men act more normally?

ALI: Well, the men act the way that society expects men to act, but the women go above and beyond. And you're like, oh, if men could sleep around with women, I can do it too. They're like—I don't know how to explain it.

FELICIA: They want the power that men have. They want to be able to sleep around with men without being called a whore or anything like that. Because men can do it and they're like, oh hey, we're just getting a lot of chicks. But when girls do it, I'm a whore. I'm doing it but you know like, guess what? I'm enjoying the shore, and I can do all I want to and I'm not going to be called a whore because I'm on TV.

PRESS: And so do you think that's not going to happen for them? That they're not going to get the power?

ALI: I mean, I think they're trying to fight a double standard in the wrong way.

PRESS: How would the right way be to fight the double standard?

ALI: If they did anything normal or I guess right, I guess they would maybe have a filter or some kind of boundaries because as many times as I've watched the show I don't see that any of them have boundaries for themselves or others at all.

FELICIA: But the only one that I can actually say that I kind of respect in a way is . . .

ALEXIS: JWoww, or whatever?

FELICIA: Yeah, I respect her because she was in a relationship with a guy for a while when she was on the show and she was faithful to him, until he cheated on her. That's another story.

PRESS: Right, he cheated.

FELICIA: Of course, he cheated on her or something like that. And she was like, oh, I'm so heartbroken. She was actually the most realistic one. She was like, I'm heartbroken, I feel—. Oh, blah, blah, what a normal girl would do, and everything like that. I mean everybody else, like Snooki, she just goes around and she dabbles with everyone.

In essence, Felicia's position is that there is a "normal" everyday sexism, and that it deviates from Angelina's activities. In fact, it rather accords with the "double standard" perspective on women's sexual activity. Rather than use the lens of an assumed feminism to describe Angelina's hypersexualized behaviors, she refers to a presumed sexist "normal" standard, according to which women must guard their reputations.

For Felicia and others in her group, a sexual economy still exists, mandating that women factor concern about attracting respect and good behavior into their calculation of acceptable sexual behavior. *Jersey Shore*'s departure from what they perceived to be the norm was upsetting. Women spoke of getting men to respect them and of the need to act like a "lady" rather than a "dog," which was a term one woman used to refer to "loose" women. Essentialist thinking also emerged: one woman claimed women needed to behave well in order to bring out the best in men who might otherwise behave badly, like "pigs" or animals. The arguments of the working-class members of this focus groups, in other words, parallel JWoww's admonition to Angelina that her sexual behavior was very naturally "giving [men] a reason to humiliate [her]" and reject Angelina's more egalitarian sentiment, "I hate that whole thing that a guy can do it but girls can't," a discourse taken more seriously by the middle-class college students whose reaction to Angelina and her behavior was more conflicted.

These differences in the responses of members from various socioeconomic positions reflect the nuances of feminist expression and reception. It was clear from the focus groups that a different sense of their life prospects as well as different perspectives on women's sexual freedom exists and that media portrayals that "push the boundaries" are conceived as misguided attempts by those whose status position is more precarious. For the first-generation respondents, college attendance presented an opportunity to exceed the life outcomes of their parents. Squandering that opportunity for class mobility through hooking up was behavior that women in these groups considered very seriously, finding it potentially damaging and ultimately rejecting it. More of the working-class women had seen their mothers and relatives struggling with ill-paid jobs and dependence on men who were often unreliable and at times disrespectful. Their concerns therefore speak to issues they quite possibly thought would be central to their future success and prospects in life, concerns that did not come up in quite the same way in our discussions with young women who already understood how to navigate the college environment and expected positive outcomes from their educations and their jobs, and assumed their own ability to attract desirable, respectable partners.

Likewise, the working-class women exhibited a kind of "toughness" that many might call resolute, a form of feminist independence whereby they would always have to work hard to take care of themselves. This conflicts markedly with the idealized image of the stay-at-home mom of yesteryear that still characterized the dreams of some of the middle-class women—dreams that often coexist with the more independent, career-oriented paths imagined by the popular feminism women have also internalized and that for these women is enabled by their privileged educations, which is discussed in more detail in chapter 3.

Conclusion

Despite abundant evidence that the sexual double standard still exists, the idea of sexual "liberation" is largely a concern for women who have less to lose when it comes to how their sexual encounters will be judged by society. While popular culture supports the idea that women are "allowed" to have "too much" sex (Attwood 2005 and 2009, cited in Farvid, Braun, and Rowney 2017), the performance of (hetero)sexuality is still regulated—there is a "right" way to perform sexual liberation, and a "wrong" way. Likewise, the meaning of feminist sexual expression varies when one considers the class position of the audience. As our focus group data illustrate, class positions muddy the waters when it comes to the way feminism and (hetero)sexuality are discussed and experienced.

Middle-class women's responses to the classed and gendered sexuality represented in this *Jersey Shore* episode demonstrate how women who are secure in their status positions (white, cisgender, heterosexual women) are open to playing with sexual liberation and empowerment narratives of sexuality as presented in this media-ready feminist vignette.

While they are more likely to embrace this form of popular feminism, they nevertheless acknowledge the contradictory persistence of a double standard, and they were hesitant, unable, or unwilling to fight the contradictions inherent in the way their behavior would be judged differently than that of their male peers. Even when those contradictions became visible through media-ready feminist representation, as was the case in the "Dirty Pad" vignette, women who occupied higher socioeconomic (SES) positions tended to push back against this representation, accepting that a double-standard was just inherent in society. For them, media-ready feminism is about working with this tension to determine the extent to which women's empowerment via sexual expression might go "too far" in a way that could jeopardize their partnership potential. They were more comfortable accepting the everyday sexism of the double standard than fashioning an assertive criticism of it.

On the other hand, first-generation students and women of color articulated that they had more to lose when it came to the question of "free" sexual expression. These women had worked hard to establish their position in society and wanted to leverage their college degrees so that they were not financially dependent on anyone, and they anticipated difficulties ahead. Although they too were torn between the pull of feminist freedoms and the persistence of more tempered cultural norms recommending conservative sexual behavior for women, working-class respondents bought in less to popular feminism than did others, as prior research (Press 1991; Press and Cole 1999) also indicates. They explicitly criticized the idea of sexual freedom, considering this not particularly applicable or desirable for them as they pursued their own goals.

In the end, no one supported Angelina's attack on the double standard. Despite the differences in perspective toward a feminist framework asserting that empowerment could be achieved via sexual conquests and through achieving sexual equality with men, women from both groups repudiated Angelina's perspective, though for slightly different but related reasons. Class and ethnic differences came into play in how vociferously the double standard was embraced or accepted. Women with "less to lose" seemed open to criticizing the double standard, although they were hesitant to embrace a stance that could ultimately hurt their chances of forming a relationship with men of equal status. They wanted to remain plausible romantic—rather than merely sexual—partners. On the other hand, women who were more apt to use their college education for purposes of social and economic leverage were much more outspoken in actually supporting the double standard, criticizing the behavior of heterosexual women who were too free in their sexuality in a way that would hurt their life chances and paralleling the female cast members' criticisms of Angelina in the vignette.

Our discussions with young women point to the need for media scholars to explore feminism through a more intersectional lens, as we attempt to make sense of how media hegemony may still operate in the age of niche media. Our findings also speak to the persistence and strength of media-ready feminism. Even women who generally embraced a popular feminist view that women's sexual expression was a kind of individualized empowerment were hesitant to support a rather tepid representation of gender equality in the bedroom or to embrace the everyday sexism that reproduces the double sexual standard. They may feel compelled to accept it, but they do not uncritically embrace this position.[11]

While ongoing feminist movements have attempted through their critical discourses and politics to open up a much broader range of sexual behaviors deemed acceptable for women, our research shows that this has never been entirely accomplished. Second-wave feminism made a start at addressing women's varied sexual identities and concerns, and at developing a political or theoretical stance capable of encompassing this broad range; however, as many critics have shown, its mode of address favors the life position of white, cisgender, heterosexual women who occupy a higher level of socioeconomic status than their cisgender, heterosexual peers. Critics of second-wave feminism have long noted that a white, middle-class, heterosexual bias persists, even in representations and discussions of the supposedly liberated postfeminist sexuality.[12] In this chapter we've illustrated some of the unfinished legacies of that movement as they are lived by members of different social classes and ethnic groups today vis-à-vis issues of hookup culture, the "double standard," and more generally, gendered sexual inequality. Women's almost uniformly critical response to Angelina's feminist assertion of women's equal right to sexual freedom illustrates the theory of media-ready feminism: responses to feminism in the media are bound to the everyday sexism that persistently structures the life experiences of the audiences who absorb them. But this everyday sexism nevertheless troubles women who are subject to its strictures and to the unequal culture it creates.

3

Balancing Work and Family

What "Choice" Conceals

Introduction

In US cultural discourses, achieving work-family balance, or choosing between work and family, is routinely framed as an individual problem specifically faced by women. This individualized perspective obscures the structural conditions—inadequate maternity leaves, the absence of regulation mandating paternity leave, standard work hours incompatible with school hours, and the scarcity of quality daycare options—that make "choosing" between work and family a difficult task for even the most economically privileged women and an impossible one for others. Yet women commonly personalize their own difficulties combining work with family while achieving balance, thinking their inability to balance family and career is a personal failure (Orgad 2019; Tripodi 2019). Collins (2019), Arruzza, Battacharya, and Fraser (2019), Orgad (2019), and others (Hochschild and Machung 2012; Rottenberg 2018) detail the need for the specific structural changes necessary to ease this burden, including most prominently changes to the organization of work and to the availability and affordability of day care. While the widespread belief that women have been liberated from their demonstrably mythical prefeminist "family only" identity is widely accepted in the United States, statistics show that women continue to perform almost twice as much of the housework as do men in most couples, and substantially more in couples with children.[1] Despite a growing number of studies that document that men feel pressured to achieve more "balance" in their lives, women still typically assume more work in the home. In addition, the notion of a balancing act when it comes to the demands of children and the office is still primarily felt by women or, in the case of same-sex couples, by one member of the couple more so than the other.

Despite the challenges women face, most in the United States believe that the opportunity to pursue a fulfilling career and to earn money in the labor force must take family needs into account (Newburger 2018; Rivers and Barnett 2013; Gerson 2009). Yet the primary responsibility for children's care usually falls on "mothers" who are most often (but not always) defined as female. This is a worldview so firmly entrenched that it is even surfacing in same-gender couples as they often (though crucially, not always) delineate responsibilities according to traditional gender roles (Goldberg 2013). Such "maternal" labor includes not only the bulk of visible childcare and housework tasks, but also often multiple invisible jobs ranging from scheduling dentist appointments, refilling the toilet paper, sending out thank-you cards, and buying gifts for teachers and extended family (Wade 2016)—the "executive director" function of the emotional and physical labor demanded by families. Women must also balance both their visible and invisible family labor with emotional labor performed in offices as well as in families, all the while taking care to position themselves as employees who are not distracted by their children (Hochschild 1979).

Popular feminism has canonized the "balanced life" as the apotheosis of liberal feminism. Some theorists (Rottenberg 2018) argue that this is the central tenet of popular feminism. This cultural script follows a consistent narrative: should women "choose" to work *and* have children, they must at an individual level balance these responsibilities. Media representations of this dilemma focus almost exclusively on the lived experiences of white, straight, upper-middle-class, cisgender women; poorer, less affluent women have much more limited choices, yet "choice" itself is represented as equally available to everyone, a belief that universalizes the experience of heterosexual, white, middle-class women. Even for these privileged women, data show that the difficulties inherent in choice are real (Orgad 2019). On one side of the coin is the perspective that, no matter how hard they try, women can't really do both—they can't have it all (Slaughter 2012). On the other side are figures like Sheryl Sandberg, who advise that if only women will *Lean In* they can both find career success and, with the right individual choices, combine the kind of outsized achievement embodied by Sandberg herself with a fulfilling family life.

Yet the cultural script of what Hays terms the "cult of intensive motherhood" remains strong, and remains in direct conflict with Sandberg's interpretation of a second-wave feminist legacy urging that even mothers deserve full equality in the workplace. The "cult of intensive motherhood" (1998) mandates that enrichment activities, "mommy and me" classes, and so on, are all considered necessary for children's successful development. This multiplicity of nurturing tasks fall inordinately on the shoulders of mothers. Hays argues that the sensibility of intensive mothering is ubiquitous.

Others document the classed and raced nature of this belief system. Lareau (2003) demonstrates that commitment to the cult of intensive motherhood, and the opportunity to practice this sort of mothering, varies dramatically by social class group. She argues that working-class women prioritize other values in their mothering styles, giving children more freedom from activities and supervision, which accords with the demands of their own jobs. Dow (2019) discusses the middle-class norms that are specific to Black mothers, adopted as they attempt to cope with the strictures of racial oppression. Hays anticipates these critiques by noting that the ideology of intensive motherhood "persists, in part, because it serves the interests not only of men but of capitalism, the state, the middle class, and whites" (1998, xiii).

Nevertheless, the cultural dominance of the ideal of intensive motherhood is widely represented in media depictions of mothers. The cult of intensive motherhood comes into direct conflict with women's attempts to achieve in most workplace settings, which generally in the United States do not offer the structural supports necessary for working parents, support that is particularly necessary for those who are intensive mothers. Yet our cultural script individualizes these conflicts, conceptualizing them as problems of individual failure and eschewing a language that would help describe work-family conflicts in structural terms. Class and racial issues that make the achievement of work-family balance so much more difficult for working-class women and women of color, and that might introduce alternate ideals in direct conflict with the image of the intensive mother, are often omitted from this script altogether.

Popular television has a long history of representing motherhood and promoting the specific cultural images and ideals surrounding it. Early television was known for its universalization of the white, affluent, suburban middle-class family (Haralovich 1989; Spigel 1992; Press 1991). Yet television's representation of motherhood has diversified dramatically in recent times. Over the last several decades a plethora of popular television shows including CBS's *The Good Wife* (2006–2015), Showtime's *Nurse Jackie* (2009–2015), CBS's *Blue Bloods* (2010–present), CBC's *Workin' Moms* (2017–present), and FX's *Better Things* (2016–present) have directly or indirectly been addressing the conflicts of work-life balance in a variety of family forms. While most representations assume the centrality of "choice," recently some representations push the boundaries of prevailing assumptions as they address some of the underlying structural issues that give rise to this turmoil.

Specifically, we selected a television series that explicitly pushed back on the popular feminist idea that work-family balance can be achieved through personal choices and that its possibility is unfettered by structural barriers. Although the once extremely popular television series *Desperate Housewives* has long been off the air, examination of its text nevertheless demonstrates that media *can* challenge popular feminism. It began a trend. We would argue that the more recent "dramedy" series *Workin' Moms* continues the tradition started by *Desperate Housewives* of treating the norms of intensive mothering with irreverence and mockery. The television drama *Nurse Jackie* also featured a working mother who is driven to drug abuse as she attempts to confront the demands of her children, her job, and her failing marriage. Although each of these series focuses primarily on white, relatively affluent mothers,[2] they all focus as well on the need to cultivate a form of intensive motherhood while trying to balance one's career goals—a popular feminist narrative that is continuously pushed on women, ignoring the fact that working-class women's long and inflexible work hours often make intensive mothering much more difficult—if not impossible—than it is for middle-class women, for whom it is nevertheless also quite difficult. While it is clear that the demands of motherhood—particularly for working mothers—are *beginning* to be critiqued in media representations, we still know little with respect to how these narratives are received.

To investigate reception of this critical trend in television, for the research in this chapter we selected a particularly relevant media-ready feminist clip dramatizing these issues from an episode of *Desperate Housewives*, screening it for women of various ages. Through a detailed analysis of the critical way in which balance is represented in this clip, we demonstrate how the show both reifies the expectations put on women and makes visible the structural contradictions of women in the workforce, illustrating their incompatibility with the persistent demands of intensive motherhood. We juxtapose our interpretive analysis of the clip with data from focus group interviews.

After recounting how this media-ready feminist moment provides critical insight into popular feminist culture, we unpack how it was received by women of different groups with contrasting life experiences (e.g., generational, racial, socioeconomic status). We find that in this instance, television's insightful representation of the impossibility of work-family balance was received with critical insight by some women whose life experiences play into their recognition that this structural flaw exists in the capitalist workplace as presently structured—but such insights were not shared by all women with similar experiences. In addition, media-ready feminist reception took yet a different form for others who are not white or middle-class, or are simply too young to have had experiences relevant to the issue.

Many women understand that gender inequality persists in the workplace. Older women in particular draw on their own personal experiences of divorce—returning to the labor force after childrearing, and being overlooked for promotions at work because they were "mommy-tracked"—and glean genuine insights into this issue. Also, many women at work are quite aware that they are not being judged according to the same standards as are men, who easily and regularly pass them by in the labor force, and this engenders conflicting attitudes toward work and career for women. Working women are also aware of continuing sexual attention from superiors to themselves and to other, often younger, women which further supports a negative and often cynical attitude toward the workplace, with the #MeToo movement bringing further evidence of this awareness. Finally, working women with children are particularly aware of the ways in which norms of mothering behavior have negatively affected their progress in the workplace. Nonetheless, women's awareness of inequality is still limited by the taken-for-granted nature of the everyday sexism that produces a general acceptance of these inequalities, and pushes back on the media-ready feminist insights of this depiction.

Despite being able to articulate—at times quite eloquently—their struggles with gendered inequality, many women overall lack the analytic vocabulary necessary to describe the problems they face in structural terms. The most remarkable features of our data are the simultaneous yet conflicting perspectives generally held—that mothering is and should be intensive, indeed some believing mothering is more biologically natural for women than for men, and that female mothers can nevertheless successfully and equally compete with men in the workplace without being disadvantaged by their mothering role. This indicates widespread inability to grasp that structural change would be necessary simply to achieve equity, and that the lack thereof initiates a set of circumstances whereby many women feel like they are failing at both all the time. None of which begins to address how socioeconomic and racial inequalities factor into mothering pressures—to what extent do the pressures of intensive mothering and balancing career intersect with race, ethnicity, and socioeconomic status? By understanding media-ready feminism via our reception analysis, this chapter explores how expectations regarding work-family balance persist and discusses the continuing ideological struggle for women in different social positions to reconcile the culture's ideals of professional success with its ideals of intensive mothering.

In our media literature, how audiences make meaning from media depictions of challenging work-life situations that problematize choice while nevertheless overrepresenting the dilemmas of the heterosexual, white, middle-class women presents an interesting and little studied problem. In this chapter we address this gap, interviewing audiences as they watch selected televisual breakthrough moments where women are forced to recognize the bind they find themselves in, yet are unable to articulate the challenges they face as structural opposition. We hope overall in this chapter to illustrate the inherent complexity of analyzing media reception, which varies across age, social class, occupation, and life experience, among other variables, while at the same time addressing conflicting representations and beliefs about work-family balance.

Desperate Housewives

The popular television show *Desperate Housewives* ran for eight seasons from 2006 to 2012. As is customary in the media world of popular feminist images, the struggles the housewives face are often posed as issues of personal dilemmas and choices, and the individual personalities of the housewives are minutely drawn. Overall the show failed to engage systematically with the larger structural barriers that make it difficult for most women to both work and have a family. Instead it focused on the problems of primarily white, middle-, and upper-middle-class women in primarily familial rather than workplace settings. In many ways the opulent fictional suburbia it depicted served as an example of television's strangely persistent idyllic image of the life of the suburban housewife, which scholars have argued endures despite the somewhat odd fact that it depicts a life that was never lived by most in the United States. In this respect *Desperate Housewives* falls into what Coontz terms the "nostalgia trap" (2016), which applies to US culture more generally. Nevertheless, the show attracted a transgenerational and transnational audience, generated a substantial critical literature, and remained popular for almost a decade, indicating that it touched on important currents in the culture regarding the role of women, housewives, and mothers.

Given its popularity, many feminist scholars have written about the show in detail (McCabe and Akass 2006; Wilson 2006; Olsen and Morgan 2010). In this chapter we focus primarily on what we argue is a salient media-ready feminist *moment* in the show: its depiction of the character of one of the housewives, Lynette Scavo (played by Felicity Huffman, who won an Emmy in 2005 for her performance), at a particular juncture in which she returns to the paid labor force after staying at home to raise her children, one of whom is still an infant. We analyze audiences' complex reaction to this back-to-work moment, paying close attention to how they grapple with and connect their own experiences and beliefs about women and mothers to the images they're seeing on the screen.[3]

Episode background. The scene selected was the season premiere episode of the second season, which was entitled "Next." At its premiere this episode ranked number 2 among 113 programs, and was viewed by 28,360,000 viewers.[4] Although this clip first aired in 2005, we assert that the work-family balance issues facing working parents are if anything more pressing today, and recent feminist literature backs up this assertion. In her 2018 book, Rottenberg foregrounds this issue directly and asserts that work-family balance is *the* central issue for a dominant neoliberal feminism. Orgad (2019) offers support for this notion as well.[5]

In the scene we chose, Tom (Lynette's husband) informs her that he has quit his job and wants to remain home with their four children so Lynette can resume her career. Lynette therefore must find employment, but as she is getting ready to go to an important job interview she's lined up, Tom's back gives out and he falls on the floor, seemingly unable to get up. As Tom is subsequently too injured to watch all four children while she is gone, Lynette must take the baby with her to the interview.

Arriving at her job interview infant in hand, Lynette attempts to leave the baby with the male receptionist, who simply places the child on the desk and ignores her while the infant comes close to falling off the desk. Realizing she will need to take the baby with her into the interview room, Lynette scoops her up and faces the obvious scorn of female executive Nina Fletcher (played by Joely Fisher in what becomes an ongoing role as Lynette's boss), who begins the interview with a series of snide remarks about how women cannot be effective at their careers if they are trying to combine family with career, a path she herself very clearly—and quite militantly—has not "chosen," following through on the theme of individual choices structuring women's lives. Lynette follows her into an inner office to meet the executive's male boss. Preoccupied and about to head out to an important basketball game, big boss Ed Ferrara (Currie Graham) keeps playing with a little basketball and hoop he's had installed in his office as Lynette "pitches" her ideas about how to upgrade the company while simultaneously changing her crying baby's diaper, making her own "shot" as she throws the diaper into the wastebasket. Ed hires Lynette immediately, much to the chagrin of the disapproving and seemingly jealous female employee.

This episode is a good example of a pervasive assumption in the post-second-wave literature, which is that women bosses who have presumably chosen to prioritize career over family tend to be hostile to other women—particularly those with families—and impede women's progress more than men. While some of the sociological literature points us in this direction, arguing that women employees operate as though there were a delineated and limited number of female "spots" in a given firm (Khazan 2017), a theory that might explain the conflicting relationship we see playing out in this vignette, most literature does not bear this out. In reality, the presence of other women executives in a corporation tends to contribute to the success of all women in the organization (McNulty 2018).

The show also promotes the idea that men are less competent than women when working in the home—both with regard to childrearing tasks as well as cooking and cleaning (a narrative trope that has been in circulation since *I Love Lucy*'s famous "Job Switching" episode of 1952). Persisting ideas of gendered incompetency make the unequal division of gendered labor in the home seem natural or inevitable. In fact, studies over the last five decades have repeatedly shown that women continue to do more work than men in homes populated by heterosexual couples, despite an increasing number of women entering the workforce (Cerrato and Cifre 2018) and despite slowly but demonstrably changing attitudes toward the responsibilities of male partners in heterosexual couples (Leopold, Skopek, and Schulz 2018).

However, the character of Lynette also repeatedly pushes the boundaries of popular feminism. Her character frequently criticized the inequitable expectations she faced at home and chafed at how evaluations and judgments made in the workplace were biased because she was a mother. While Lynette had at one time reached the top of her profession, winning several prestigious awards, we also see the difficulties Lynette as a mother encounters in order to maintain this level of professional success, giving up both her top-level of success and at times sacrificing time with her children. Given the complexity of Lynette's character, which both documents the struggles working moms face while simultaneously addressing how these are related to larger structural issues—this vignette provided the perfect opportunity to unpack the meaning-making processes of audiences from various backgrounds in relation to the conflicting demands of work-family balance, professional success, and intensive mothering.

Methods

The sections that follow draw from a series of ten focus groups conducted by Press with both older and younger women, and three earlier groups (predating the show but included for a brief longitudinal comparison of attitudes toward the issue) conducted with approximately forty-five young women in 1999 when Press first began researching the issue of work-family balance. Discussions took place with women of varying generational, racial, ethnic, and socioeconomic groups. The participants included college-aged women attending a large midwestern state university, a large southern state university, and a smaller southern state school frequented by first-generation college students. The sample also included two groups of older women whose ages ranged from thirty-two to sixty-five, one a group of divorced older women working in various professions, the other a group of teachers and guidance counselors. One group of college students allowed Press multiple visits to observe their weekly gathering to watch the show. Another group of college students was entirely African American, and yet another was a group of first-generation college students of varying racial backgrounds. A graduate of the large southern state university was interviewed with her mother. The data, collected over a decade and a half, in total includes approximately two hundred individuals.

In what follows, we focus on women's discussions of their own lives and their direct responses to the vignette from the episode described earlier. In particular, respondents were asked about their views on the issue of discrimination in the workplace, the impact of family responsibilities on women's ability to perform in the workplace, the division of labor in heterosexual nuclear families, reactions to how specific characters were portrayed, and how what they watched related to their own stories and experiences. Because the nature of the respondents was so varied, we were able to analyze how expressions of media-ready feminism differed with regard to age, social class, and race/ethnicity.

Generational Differences

We begin our discussion of responses to Lynette's vignette by focusing on the generational differences that emerged saliently in the mother-daughter pair interviewed in depth. Their experience exemplifies the generational differences among white, middle-class women uncovered in this research and sets the stage for the later analysis in important ways. The two women—Janine, a sensitive, thoughtful, ambitious white, middle-class university student, and her mother, Linda, a hardworking white nurse who had been in the field for decades—reflected for hours on their family history, current situation, and thoughts about the future. In many respects they articulated their positions from a standpoint of both racial and class privilege.

An ambitious student who excelled in her courses and was a campus leader, Janine was focused on obtaining the highest GPA she could in college, securing internships and a lucrative job following graduate school. Though she expressed a sincere and strong desire to combine career with family, like many other white women of her generation whose parents had gone to college, the idea of family was secondary to her life plan following graduation. Janine had not given much thought to how family would fit in with her career plans. Having been raised in a privileged environment, the idea of juggling, or balancing, was not really a salient thought. She just assumed, according to a popular feminist script, that work-family conflicts are easily resolved on a case-by-case basis. The fact that Janine had no definite plans about how she would cope with these issues and lacked insight into the social, economic, and cultural mechanisms that contributed to them is at the heart of the problem—both individually and culturally—for even similarly privileged young women facing this issue. Janine's attitude reflects a popular position, one that assumes that work-family conflicts are resolved and that no further political action or reform is needed.

However, Janine's lack of attention to issues she might later experience in combining work and family came into play during our interview when she learned of her mother's own difficulties in combining work with family. This is first noticed when Linda shares a story about how, although she went on to have a long career as a nurse, she had once toyed with the idea of becoming a physician:

> LINDA: I got married young by today's standard. [Janie's dad] was three years older, and he was here doing his master's. And we met as I was graduating from undergrad. So we dated for a year, and then we were engaged for another year. So I was twenty-three and he was twenty-six.
>
> PRESS: So you were graduated. When you made the decision not to become a doctor . . . do you remember discussing it with your husband?
>
> LINDA: I remember him having strong feelings about me not doing it.

Hearing this, Janine was shocked that her dad had stymied her mom's career ambitions.

> JANINE: What were Daddy's arguments? Was he just like, no? Was he kind of hinting at it, or was he just like no?
>
> LINDA: No, I think he was as strong as, okay, if you want to do that, fine, but you and I are not going to last. . . . and I really, really wanted a family.

A few main observations we would like to make about this exchange illustrate some of the general trends that we also found in the group interviews. First, in order to pursue her dream of becoming a mother, Janine's mother had to "make a deal" with her husband, promising that she would not pursue the goal of becoming a doctor in exchange for having children. Janine's mother also seems devoid of resentment at giving up any further career advancement in exchange for the promise of a family, while her daughter, as a child of popular feminism that recognizes no conflict between work and motherhood, is shocked at the mention of this bargain. It's interesting to look at generational differences when attitudes toward white, middle-class women working in the paid labor force have shifted so dramatically across generations. Janine and her mother's middle-class privilege and their whiteness is an integral part of this dynamic, as we will see later, since the notion of the mother who stays at home was more alive in the white cultural imagination than it was for the African American women we spoke with, or for the working-class white women in our study.

Second, it's worth noting in this instance the seeming lack of communication between the generations on this issue of work-family balance. Janine seems never to have heard her mother's story of how she decided not to become a doctor and how it was related to her husband's apparent ultimatum that if she pursued this path, they would break up. Clearly this mother-daughter pair, though evidently close, communicative, and supportive of each other, had never discussed the impact having children—even Linda's desire to have children—seems to have had on Linda's life and work trajectory. Upon hearing it, Janine is silenced—deeply affected by the story. Following Linda's shared history, Janine considers how these events had changed the contours of her family of origin and their possible relevance to her own future path and decisions. Returning to this incident later in the interview, Linda underscored that she considered this a *personal* decision by saying that she never pushed the issue—she appeared to defend her husband by saying that if she had, he might have been more supportive.

Generational differences were also salient when Press discussed these issues with the two majority white, middle-class, mixed-race groups of older women who had worked as teachers and guidance counselors in public schools. When the older women's responses are compared with those of younger, college-aged women, the generational divide in the cultural context within which work-family decisions are made is dramatic. Examining their lives from the other side of having a family, the older women were often painfully aware of the career opportunities they had missed, which they often attributed to the lack of good "career-woman" role models, many specifically mentioning that their mothers had not provided them strong models—again putting the failure to achieve success on women themselves, rather than challenging the broader structures that made career opportunities for working mothers so difficult to pursue, particularly salient in their own mothers' generations.

One of the older-women groups, a group of teachers, included a Latina woman who expressed very different expectations and described a very different life situation from those of her peers. The child of immigrants, she was still living in her parents' home as an adult and was expected to do so until she married—as mandated by her father, even though she was now an adult. She felt torn between her desire to obey, and in fact to help her father by continuing to pay him rent, and what she identified as her more modern and American identity as an independent and ambitious career woman with a demanding job. Her mother had not held a paying job. In her case she was experiencing firsthand the conflict of cultural expectations in the more traditional society from which her parents had emigrated vis-à-vis current US society, which would judge her father's expectation that she live at home until marriage to be old-fashioned, and would similarly judge as old-fashioned the limitations he placed upon her freedom of movement.

Younger, college-aged, middle-class white women in our study often could not perceive any workplace difficulties in their mothers' work experiences, despite a vast literature that reveals the continuing presence of these difficulties, doubly so for their mothers' generation. Race seems to play into this perception. We will see a notable counterexample in the case of a middle-class Black woman in our study, whose mother had consistently forced her to discuss the difficulties she might face when attempting to combine her planned career as an attorney with her often-stated plan to have a large family of six children, using her own experience as evidence. Interestingly, we heard no such cautionary tales repeated by the white middle-class women in our study. This helps to explain why focus groups of these women interpreted their mothers' experiences in the labor force as stories of triumph and success, rather than difficulty and limitation. White middle-class mothers did not seem to communicate to their daughters that work-family balance was a problem. Perhaps this, together with other cultural factors, failed to sensitize young women to work-family conflicts they might be facing later in life (Gerson 2009). A failure to perceive these difficulties was particularly striking in the 1999 focus groups, as these were women whose mothers had had even fewer opportunities for resuming their careers after time out for children. But we observed these attitudes in the more recent focus groups as well, which continued this discourse almost without break.

Press's discussions led into other topics for the older generation of women, who quite often bring up a series of gripes about the way they've been treated at work, particularly in the context of their responses to the vignette about Lynette's job interview used to prompt discussion in our interviews. The teacher/guidance counselor group spoke repeatedly about the way men are often quickly promoted into positions of power in their profession over women who have more extensive experience and even more stellar job performance. Members of the divorced women's group similarly claimed constant differential treatment and discrimination at work, issues they connected to the fact that they were plagued with more childcare responsibilities throughout their careers than were their male contemporaries, particularly following their divorces.

In the *Desperate Housewives* clip we used, Lynette is shown as technically "having it all" in that she has a partner willing to stay home with her children while she is ostensibly free to pursue her career. Yet the breakthrough feminist vignette we show illustrates that "having it all" comes only with great difficulty, if at all. Lynette is shown to triumph at least momentarily in that she obtains a prestigious advertising job despite having to diaper her baby during her job interview. Yet her work-family conflicts are clearly going to persist as she occupies this demanding job.

This aspect of the show's breakthrough feminism was discerned and embraced by many of the older women we interviewed, whose perspectives offered a clear contrast to the sometimes unbridled optimism of most younger women of all races and classes. For example, the African American daughter mentioned earlier who planned to combine a career as an attorney with a family of six children resented her mother's warning that such a combination might be difficult. Younger white women, whose mothers had not "had the talk" this African American woman experienced, similarly failed to connect Lynette's struggle to their future lives, believing that such work-family conflicts would not affect them. As we describe in more detail later, these women responded to the clip in a media-ready feminist manner that overlooked the real-life conflicts actually highlighted in the vignette.

Older women in our study reacted differently to the vignette, consistently mentioning the difficulties they had faced in their own lives in this regard. They felt the show's representation of Lynette's difficulties was in part a vindication of the struggles they had faced, which they brought up in response to the show. For example, in the divorced older women's group, one participant recounted the way opportunities were closed to women when she was starting out, working in a bank. Another group of older women overtly and repeatedly complained, with feminist insight, about the way the men in their workplace were promoted much more quickly than were the women and rose to positions far above them, even when the men involved were much younger and more inexperienced.

> AMANDA: When I went to work at City Mutual Bank, there were four of us put in together. It was the President, the Executive VP, I was Senior VP, and the Controller. When the Executive VP was hired away from NBW . . . He was offered $50,000 more, I was offered $5,000 [in her counteroffer] . . .
>
> (Gasp.)
>
> DEE: Stop, I know.
>
> AMANDA: I got—I'm serious. That's what happened. And that was 1987. That's not too long ago.

In retrospectively discussing their difficulties moving up the career ladder, older women tended to be pessimistic even about younger women's future prospects in the labor force (certainly they were more pessimistic than were younger women themselves).

In one example, they felt young women would be hindered by the presence of older women in the workplaces they would occupy, as the clip represented. Older women seemed to expect this kind of negative reaction from female workplace bosses even though, as we have demonstrated, the literature indicates the opposite is true. In the older women teachers' group, a woman went so far as to identify other women in the workplace as the *main* obstacle to women succeeding:

> Alexis: Some women are . . . leery of assertive women. I don't think that all women are kind to other women. I think that's the greatest problem we have as women that women do not promote other women. They're not kind to each other. It seems as though there's always this competition going on that really has held women down. It's not men in our world; I think women hold other women down. I think that's our problem. There are too many insecure women who are not strong enough to be with assertive women and to take that charge. I see women being challenged by other women.

Alexis goes on to say: "Did you see how the man was much more, like women really do better with men. I don't know if there's a sexual thing going on. There's something going on with the chemistry between men and women. I do believe that." Janet supports her statement:

> JANET: He was more interested in what she had to say. He was just zoned in on what she was going to bring to the company, where the woman was more concerned about what was going to interfere; was she going to be out sick a lot because of the babies, or if she's going to be late.
>
> ALEXIS: Power. The woman is more concerned about power.

Discussing the "survival mode" women often find themselves in at work, the divorced women's group felt this situation would continue to pit women competitively against one another:

> SANDRA: I felt that the women didn't pull us up either for different reasons. But I also felt that we were the first to judge other women. And I felt that it wasn't a "let's have more women at the top," and push the men out. That's not a movement yet, it was "there are only three slots for women and I want my one. And I have to keep my one."
>
> ARLA: So I still don't think when I was working even in the late eighties and early nineties that it was, Oh, you mean there are ten slots, let's make sure all ten are women. And it wasn't a "lift up others." It was a survival skill I think. I don't know what it is like . . .
>
> DEE: I don't know that it will ever be not a survival mode for women.

These remarks resonated with *Desperate Housewives'* depiction of the antagonism between Lynette and the female executive who codirected her interview with the male boss.

Although these interviews predated the new salience of sexual harassment heralded by the recent visibility of the #MeToo movement, older women also mentioned sexual harassment as a common occurrence that regularly limited women's workplace opportunities. Returning to the Linda and Janine mother-daughter interview, mom Linda discusses the tough climate that included multiple instances of harassment that she faced when she began working as a nurse. Better treatment by physicians is now legislated by most hospitals.

In contrast to the challenges older women faced at work, younger women had yet to experience as much discriminatory treatment in their school careers. There are a few exceptions to this perspective: some college-aged women note that male students are free to attend class in sweat pants and exercise clothes, while they themselves feel more pressured to dress up relative to this for class. They also note the use of the epithet "slut" (discussed in more detail in chapter 2) as a means of controlling their sexual behavior—they live in some fear of being the object of this label, which they feel can still be applied to them for the same behavior that might garner praise for their male counterparts. The fear curtails their freedom of action vis-à-vis their male contemporaries. Current research and certainly the #MeToo movement and its continuing revelations back up this assessment.[6]

Lynette as unlikeable and irrelevant. Generational differences also strongly structured women's responses to Lynette as a character, and to her experience at her job interview in the vignette we chose. Women young and old viewed Lynette as a more realistic figure than were the other housewives, and some women in preliminary conversations liked her portrayal best because of this (leading us to choose a vignette in which she was central). Younger women were not especially responsive or critical in response to Lynette's situation, often reacting to it with stories of their mothers' triumphs over the challenge of combining work with family. Quite a few younger women expressed ideas that their mothers had managed easily, believing that their decision to take time off from work to care for young children, and then to resume work with no penalty, would be effortless. This is not borne out by research.[7] Despite an episode indicating the reality of these struggles—which resonated with older respondents—younger women denied its relevancy. So while the portrayal of Lynette functions in part to challenge the popular feminist framework that asserts women's workplace triumphs, through the lens of media-ready feminist reception we capture how young, white, wealthy college students have trouble believing in the seriousness, the reality, and the relevance of the continuing problem of work-family balance. For us, this was a clear media-ready response to the vignette.

Interestingly, for personality reasons, Lynette's character at times became a somewhat controversial figure in our interviews. Though the young women tended to find her the most believable of the housewives, she was deemed not especially likeable, which is interesting and somewhat predictable from the perspective of recent feminist theory (Argarwal 2018), which notes that "forceful and successful women are not deemed likeable" (Cooper 2013). Lynette is the most assertive of the "housewives," the one most clearly associated with career success. In addition she is the most assertive mom, fiercely arguing for and protecting her children—and revelations about Felicity Huffman, who plays Lynette, having gone to great and dishonest lengths to gain admission for her daughter into an elite college make one wonder if interviews today, in the wake of the college admissions scandal, would indicate even more negative associations with the character of Lynette Scavo.

It seems that Lynette's forceful character was largely unacceptable to viewers. Lynette faces concrete problems in her life, including recalcitrant children and, later, teenagers; a husband not fully able to contribute to meeting the dual demands of work and family; a career put on hold due to the birth of four children and subsequently taking a measurable hit. These problems were illustrated by the show in a quite critical media-ready-feminist fashion. Yet younger women did not receive her character sympathetically overall. They blamed Lynette at least in part for her problems, failing to see how the lack of support structures for working mothers contributed to her frustrations. We believe that this is well illustrated when her character was frequently criticized by younger viewers as "bossy," which directly channels Sheryl Sandberg's pet peeve in her *Lean In* campaign against the epithet "bossy" as applied to assertive women.[8]

One young woman, a white college student, notes:

> CANDY: But [Lynette] is so constantly, like she always needs to be in charge and she won't listen to other people and she always has to have her way. It just annoys me so much because you could never reason to her. Like, I'm always on Tom's side, and Tom never wins. . . . Poor Tom, *I feel so sorry for Tom* a lot of the time. . . . No, I blame Lynette for her kids.

In this quote we see how young respondents deny that inequalities persist within the home (though research demonstrates that they do). In the focus groups of young women, respondents would frequently comment on how Lynette is simply too domineering to be likeable, even while they note that she is the most realistic and "relatable" of the housewives, partly because she is rather continually preoccupied with this problem of combining work with family.

> FRAN: She [Lynette] is the one who always thinks she is right. She is not my favorite, but I do like her. And she is the most believable, sort of.
>
> MARY: Yeah, she is easy to sympathize with. She is the closest to reality, like the middle-class working mom.
>
> FRAN: [Paradoxically:] That might be why I dislike her the most because she is the only one I feel like I can imagine is a real person, so I can imagine knowing her and hating her. . . .
> But if it's Lynette, it's like, if I knew someone who was like that, I would—she would always be on my nerves, so, 'cause I do know people who are like Lynette, and they really bug me. I have a neighbor who Lynette reminds me of. I don't dislike her; she just annoys me a lot. I don't like that Lynette is really stubborn and I feel like it comes out a lot.

Interestingly, none of the young people in this study addressed *why* Lynette might feel so stressed. Lynette is criticized for prioritizing work as well as family—and it is this more than anything that seems to make her unlikeable.

In fact, this ambivalence that younger women show to the character of Lynette is the *moment* of media-ready feminist reception: they draw back from the show's foregrounding of this strong character and retreat into an everyday sexism that sees powerful women through a negative prism. This everyday sexism that prompts these criticisms of Lynette, and which predominates in our culture, is so powerful that it can preempt women's *own experiences* in determining their worldviews.

Consequently, we thought that women of the older generation who had experienced the stresses Lynette faced firsthand might be more sympathetic to her character. In fact they were more sympathetic to a point, yet in their responses they often mirrored young women's criticisms of Lynette's personality. This indicates the power of the cultural stereotyping, in that even women who have themselves experienced problems maintaining their "balance" between work and family, criticize the fictional image of a woman who responds strongly and assertively to these conflicts in an attempt to take charge of her life in this regard.

It's interesting how consistently, even in these female focus group interviews, a woman perceived as "domineering"—such as Lynette—inspires critical reactions. This carried over into women's interpretations of the interview vignette they viewed, in which the female executive was represented as being so critical of Lynette's unfortunate need to carry her baby into the interview, and critical of Lynette's desire to combine a high-powered executive position with mothering small children. And though the older women were sympathetic to Lynette's having to face this situation, they remained critical of *her* personality in addition to criticizing her female boss. Again, we witnessed a critique that seemed to be kicked-off by a biased, generalized cultural dislike of assertive, "bossy" women. Ironically women mentioned this dislike of successful and outspoken women as a cultural stereotype they themselves had to buck at work, at the same time they mentioned finding Lynette unlikeable.

Partner Expectations

Desperate Housewives' portrayal of an everyday sexist inequality in the workplace is apparent in its representation of Lynette's husband, and in viewers' responses to him. Tom reifies everyday sexism by embodying the age-old concept that dads simply cannot do what moms can. This was a common trope in the golden age of television, iconically present in that 1952 *I Love Lucy* episode in which the husbands are shown to be incapable of performing the most basic household tasks.[9] It continues in *Desperate Housewives* (and notably in the more recent *Workin' Moms*)—yet each of these shows picture women responding differently and more critically to this notion than did 1952's Lucy Ricardo, who gratefully returned home after a day unsuccessfully trying to labor in a candy factory, happily cleaning up the mess her incompetent husband had predictably made while attempting to cook and clean.

Upon viewing the *Desperate Housewives* clip, women both young and old were not surprised by Tom's seeming inability to care competently for his children. The "Tom flat on his back" vignette rang true for women young and old, and it came up in interviews with African American and with Latino women. Women expected fathers to lack the capacity of mothers to care for their children. However, some young viewers do seem convinced that by the time they found a partner, this unequal gender pattern will have ceased—yet paradoxically they did not think the role of mothering would change that much.

In the interview with Janine and her mother the clip prompts not entirely sanguine thoughts about what Janine expects from the future dads of her own generation. Though she *hopes* for a more competent partner, she cannot imagine or describe one. Her comments followed directly from her mother Linda's story, which noted that Janine's dad did not put in as many hours as she did into child care; he tended to see his participation as "babysitting," while when she stayed home to watch children she was seen, as she says, as "doing her thing." Linda's tone is annoyed as she recounts these events, and Janine seems rather cognizant of this annoyance. Again, she hope for a more equal partner yet expects to encounter the same male incompetence.

> INTERVIEWER: Do you think the guys in your generation are going to be like Tom or are they going to be more aware?
>
> JANINE: I think they probably will still be a lot like Tom because I try and picture even my good guy friends with a child or raising children. And it almost seems funny. Like ooooh, that would be dangerous to give him a baby to watch. You know and that boy who just let Penny roll around on the table. You know I think there's some fear there.

Older women agreed with Janine's assessment of young men, believing that while men seem to be doing more around the home, they believed women will always put the child's needs first in a way that men have not and won't, even in the near future. New research on the "third shift" of work bears out this reality (Bolton 2010; Kumar 2015). Unlike younger women, older women invoked the role of nature to explain these continuing inequalities—arguing that women are "naturally" better at multitasking and have the ability to see what needs to get done around the house in a way that men can't:

> NICOLA: I don't think it's going to change. I think women with children, regardless of whether they identify with the feminist movement or not, if they have children they will make it a point to make the children a priority. If they are lucky enough to have a partner who believes in the equality and that you are

both responsible for the children, and you're both responsible for the household, and you're both responsible to each other, all the more perfect that would be.

DEE: We are able to multitask. Men are goal oriented. This goes into Psych 101 again, I'm sure you know. This is the problem. This is the solution to the problem. It's the internet thing that goes around periodically that says the man says I'm coming to bed, and he goes to bed. And the woman says I'll be right in. I'm coming to bed. And on the way into the bedroom she makes lunch for the next day, and puts the laundry in the dryer, and puts this away, and something else. And I live with a wonderful man. My husband is terrific. Nancy will tell you that.

AMANDA: I'll say I'm going swimming this morning. And he'll turn around forty minutes later and say you're still here? Well yeah, because on the way I did this, and this, and this. And this had to get done. And I saw that was out of place, and this needed to be done. But you're going swimming this morning. Yeah, I'm getting there, you know. Whereas when he gets up in the morning and he says I'm walking now, he gets up, he gets dressed, and he goes out and walks . . .

However, the women of the older generation, though many mentioned their belief that these differences in attitudes toward care might be due to biological gender differences, were actively critical of Tom's behavior and could relate to this depiction of his "opting out" of his responsibilities and the resultant difficulties this causes for Lynette. They accepted the media-ready feminism of the vignette we showed them. For example, among the teachers' group there are many comments expressing disgust at Lynette's husband Tom hurting his back at the last moment just as she is leaving for the interview. Women chuckle knowingly as Tom claims to be unable to care for the baby along with their three other children, and Lynette is forced into the uncomfortable and somewhat comic situation of bringing her baby to her important job interview. In fact, some thought this episode's critique did not go far enough in that it naturalized this occurrence and situation, letting Tom off the hook (although earlier several women in this group expressed their belief in precisely these biological gender differences):

KATE: You know what I didn't like about the message? I didn't like that he was failing miserably at staying home. Somehow we're all laughing at that, but wouldn't it have been nice for him to succeed and be doing a knock up job at it?

ALLISON: I felt badly for him to be honest with you because he was clueless.

KATE: Maybe it wouldn't be as entertaining though.

LAINE: That's part of the television industry is why are we laughing at people struggling?

One older woman in the divorced group told how Lynette's vignette resonated with her own experience:

SANDRA: When I was two weeks past due with my first child we went two, two-and-a-half hours outside of New York City, to a family gathering and I beached myself on the beach, but I was out to here. And my husband put his back out, couldn't drive home. I could barely fit behind the wheel to bring him home but he was so injured that he had to go to the hospital and get one of these things, and the whole thing. And the next day I went into labor and we're in the room, and he had to go leave the hospital to get meds. So that's why I felt it was realistic.

As these comments demonstrate, older women tend to relate Tom's behavior to that of their own husbands; he strikes a chord as a realistic figure for them. Tom is real because he exhibits the natural incompetence of dads; Lynette is real because she continues to put family first, even when she enters the role of sole breadwinner.

Yet further responses to the clip reveal that older women actually do believe the more conservative interpretation of Tom's behavior—that it is rooted in the biological basis of gender difference in competency. Most seem to accept this despite the criticism of one women who targets this precise issue, as recounted earlier. We see this not only in their response to Tom's inabilities to take care of the children, but also in their response to the male receptionist, who tries to watch Lynette's baby but whose incompetence puts the baby's life in danger:

MARIE: He [the male receptionist Lynette handed her baby to] was clueless about how to take care of the baby. He didn't understand the baby would roll off [the table].

ALLISON: That's interesting now that you mention it. All of the men are kind of clueless in the show.

INTERVIEWER: So what I'm hearing, it sounds like you all believe that men and women are pretty different.

ALLISON: I think they are.

MARIE: Biologically, emotionally.

This belief in natural difference between the genders vis-à-vis childcare competency sets the stage for women with families to continue shouldering the bulk of childcare responsibilities, rather than demanding the structural support to help equalize this burden that would enable further workplace achievements.

Despite transgressing the boundaries of popular feminism and laying the groundwork for a social critique of these beliefs, the vignette doesn't seem to prompt an overall *rejection* of the everyday sexism inherent in these differential assumptions about biological gender differences being the basis for different gender roles. Even among most of the older women who have direct experiences with these issues, their belief in inherent biological difference is prioritized. No one brought up the concrete social policies necessary to ascertain whether the differences are biological or cultural, as feminist sociologists have long argued (Williams 2010; Fausto-Sterling 2012). None in our study critiqued the structure of a workplace that patriarchally privileges male achievement and differentially penalizes women who assume the bulk of family responsibilities in the absence of company-based or government-based support. The seeds for this critique were present in the media-ready feminist television moment we showed them, but the critique remained unspoken in our interviews.

The overall tone in these comments is one of mild amusement, shading into disgust, rather than a critical anger. Older women sound tired, tired of being left behind to "run the business" while occupying a low-status position, to do the work of teaching in the trenches, to shoulder the major burden of labor in the family. They notice that the higher-status man in the vignette, who quickly hires Lynette without being bothered by her baby, is simply free to be off to his basketball game, leaving the women behind to mind the store—and, in most of their own cases, to combine these work duties with heavy family responsibilities as well. As Hochschild and Machung noted about working mothers (2012), they talk about sleep as though it's a luxury working women cannot afford.

In the case of this vignette, *Desperate Housewives* rather starkly portrays a real inequity in the expectations placed on working parents. These expectations are intensified by the ideology of intensive motherhood that continues to dominate cultural ideas of proper mothering, despite television's ongoing critique and mockery of these ideals that are impossible for all women to achieve. They are even more difficult for working-class women and women of color, who face additional stresses not experienced by white middle-class women.

Responses to this episode shed light on the fact that women both young and old are able to see the impossibility of achieving each of these goals yet aren't able to articulate even a narrow path toward a solution, true even when the problem of gender inequity confronts them in a representation as stark as this media-ready feminist episode. Our interviews also demonstrate how young women are unable to see the inequalities the older women are quite aware of having faced.

Imagining a more feminist future is difficult for young and old alike. None seem able to articulate a utopia of men and women in heterosexual couples equally shouldering childcare duties. Janine's mom relates some of the continuing social prejudices faced by men who try to buck gendered inequality by being more active caregivers:

> LINDA: There was an interesting conversation the other day because one of our doc's husband stays home with their toddler. And one of the other female physicians said, I just don't think that's really cool in a man for him not to have any kind of a job outside of the home. And I was like, well if she's the one that—they've decided this together. And she's like, yeah, but I just wouldn't want a man who is into that . . . another woman physician commenting that she just didn't think that that was very masculine, or interesting, or cool, or whatever word she used. I can't remember exactly. And it was really none of her business. I mean she's married to somebody who has a career, and she married late, doesn't have children just yet, but I don't think she would ever envision that her husband would stay home with their children if they had them because she just

doesn't think that's. . . . And then other people, yeah, chimed in about, yeah, they didn't think that was very attractive in a man if all he wanted to do was stay home.

JANINE: See maybe I'm—I don't know. I feel like that's a good quality that I would look for in a partner; like a guy that would be able to contribute to the family.

Perhaps Janine's concluding remark indicates the way forward for younger women: that women will seek caretaking qualities in their partners (whether male or female), and that heterosexual men will concomitantly seek women with greater breadwinning abilities, and that each of these qualities will actually increase the desirability of each gender as they acquire them. As we move to a world beginning to reject gender binaries, gender-connected polarization of skills may slowly fade from our cultural norms.

Class- and Race-Based Differences

Of course, social class and race-based differences also factor into how women conceive of the way a search for work-family balance will factor into their life plan. While the opportunities afforded women to combine work and family ambitions have been improving, scholars believe these considerations are still a factor in the continuing dynamic by which women are paid less and promoted more infrequently than men, even following equivalent work and performance (Dishman 2019; Webb 2017). As the responses of the participants in the focus groups have made clear, however, and as recently underscored by Orgad (2019), the generational divide is very class specific and intersects with other axes of oppression in insidious ways.

Racial and ethnic differences between women's experiences interact with how age and socioeconomic status create distinct experiences of what constitutes work-family balance. Cottom (2016) and Gandy (2014) speak directly to advice given in the more popular feminist literature (Slaughter 2012; Sandberg 2013) about how women can both get ahead at work by overcoming gender bias and how they can achieve the ever-elusive work-family balance. Both counter that the experience of women of color is quite different and simply noncomparable to that of the white women this literature addresses. Race theory illustrates how Sandberg's response to these issues—that women of color must simply "work harder"—is not only insufficient but entirely off track. Cottom invokes Angela Davis's classic book (1983) discussing how race structures the gendered and classed experiences of African American women from both ends: working mothers of color experience more discrimination and disadvantage in the workplace, and their children face the challenges and dangers of growing up in a society fraught with racial oppression, a situation mothers of color must address with techniques aimed simply at keeping their children safe. And as Cottom beautifully illustrates, in direct contradiction to Sandberg's "lean in" advice, Black women have always "spoken up" but rarely is their voice recognized as valuable in the boardroom.

The cultural discourse about work-family balance has been, quite problematically and like so much else in our culture, overwhelmingly centered on the experiences of white women. This was true also of the vignette picturing Lynette's job interview and her family. All of the characters in this vignette were white and appeared to be highly educated and of middle-class background, although as the show moved on, *Desperate Housewives* did incorporate a Black housewife and a Black family into the core of its characters, in a representation that was, however, far from flattering. Other shows about working mothers are becoming less centered on the experiences of white characters as well; for example, *Workin' Mothers* has incorporated a more diverse cast as this show has developed in recent seasons.

Not surprisingly, race-based differences in attitudes toward work-family balance, and in the reception of its depiction in popular media, did emerge in our data, though the responses to *Desperate Housewives* were limited as we found the show not to be as popular with the women of color in our sample. The more general attitudes toward work-family balance of first-generation college students, many of whom in our sample identified as a person of color, contrasted in many ways to the white students we spoke with. For most of the former, the very idea of "choosing" between work or family was ridiculous. Their expectations were that they would always work, and so questions of "balance" were not part of their decision about having a family. Among the less privileged, most were already working in the full-time jobs they intended to keep after they'd finished their degrees, jobs such as one respondent's apprenticeship in a hair salon, where she had been working since age nine. Yet this finding was true of respondents who identified as a person of color and occupied more middle- and upper-middleclass positions as well.

A focus group of African American college students uniformly mentioned what strong role models their professional mothers were. Some mentioned how they rarely saw their moms, who in these cases had very demanding professional positions. Similarly to the white college students, none mentioned any trepidation when it came to their own plans regarding their intentions to combine work with family. All stated their intention to both work and have families. One woman stated that despite her desire to be, as she termed it, barefoot and pregnant, she nevertheless desired a demanding career. Gabriella noted, "I want to get married and have a career. I wouldn't mind being barefoot and big as a house in somebody's kitchen, you know." Several African American women in our sample stated that, for them, feminism was about "choice," yet none indicated that the choice of not entering the paid labor force seemed at all desirable or possible for them.

Unusually for our African American sample, one woman mentioned that her mom had stayed home temporarily when she was small, returning to work when she was about thirteen years old. Interestingly, and unlike any of the white college students we spoke with, the student recounted an ongoing dialogue with her mom about how difficult it was going to be to pursue a high-powered career and have a large family. The student mentioned that she had had a continuing and very serious discussion about this issue, given that she planned a career as an attorney that she hoped to combine with having a family of six children. Allison felt the need to actually research corporate attorneys in order to prove to her mom that this combination was possible, which she felt she had proven when she uncovered the story of an Exxon corporate attorney who had a large family:

> INTERVIEWER: So are these issues you've talked about with your mom? Family and work?
>
> ALLISON: Yes. All the time.
>
> INTERVIEWER: All the time?
>
> ALLISON: She knows that I want six kids and she's just like, how are you going to do this and also be a lawyer?
>
> INTERVIEWER: You want to be a lawyer?

ALLISON: Yes. I mean I feel like I researched a lot of people, especially when I was little because I wanted to be a corporate (inaudible), a corporate attorney from Exxon. She has a family. . . . I was looking it up. I'm pretty sure she does. I just tried to argue with her. I'm just that type of person who is going to go research to pull up a good case. I'm not necessarily saying that I have to work when I get older or when I have kids, but I want to have that option if that's possible. If it's not I will work, but I do want to raise my children as well. I feel like I had valuable time with learning, oh my goodness, I take advantage or I take my mom for granted. She does pick up behind me. It's useful in a sense. I do wish my mom had more time to be at events and things like that. Now she does. When you get older you get settled into your career. My mom is at my sister's, every cheerleading competition.

INTERVIEWER: It sounds like you've taken this issue pretty seriously. You've researched corporate attorneys. That's a first in my groups. So what have you found? Have you found that it's difficult for these corporate attorneys to have families?

ALLISON: Well, now, I guess when you get established. She works from home. A lot of these women work from home and just go into the office once or twice a week. That's what I strive to do. . . . I mean, after a while, if you get established and you get like all these contracts and you know your clients and things like that, you don't really have to leave if you have a computer and accessibility.

Allison's experience in having this ongoing argument with her mom bears out the idea that Black mothers must often problematize issues white mothers can take for granted. In this case, while the issue of balancing work with family seems to have been very problematic for most of our older white informants, the younger white women in our sample do not seem to have discussed these problems at length with their mothers or other older female relatives. These moms were content to adhere to the strictures of a popular feminism that simply takes the inevitability of work-family struggle for granted and assumes that this is an issue that, in the wake of second-wave feminism, has simply been solved and will be unproblematic for women. This *despite* the fact that almost uniformly, the older white women in our sample could identify many problems they had experienced in attempting to combine work in their families with work in the paid labor force. There was an unquestioned assumption that problems they had experienced had simply "gone away" in the wake of second-wave feminism, and that their daughters' experiences would be different—this despite the fact that in the case of the teachers' group, multiple women mentioned the gender-based discrimination they were *still experiencing* in the workforce. In media-ready feminist fashion, however, they did not feel these experiences demanded organized, systematic critique or response that they could hand down to their students or daughters.

This African American woman, however, who had the experience of being both a stay-at-home mom and working mom, *did* feel that the problems of working mothers merited conversation—and ongoing conversation and focus—as she parented her daughter. She strove to sensitize her daughter to the problems working mothers, in her experience and from her perspective, still face as they strive to combine work and family. Her response to this problem did not fall into a media-ready feminist pattern but set the stage for a more critical feminist response to a set of workplace and family norms and structures that consistently make it difficult for working moms to achieve work-family balance. She sought to prepare her daughter for what she was to face, in accordance with race theory that stipulates that African American mothers find it necessary to offer their children extra preparation for the multitude of problems they will face as persons of color in a white-dominated culture.

Conclusion: Working Mothers and Generational and Intersectional Feminism

A slightly older Janine, the daughter in our mother-daughter pair, might be Lesley Staal (2011)—a former college student who "rediscovered" the great books of feminism upon the birth of her first child (Press 2012a). The experience of becoming a mother made her a feminist and sent her back to reread the feminist texts she'd read in college, which had lacked meaning at that time in her life. Staal's position is similar to the one discussed by Barnard president Deborah Spar, who describes herself as an "interloper in the area of feminist theory" (2013, 11). Like Staal, Spar grew up in the era *after* feminism had reputedly already succeeded and was no longer needed. As Spar puts it, she got a lot of "trickle-down" feminism that was transmitted through the cultural ether (24). This is precisely the situation Janine is describing. In Spar's case, she experienced what is common for many women of the current generation. While not an explicit "feminist" growing up, she began to see the need clearly, and urgently, upon leaving school and assuming her first series of professional positions. Upon becoming president of the all-female Barnard College, Spar found the need to address feminist issues so urgent that, though not a feminist scholar herself, she proceeded to write a book, *Wonder Women*, addressing the issue before the #MeToo movement brought these questions to the forefront of cultural discussion.

The problem both Janine's experience and Spar's trajectory present is the apparently overwhelming message common to both, and emblematic of the current popular feminism: that the most fundamental feminist struggles have been won. This cultural assumption among young, upper-class white women is so strong that even when media depicts characters struggling with such gendered oppressions, they are met with opposition and disbelief, spawning attitudes that frame the women who try to confront such obstacles as too bossy or demanding, and maintaining the idea that their future male partners will be incapable of providing the necessary task of taking care of children should they decide to work. The recent debacle over sexual harassment and assault, and its attendant publicity, have changed the way women look at these particular issues. It remains to be seen if these events will usher in permanent changes for working women. The impossibility of a gender-equitable work-family balance under our current system remains an obstacle so fundamental to women's advancement in the workplace that women have made little measurable workplace progress over the last decade—and have even lost some workplace gains of late (Kramer and Harris 2019a, 2019b).

Tales of the older working women in our study are rife with the difficulties they encountered both in combining work and family and simply in getting ahead at work. In this respect they contrast with published authors Staal and Spar, both of whom come from unusually elite backgrounds and have succeeded professionally to a much greater degree than is the norm for working mothers.[10] The women teachers and guidance counselors' group made many comments about single motherhood and abusive husbands and stepfathers, and they discussed women "having two full-time jobs" (as sociologists such as Hochschild and Machung [2012] have documented). Yet few were able to make the leap in order to identify with Lynette. While they did find Tom to be relatable with regard to his incompetency, and felt that Lynette's character was the most "real" of those featured on the show—and while some spoke positively of her—most distanced themselves from her character, believing that she was too demanding in the home and too bossy at work. While for some their experiences allowed them to break through the more conservative media-ready feminist mode of response to a breakthrough image, most retained skepticism when confronting this critical media-ready feminist representation.

For women young and old, the media they consume do not necessarily help them garner a more realistic vision of their future. Decoding the messages via media-ready feminism, different groups found themselves unable to sympathize with Lynette. For women who occupied more privileged positions (youth, whiteness, wealth), the desire to have a family seemed like a compatible part of having a career, something that would simply work itself out after college. Repeatedly, these women expressed the desire to have families and the belief that combining work with these families would not present difficulties that they couldn't surmount. Moreover, they pointed to their mothers as role models and noted that these women they respected had taken a hiatus when they or their siblings were born but had successfully taken up their careers again after a certain period of time (which varied from respondent to respondent). Daughters' perceptions were almost uniformly positive: their mothers had managed the "break," with little cost to their careers. Almost all saw their mothers as "successful" and happy, with good—or good-enough—careers. Young women saw work-family balance as desirable, achievable, and a component of their future. As a result, they felt Lynette was a nag. Seeing a woman prioritizing work over family was jarring for these respondents who felt that women should take breaks to stay at home with their families. These accounts contrasted dramatically with the stories of older, white, relatively affluent women who frequently described how they scaled down their ambitions to meet the expectations of men who surrounded them (both romantic partners and coworkers).

These findings were in stark contrast to women who were not afforded the same structural opportunities. Women of color *and* working-class women of different races in our study conceptualized their future lives in a completely different way and, as a result, found Lynette's character unrelatable specifically regarding the idea that she went "back" to work, because the idea that she ever would stop working was not in their thoughts—even for those who planned large families. Her story did not speak to them. They tended not to frame the problems of work-life balance in terms of choices because they were not raised in an environment where opting out of work was considered an option or even functioned as an ideal. Given the struggles they faced, they did not resonate with the problem as framed by *Desperate Housewives* as one of balance, or of prioritizing work "over" family, or vice versa. Their thinking was not focused on choice, and they seemed much less governed by the ideology of intensive mothering, which did not come up in our interviews.

Dow discusses how Black mothers, when attempting to achieve middle-class ideal mothering, must navigate what is often a largely white, middle-class world and must make decisions about the kind of environments to provide for their children, sometimes choosing between elite schools and activities that often include only a small number of children of color and those that are more integrated but offer less "elite" opportunities (2019, 23). So many of the choices Black mothers face in our culture have to do with navigating a world dominated by a vison of culture that is hegemonically white and middle class—in this case that means replete with the vision that women have high-powered careers, like Lynette, that they can choose to leave at will. Black mothers want their children to be familiar with this culture while at the same time tuned in to the idea that they themselves do not inhabit it in the same way white women do, even when they achieve class privileges such as a good education and high-status job.

The *Desperate Housewives* vignette does not begin to address these issues of racial and class difference; rather, it smooths them over into an idealized world of privileged whiteness. This is something television is just beginning to address with more racially and social class–varied programming. *Workin' Moms* began to do this as the series progressed, and *Black-ish* has had some shows focused on mothering—though the notion of achievable work-family balance is so entrenched in our culture that even newer shows focused on mothering are resistant to the many issues and complications that considerations of ethnic, racial, and social class diversity introduce. It remains to be seen whether the new #MeToo furor over workplace sexual harassment will lead to a broader and more honest confrontation, in media representations and in reception of them, of the structural changes necessary to alleviate the work-family conflicts persisting for most women, and to a broader feminism applicable and relevant for all.

Figure 4.1. Photograph of a Tinder billboard advertisement in Madison Square Garden (corner of Thirty-Second Street and Seventh Avenue). Photo by Francesca Tripodi, taken on November 1, 2018.

4

Swipe Right for Consent

Hookup Culture, Tinder, and Structural Sexism

Amid the crowds of people spilling off the trains at Penn Station, we hustle for the exit, caught up in the pulse of New York City. Riding the escalator out of the bustling hub into the frenzy of Madison Square Garden, the cool air hits our faces as we are confronted by a sea of high-rises. Stepping onto Thirty-Second Street, we are immediately met with a large billboard promoting #SwipeLife—"Single does what Single wants." In the advertisement a beautiful, skinny, white-presenting woman with blond hair and high cheekbones looks powerfully into the horizon. This is her city—singletons of Manhattan are at her fingertips.

Using a simple slogan, "Swipe, match, chat," Tinder asserts in this billboard that women hold as much power as men to control the future of their relationships. As part of its terms of service, Tinder requires users to adhere to a set of standards on conduct—no nudity or sexual content (in the words of Tinder, "Keep it classy and appropriate for public consumption"), no inappropriate behavior ("Be respectful with anyone you interact with in the Tinder community"), no violent or graphic content, no pictures of children ("even if it's you as a kid"), no copyright infringement, no scamming, no harassment ("stalking, threats, bullying, or intimidation"), no private information, and no hate speech. Those who violate these terms on the app may be banned from future use. The ad and the terms of service promote an expressive individualism—encouraging users to see their place in the dating scene as a personalized, unique experience, more real than their social responsibilities within it. Users decide who they are interested in ("swipe right to like") and then, only after another user makes the same choice (what the company refers to as "matching"), can users message one another.[1] Other apps, like Bumble, claim to foster an even greater sense of female empowerment, since only women can initiate the first round of contact. In short, apps like Tinder and Bumble are complicated. In some ways they operate under a "popular feminist" ethos stressing the importance of female empowerment but remaining within the framework of cisgender heteronormativity. However, they also provide an opportunity for women to initiate intimate relationships.

Analyzing people's engagement with these apps offers a prime example of media-ready feminism. The empowerment frame utilized by these apps is a modern manifestation of female-initiated sexual encounters. Yet they are built for and focused on the privileges of a relative few and ignore the underlying structural sexism that predicates the dating scene altogether. Drawing from data we collected as part of a larger study on how college students cultivate consent, in this chapter we discuss how college students use apps like Tinder as a form of empowerment (i.e., "playing Tinder") but also fail to recognize how "swiping right" can act as a form of tacit consent, fueling the everyday sexism of the hookup culture in which dating apps are embedded.

In our research, we observed that while Tinder might facilitate matches under the guise of empowerment, should users decide to meet up, they are thrust into a situation in which consent has already been implied. This assumption helps to explain why women feel disproportionately pressured to engage in sexual activity, often against their own desires. Our data suggest that many heterosexual women change their minds yet do not feel like they can say "no" once a certain level of sexual engagement has begun. Such interactional asymmetry has been studied by other prominent sociologists investigating "hookup" culture (Armstrong and Hamilton 2015; Wade 2017). However, this chapter offers an in-depth discussion of how dating apps perpetuate the ambivalence of media-ready feminism whereby young women feel both "empowered" by a smartphone-enabled dating environment, yet, as they respond to and use these apps, they feel unable to navigate beyond an initial yes, even if they are thrust into situations where they no longer feel comfortable. To illustrate this assertion, we offer an in-depth discussion of the operation of implicit consent in Tinder-structured situations and the role this plays in perpetuating everyday sexism.

During the 2016–2017 academic year we led a team of undergraduate researchers who conducted participant observation, focus groups, and interviews with their peers. The goal of this research endeavor was to gain insights into undergraduate life typically limited by older researchers' distance from these subjects. Through this research we found that, despite undergraduates' relatively large dating pool, most use Tinder in a plethora of ways, including what we term Tinder "play." The Tinder "game" facilitates the opportunity for students to gain an ego boost or rate the "hotness" of the guys or girls on their campus. At the outset, online Tinder encounters may be quite pleasant. However, our findings reveal that if students were to decide to meet up with their matches, their encounters follow the same cultural tropes as other "hookups" (Wade 2017)—quick, disengaged sexuality—rather than facilitating opportunities for more long-standing relationships. Offering a promise of more agency to female participants, Tinder's structure is compatible with a hookup culture that has been widely criticized for enshrining everyday sexism. By unpacking this structure, we explain how the implicit (rather than overt) consent of Tinder's structure is bound up with a swipe, substituting for the more active assertion of consent that is possible in in-person meetings, and leaving the in-person exchanges that result open to a sexist culture of violence and misunderstanding.

We juxtapose our data with "Grace's" published account in *Babe* of her date with celebrity Aziz Ansari (Way 2018a). Despite the initial tendency to dismiss her story as unprofessional journalism documenting merely a consensual sexual encounter, our findings reveal that Grace's experiences resonated with the young women in our study. Not only were her repeated requests to Ansari to cease sexual activity mirrored by much of our own data about dating and hookups, but discussions surrounding this case also connected to our data on implicit consent and Tinder. Such a finding demonstrates how the playfulness of dating apps like Tinder are a by-product of the institutions through which they are built (i.e., those in Silicon Valley) and on which they operate (i.e., college campuses). This chapter also details how the nuances of hookup culture unfortunately remain "outside the purview" of the reappropriation of the #MeToo movement circulating on social media. It documents the domestication of Tinder's media-ready feminist moment in the mode of its appropriation and use.

The History of the Hookup

Sociological studies describing the new sexual "hookup culture" abound (Wade 2017; Armstrong and Budnick 2015; Armstrong, England, and

Fogarty 2012; Armstrong and Hamilton 2013; Armstrong, Hamilton, and Sweeney 2006; Backstrom, Armstrong, and Puentes 2012; Bogle 2008; Khan et al. 2018). Wade (2017) in particular describes a phenomenon that seems relatively new in college students' sexual behavior, in which they engage in sex without emotional connection. The progression to an emotional relationship is difficult, slow, and hazardous when it comes to maintaining a network of peers. According to Wade, these restrictions of emotion are present for both men and women, each of whom must guard against seeming too "desperate" or misinterpreting the actions of the other as indicating real interest in a relationship when it does not. Our findings mirror this reluctance to define the relationship, what college students colloquially refer to as "DTR" (define the relationship), a process requiring an explicit discussion about relationship status that normally takes place after extensive sexual activity.

Like Wade, we also find that behind the guise of egalitarian participation in hookup culture by men and women, heterosexual women feel disempowered. They feel bound to simply respond to (or ignore) male advances and find that there is a double standard continuously applied to them when they engage in sexual behavior. Many women in our study felt they did not have the power to be the "active player" in initiating hookups. A woman in a sorority focus group says:

> I feel like [at our university the norm is] very like, "Girls are passive, guys are active." So we girls don't even size up a guy until they've already come over and made a move and then we decide, "Okay yes, I'm interested," or, "No. I'm not." Whereas I think guys have to be a lot more aggressive. So I don't know, I've seen guys at bars scanning every single female that walks in the room and you can see that they're assessing them for their body parts.

In this quote she points out the more aggressive "vetting" process women's bodies go through in the heterosexual dating scene, which is not paralleled by the way women assess men. These findings echo Armstrong, Hamilton, and Sweeney (2006) and Armstrong and Hamilton (2015), who also found the hookup scene to be profoundly gendered, and profoundly unequal, predisposing the women who participated to sexual violence and nonconsensual encounters.

This heteronormative assumption of power in hookups is not exclusive to sorority and fraternity environments. Another example of gendered power roles comes into play when a woman not in a sorority discussed how women must work hard to avoid the stereotype that they automatically want a relationship rather than a hookup and describes the imperative women in particular feel to avoid being seen as "desperate" or "thirsty":

> [Women] do not have power . . . if a girl has feelings for a boy, she doesn't get to be the boy's girlfriend until the boy decides she's worthy . . . after she . . . like jumps through hoops to do it. That to me is what the very core of hookup culture is. . . . It's not fine for a girl to want exclusivity or to be someone's girlfriend or boyfriend, because that's desperate, and that's not cute. Like don't be clingy. I don't know.

As these quotes demonstrate, and as we illustrate with our research in chapter 2, the "double standard" is still active even in a seemingly egalitarian hookup culture. As widely reported in our research, women's participation in sexual activity is judged differently than that of men. However, as Wade (2016) indicates, opting out of "hooking up" is not an option for most sexually active young people. Even those who do not want to engage in casual sex are swept up into a culture where intimacy other than the explicitly sexual is shunned and avoided. So despite the continuous pressure to have casual sex, and not to be judged as someone who avoids hooking up, they must both participate in sex *but also be selective* in their hookup activity. This selectivity helps white, heterosexual women ensure they do not incur the "slut" label while at the same time solidifying their desirability. Such selectivity is bound to both gendered and racial inequality. Wade (2016) and our own data both suggest that African American women and Asian men were rarely afforded the opportunity to hook up on college campuses, racial judgments infusing the assessments of sexual desirability and pointing to an objectionable ranking system that is demonstrably racist as well as sexist.

What we also found is a lack of linguistic facility with the new system. White, straight, cisgender women are not sure how to conceptualize or label the normative demands of a system wrought with contradictions. The opportunity to hook up is therefore mixed: it is capable of conferring sexual agency that, when actualized, can potentially damage women's status. Lack of familiarity with its terms, or with its proper, specialized vocabulary, leads heterosexual women to feel uncomfortable communicating their sexual desires and preferences. There is a complicated system of the nonverbal affirmation of status and consent operating here, which nevertheless may not be universally understood in the same way by all who participate. What is clear is that a failure to know or feel comfortable sharing sexual desires may contribute to what has been identified as the gendered orgasm gap, a term referring to research that demonstrates that women rarely achieve orgasms in hookup encounters (Wade 2017). It is also clear that women do not always feel comfortable saying "no" when this involves expressing the desire to halt already-begun sexual activity, particularly if they were the ones who initiated sexual acts or even meet-ups.

Women's proclivity to understand their power as limited—for example, to underestimate their ability to exercise agency—is particularly problematic when we examine conversations during which consent to sexual activity is granted or withheld. Recent debates about consent illustrate that it is important to determine when consent is given and when it is not, and that there should be no gray areas when it comes to granting consent (Kimmel and Steinem 2014). Yet, in our interviews, we found that few undergraduates engage in any type of conversation at all during sexual encounters. Many described how it "ruins the mood" to talk during a hookup and that in order to maintain desirability, consent is often implied simply by an *absence of protest*. According to our findings, therefore, consent is rarely "active" in hookups. As a result, both granting and withholding consent become fraught with contradictions and are often indicated by tacit agreement. An implied form of consent, for example, can come from meeting someone out at a bar. Simply texting someone after a certain time means that you want to hook up, according to this white, straight college junior:

> If you text someone past 11:30, that already has a connotation, it doesn't even matter what you're saying. . . . Buying someone a drink, that had a specific connotation. It's weird trying to navigate that and still play stuff kind of ambiguous[ly] when you know everything that you do has basically been done before with the intention of getting someone to go home with you.

One focus group of heterosexual women explicitly identified the consensual tipping point in the context of hookup culture to be, in the words of one white woman, "as soon as I tell them I'll go back with them. If I don't want sex, I shouldn't go home with them. It's not universal, but I feel like I should." Another straight, white woman described how she avoided saying "no" to someone who wanted to go home with her by simply kissing another man she did not especially want to kiss: "I never wanted to do anything except make out with him but every time he'd be like do you want to get out of here and I'd just bounce away . . . to make it clear that it wasn't a thing, I made out with his friend in front of him."

If women end up going home with someone and feel trapped into having sex once they are in private, some will initiate what is called the "obligatory blow job," termed by one respondent who felt that she had to engage in some kind of sexual activity since she went home with a guy and wanted to avoid "feeling bad" or "looking bad" if she didn't have intercourse.

Often, there are potentially dual and contradictory messages involved in the various stages of a hookup. So, for example, giving out your phone number could mean "yes I want a hookup," but also "go away right now, so that I don't have to talk with you." In each case, however, the woman who is involved in this interchange (a) does not initiate the encounter, and (b) expressed a lack of agency regarding how the exchange would proceed. Even a woman who wants a repeated encounter cannot ensure that her phone number will be used; it might have been sought simply to end the current encounter. In different contexts, the same act can mean one thing as well as its direct opposite. So while giving out your phone number to someone at a bar means that you could be interested in hooking up with them, it is sometimes a mechanism for halting an unwanted encounter, as in this example:

> So if you talk to someone at a bar for a while and they don't ask for your phone number then like, okay you've just gotten closer with that kid in your discussion. Whereas if they ask for your number at the end of it, then it's like oh, you know that something's up. But I also think that people just give out their phone numbers because they don't know if the person wants it, just because or if they want it to contact you later in the night or if they gave it to you because they didn't want you to bother them anymore. So it's not like, "I got the phone number, I'm golden." It's like if you don't get the phone number, then where are you?

Expectations increase if women say "yes" to a formal date or accede to a request to accompany someone to an event, and women we spoke with weigh these expectations when deciding if they should accept invitations.

Such a consideration is amplified if the woman doesn't really know the guy that well. In the words of Emily, a white, heterosexual freshman at college: "When I weighed if I was gonna say yes to him or say no to him, my question was, "Am I willing to hook up with him or am I not?" Dimensions of consent become complicated on dates, as the sexual considerations and demands might differ depending upon who will be paying. One third-year, white, female heterosexual college student says:

> There's like a big controversy over who should pay, but normally if a guy is paying I consider that definitely a date. And if I don't know if it's supposed to be a date, I might not offer to pay right away and see what they do. So whereas if we're both paying that might be more of a hang out.

At the same time, public events can open women up to increased outside scrutiny, and because dates imply consent, women also must consider how being seen "out" with someone might influence their status. One student invokes the influence of the male peer group on the outcome of such an evening, implying that the man participating will be hyperaware of their expectations that this kind of event will result in a hookup for him and that his own behavior will be influenced by this:

> The dates to these [formal] functions are subject to judgment from a male's friends and thus that person you ask means more than a random hookup, for social as well as romantic reasons. This affects the relationship further in its definition once other people post questions to the "couple" on "what they are." This can be very uncomfortable to both parties when there has not been an explicit moment in which the two of them "define the relationship."

Women speak explicitly about how the underlying assumptions embedded in their decision to say yes to a date, go home from a bar with a guy, or even to give someone their phone number all complicate their ability to say "no" at a later time. Women seem reluctant overall to offer explicit rejection, period, and this seems to be an instance where the norms of hookup culture intersect with the more general norms of gendered speech patterns (Lakoff 2017). Many recent discussions of consent have been actively promoting an explicit type of consent as a safety measure for women in hookup culture, advocating an explicit "yes" rather than assuming that consent is implied by the simple absence of a "no" (Kimmel and Steinem 2014). However, our data indicate that many assume that saying "yes" is actually a continuous process, and that changing one's mind once this process has been initiated is difficult. It is also clear from our data, and reaffirmed in Grace's account in *Babe*, that if women say "no" they are often pushed to reconsider, or at the very least they feel like their "no" is not heard as a valid form of expression, since their earlier actions had apparently indicated a "yes" without them explicitly meaning to communicate this. Not only do men seem to control the progression of a hookup, but men clearly most often controlled the extent to which a relationship may be defined as either simply an extended "friends with benefits," a one-night stand, or a long-term committed relationship. We interpret this as the persistence of heteronormativity even in this allegedly feminist age, and even in the workings of the relatively new set of cultural rules by which young peoples' sexual relationships are governed. As Blair, a white, heterosexual women in her junior year of college, states: ". . . more often than not, stuff just like fizzles out here. Unless you're like exclusively dating a person and there was a blow-up fight and a reason you guys are ending your relationship, so often it's like oh the semester's over, guess we're gonna stop fucking now!"

Playing Tinder

This chapter focuses on how the dating app Tinder is a key example of media-ready feminism. Tinder is known for making online dating easier and somewhat safer with a twofold strategy: first, by making it seem like a game, with easy, geolocative swipes that yielded dates far more quickly than former sites; and second, by shielding women from unwanted attention by limiting those who contacted them to those on whom they had already swiped (Clifford 2017). Many of the students in our study focused primarily on the "game" aspect of Tinder's reputation and approached the use of the app as such. As one woman describes, she swipes just for the "entertainment value," which might lead us to think that the consequences of Tinder's structure were not culturally serious. This is not what our analysis finds, however.

Nevertheless, this is an idea shared by many of Tinder's users in our study. The idea of "playing" Tinder was explicitly discussed by Kai, a heterosexual male who described the app as a "waste of time" for students in college. He shared the widespread assumption that students enrolled in a university do not rely on the apps in order to facilitate relationships, although as we have illustrated this is not equally true for all students. The way Kai and others treat the app like a game helps to support the wider narrative that apps like Tinder and Bumble are "just for fun." Many, both men and women, speak of them that way, including this woman: "It was kind of like a game honestly, more than anything else." Another heterosexual woman claims (talking about where Tinder is organized in her phone), "Okay so, I put Tinder under games because I thought that was funny."

In a female-only focus group of straight, white, cisgender college students, we found that many "play Tinder" in group settings:

> STACI: Um, like, a lot of my friends are, like . . . when we're messing around on Tinder—I use that term (laughter)—it's more of, like, um, kind of, like, a joke or kind of like a game . . . like swipe right for someone and see who does the same as well . . . and see who, like, might like how you appear or something like that but never take it seriously. So, it's more of, like, a, um, playing like a game or something like that where it's not nothing serious, like, if you do get a match on Tinder. It's just, like, a, Oh! Okay, cool.
>
> CARLY: We always made fun of it. We said, "Playing Tinder," to make sure people knew it was a joke.

The "Tinder game" can in fact serve as a playful ego boost for those who are shy or otherwise disadvantaged in the face-to-face scene. In this vein, one heterosexual college woman discusses explicitly the kind of ego boost that can be involved when a white heterosexual woman "plays" lightly with the app:

> I think for people in general, and girls in particular, it can be a huge *ego boost* [as] over time you get a match, every time a guy messages you with some cheesy pick-up line or compliment, I am sure it just sends a rush of dopamine to your head. It sorta reinforces the fact, "Hey I am pretty and attractive and people want me."

However, the freedom and flexibility to "play Tinder" was not afforded to all that we spoke with. As we will detail later in this chapter, students of color found that Tinder, and hookup culture more generally, was a product of popular feminism. To test this theory, we launched a small experiment to better illustrate how Tinder's promise of sexual agency—its accession to popular feminism—was tempered for minorities using the app in ways that exceeded the way it was halted for white, cisgender users. Our experiment demonstrated clearly that one's race affected the desirability of one's Tinder profile, so that even the ego boost afforded white users of the app was less available to minority users. To conduct this project, a student researcher created two profiles very similar in nature. Tinder requires users to sync their profiles with their Facebook accounts, so this required the student to delete her own Facebook account from her phone and create two false Facebook accounts based on two photos that were available on Shutterstock "open" photos. She chose photos that represented the "face forward" picture that people have on Tinder. She chose a second set of photos that represented the "fun" playful picture that people also put on their Tinder profiles. We used these photos to represent two very generic-sounding people. Finding that the two most common names on Tinder are "Emily" and "Lauren," we named one Emily, the other Lauren.

Each profile featured two "selfies," one with a filter and one as a side-angle where the woman's body was in the lens. They both were "lovers of pizza" and expressed affinity for the school they were said to represent. The only difference was that skin color in one profile was darker than the other. What we found was that the lighter-skinned woman received exponentially more swipes. Emily was matched with almost twice as frequently as Lauren. Our findings here mirror the data reported in the book *Dataclysm* (Rudder 2015), which was made from scraping the OKCupid—another dating site—data. In fact, when broken down by race, we find that Asian women receive the most swipes and Black women and Asian men the least—so race and color do in fact play a large role in establishing the attractiveness of Tinder users, in large part determining the "action" and attention they receive. Tinder reproduces the structural racial inequality that racial minorities experience in the broader culture.

Framing Tinder as something silly supports the wider assumptions that the mechanisms by which people are facilitating relationships are relatively innocuous. Indeed, for those who are confining their use of the app to just the app, it supports a framework of feminist empowerment.

This is especially true for students—like Carly, quoted earlier—who used the site to find a "real" relationship: "We said, 'Playing Tinder,' to make sure people knew it was a joke. It was always kind of a running joke and then people started using it and having successful relationships off of it and it was just a very interesting concept."

Importantly, some who were in search of a "real" relationship also turned to Tinder as a way to "opt-out" of hookup culture. This was particularly useful for students majoring in degrees populated overwhelmingly by one gender (e.g., nursing or engineering). Yet when we found students interested in using Tinder for this purpose, their rationale was often imbued with misogynistic implications that the women in their classes (e.g., the women in engineering or computer science) were not "hot enough" for them to date.

One sophomore majoring in engineering described:

> I took a snapchat of my time series class and showed it to him and there's like twenty people in the class, forty people, thirty of them are guys, nine of them are completely unattractive girls, and one is like a mediocre. That's why I'm saying it's easy for guys in philosophy classes and law classes, you have hot girls in your classes. [Engineering] doesn't have the things Tinder offers you.

The existence of the dating app provides an imaginary world where presumably they can envisage a series of potential partners as much more "acceptable" according to the misogynistic standards that gave rise to these negative judgments in the first place; in fact, we might infer that the dating app prompted this type of misogynistic thinking. Using markedly less sexist language, some women nevertheless corroborate that Tinder is a "useful tool" for meeting potential partners. Their thinking about Tinder's use was more practical and did not tend to exacerbate a tendency to objectify dating partners.

While some students mentioned using Tinder to find the "hot" partners not in their courses, other students spoke of themselves as needing Tinder because they feel "unattractive"; for instance, they don't feel they meet the high appearance "standards" of their peer group. For these students, Tinder was a way to both "hide out" but also to get some positive validation, at least online, that in real life might be scarce. Students in our study reported informally that they have observed that many men speak of swiping quickly on everyone to indicate widespread interest, believing that they will get at least some pushback with this technique. This technique seems to generate at least some positive feedback for the women they are swiping on—women who are not receiving it in their real lives. And in fact, many of the women using Tinder mentioned that they did so for an ego boost, as they often felt judged exactly as the aforementioned misogynist quotes indicated, as "not hot enough" to interest the men that they met. A Tinder presence, and Tinder activity, ensured at least some positive reinforcement, as they were almost guaranteed to obtain some "swipe" interest. People who want to feel desirable describe the rush of matching with relative strangers as a reaffirmation of their physical attractiveness. However, even in the case of men who feel insecure turning to Tinder for this affirmation, we argue that once students match "off-line," the underlying cultural norms embedded in hookup culture end up taking over, shifting the power dynamics back in favor of men in most cases.

When talking about dating apps, people often bring up how they know someone who has found a serious relationship there. This is interesting because, although these comments were widespread, individual instances of Tinder leading to relationships do not seem to have upgraded the overall image of Tinder as a tool for often unserious, casual sexual hookups. An overwhelming majority admitted that their interest in Tinder was for more unserious "hookups" rather than a tool to find long-term relationships, as this remark by a white, heterosexual, college sophomore woman indicates: "He [my friend] always complains about. . . . he's like, oh I need to find a wife so I can have a family. And I was like, you look in bad places for it. Going on Tinder is not where you're going to find that." Tinder is widely seen as a device to implement hookup culture. This carries implications for the way feminism or misogynist values are embedded within the app and its use.

Tinder as the Media-Ready Feminism Moment

Tinder offers the promise of a new feminist sexual agency with its swiping-activated meet-ups. Nevertheless, the cultural context within which Tinder is used seems to bend its impact in the other direction. We find this to be particularly important regarding the assumption of "implicit consent" that informs Tinder meet-ups. For while the app might invite single women to do as they please, and initiate only the encounters *they* desire, the underlying assumptions of what matching and meeting up might mean in the context of hookup culture are not considered. Even the act of "swiping" itself merely to indicate interest already implies a tacit form of consent to sexual activity that Tinder does not explicitly discuss. While this book is not explicitly about policies, this issue would be easy to address in Tinder's existing terms of service. Underneath the warnings not to post nude photographs or pictures of children, Tinder might provide a simple statement: "Agreeing to meet with someone you match with in person does not confer consent." Yet issues of consent past the point of "matching" are not discussed either implicitly or explicitly. We argue that a failure to engage in consent as an active and continuous process can lead to problematic mutual misunderstandings. Ultimately, technologies like Tinder and other similar dating apps, whether used in search of serious relationships or in jest simply for "play" as we describe later, operate within the context of the hookup culture that, as we have documented, treats conversation about consent as, in the words of one respondent, "a mood killer," thereby implicitly advocating sexual activity without explicit verbal consent.

As a safeguard, a straight woman cautioned against what she termed an "aggressive" or too serious use of Tinder—paralleling cultural scripts that penalize "aggressive" women, off-line as well as on: "You don't wanna aggressively use Tinder, whether it's for hookups or for relationships/dates, I just don't think aggressively using Tinder is the right way to go about it, because you just have to sift through a lot of bullshit." This interesting advice to women regarding their online dating activities reflects advice that follows our cultural scripts attempting to ensure that women's offline dating activity does not seem too aggressive. Women are cautioned *not* to take the initiative in dating and sexual activity despite living in a world of active, assertive women, one in which her script is ostensibly dated yet is now recommended to women as a safety measure.

Perhaps surprisingly, a member of a popular fraternity gives voice to an extreme assessment of Tinder that supports our interpretation: "I think it's [Tinder is] a recipe for sexual assault. You have a guy's first name and a picture and you're just gonna meet him somewhere? Like if I was a girl, I'd be straight up terrified." But what this fraternity brother fails to realize is that Tinder is just a by-product of a larger system of hooking up where women have very little control over whether or not their "no" is heard, and often don't feel like they are in a position to say "no," even if they don't desire sexual activity.

Similar to hooking up by meeting at a bar or a party, Tinder simply facilitates another avenue by which women, when taking the initiative, feel they can no longer say "no" after a certain point. To avoid sex after it is implied through these cultural signals would involve an active, asserted denial, which is not always easy to give in the context of hookup culture, as we have previously explained. In this way, Tinder facilitates yet another situation in which women seem to be in charge of their sexual lives in an active, feminist manner, yet are in fact interpellated into a system that predisposes them to rape culture by structuring them into a system that does not listen to their objections to further sexual advances.

Media-Ready Feminism and Combating Racism within the Feminist Moment

In the literature about hookup culture, it is clear that students of color face more perils when participating, and more seem to "opt out" than do white students. Regardless of gender, these students feel more marginalized by hookup culture and more threatened by the college culture generally (Wade 2017). As Wade's study found, this is particularly true for Asian men and Black women.

These differences hold true in the case of how students of color navigate college life and discuss the use of dating apps as well. In our sample, students of color and LGBTQ+ students spoke differently about dating apps than their straight, white peers. Tinder is fashioned from Grindr, a dating app for the nonheterosexual (primarily for gay men). Research demonstrates that participation on Grindr, for example, which specializes in the nonheterosexual, has a highly sexual connotation (Turban 2018; Ahlm 2017; Tziallas 2015; Blackwell, Birnholtz, and Abbott 2015). A gay, white senior male in our study comments, "Grindr is explicitly for gay men and it has the connotation now—I don't know if that's how it started actually—but basically looking for hookups." He goes on to comment that even though he potentially is not only looking for hookups, he is forced to endure Grindr's raunchy content if he wants to be connected to the community:

> So sometimes I'll be on there and I'll just get these messages from these randos, which is fine because part of me is like if I'm on Grindr I'm kind of like resigning myself to get these messages, like it's going to happen. But there have been times

where it's just like, "Sex now?" And then I'm like who the fuck sent me this and I look and it's like no picture, no name, age 46—like why is that the one piece of information you chose? It's not helping. One was just like, "Threesome?" or just unsolicited pictures of dicks.

Other LGBTQ+ students who participated in our study also described how they felt "compelled" to use Grindr instead of apps like Tinder. They also speak to Grindr's explicit sexuality, mentioning that at times they nevertheless feel "compelled" to use it—and to ignore what they experienced as its demeaning and objectifying treatment—simply to be connected to the community and to obtain partners for either relationships or hookups. In this way, even though they felt less "safe" on apps like Grindr, they preferred using them to Tinder because explicitly LGBTQ+ apps provide an environment already accepting of nonheterosexual meet-ups. A gay, white, cisgender male student described it in these terms:

> I have [used them], but only at my lowest of lows . . . I've never used Tinder. I have used an app called Grindr. But it's so perverse that it makes me feel disgusted with myself . . . I know that I would never fuck a true stranger, but at the same time the fact that that's a possibility and they have means to contact me makes me feel gross.

Therefore, the sexual expectations upon which Tinder builds itself are not new, yet it parades itself as a platform for *relationships*. Moreover, its billing as an "equal opportunity" platform vis-à-vis gender, sexuality, and race also fails to acknowledge the role racism plays when determining with whom users want to match.

Women of color not only experience the "implicit consent" assumption incorporated into Tinder use more intensely than other users, but they experience even more disrespectful comments and treatment on Tinder. The following quote is a good example of where the experience of an African American, queer female student—a nontraditional, twenty-seven-year-old senior—who uses the app contrasts with the somewhat different impressions and experiences of the straight, white women students we have quoted:

> Tinder is a gross place . . . I mean don't come in my inbox with "Oh I've never fucked a Black girl before," or "Oh, are

your titties real?" or, "Oooh your ass looks fat." Straight to the point. One time, and I considered it for a second, he was like, because my Tinder profile said something like "Kind-hearted alpha, ambitious, student" whatever. He wasn't incorrect in this, but he read alpha as me being a dom, and he wanted me to fuck him, and I was like, no . . .

The queer African American woman just quoted goes on to mention that she uses a site called Sugar Baby, which sets up young women (or young men) to have sex with older and wealthier men and women who explicitly pay or offer them great perks for the service. The Sugar Baby site perhaps pushes the boundaries of media-ready feminism in that relationships are clearly defined and somewhat gender neutral, as the "baby" can be male and the sugar "parent" can be a "mama" or a "daddy." On the Sugar Baby site our informant felt that she received more respect than she did on Tinder. She attributed this to its more explicitly contractual nature:

On the sugar sites, I think because there is a clear understanding of what a mutual agreement looks like, so it's more business than anything on these sites. Of course you have the occasional disrespectful comment. But, for the most part I've had more respect on the sugar sites than Tinder.

She felt that the parameters of the relationships were simply more explicit on the Sugar Baby site, which exist to connect (mostly) younger women—but sometimes men—with (mostly) older, prosperous men—but sometimes women—willing to pay well for sexual favors. Not unlike findings of research conducted inside BDSM communities, the boundaries of consent are more explicit in nonnormative spaces (Tripodi 2017a) like this site.

A person's race or sexual orientation also hindered their ability to "play" Tinder in the same way as their white, straight female peers. While they report that playing Tinder can lead to an ego boost, others tend not to get as much interest, so the app does not function in the same way for them (Rudder 2015). In this way, the logic of popular feminism, and its media-ready feminist responses, once again structures who can play, and win, the Tinder ego boost game. And those who are white, young, and heterosexual, given the centrality of the visual to the Tinder universe—the subjects of popular feminism—are the winners. The others—people of color, non-cisgender, non-heterosexuals, those who are "not young"—those "lose" in the Tinder universe, in explicit, painful ways that mark their experiences in many other arenas of life as well. For them, Tinder can be more of an ego challenge than an ego boost.

This aspect of Tinder's operation within the parameters of popular feminism plays out in distinctive ways. As discussed earlier, we did find that straight minority women uniformly complained of the crudeness aimed their way when using Tinder; although this did happen, for some this was not the uniform experience of the straight, white women with whom we spoke. The crudeness factor was one set of objections to the app that seemed to take priority in minorities' experiences.

In our data, we also found that LGBTQ+ students feel more compelled to use dating apps designed for their community because they cannot, or do not, feel comfortable with finding people in the public spaces that are especially dominated by white, heterosexual students. However, as with in-person meetings, the opportunities Tinder might afford white women to make connections, find dates, or to simply meet one another were not shared by all users—and the tendency for Black or Asian women to receive more crudely sexual approaches and messages from males seeking contact increased the sense that Tinder use was potentially dangerous.

A white, heterosexual, female college senior—Alexa—speaks about this in detail using her friends' experiences as examples: "Actually I have some friends. . . . Like I have friends who are gay women, who have met other gay women through the dating apps that they've been in relationships [with]. But I think that's kind of different than heterosexual relationships . . ."

The different place dating apps occupy in the dating experiences of various minority groups—their importance as well as their dangers—can be witnessed firsthand in this discussion between two queer-identified women in our study. One student—a white woman, Sarah, who is a first-generation college student and the child of immigrants—states how Tinder is very much used in the gay community, especially in the small city in which she lives.

> I feel like maybe in places like New York City, or San Francisco . . . where there's like a bustling, active gay community, you don't necessarily need online dating, but in [her small city] it's like, where are you going to meet gay people in real life? . . . the dating pool is so small . . . you have to find people you're attracted to, and that are also attracted to you. . . . The only way to do that in person if you're gay is to go out in

the middle of the street and shout, "I'm gay." And, like, that probably won't work finding a partner. So like, yeah, for sure I would say that online dating is a big part of being gay in a place like [here].

Renata, a cisgender, queer female student, also white, echoes these words as she describes why she got Tinder: "Part of it was I felt so isolated at [my university]. I didn't know people. I didn't know queer people. And I was just like wanting to meet new people. I think that was a big part of it. More so than, like, the desire to have a relationship with someone, a serious relationship." Her words illustrate how LGBTQ+ students seek out online communities to build relationships, especially when they do not feel comfortable on their campuses. In addition, the marginalized populations in our study, both racial and sexual, seemed disproportionately affected by questions about Tinder's anonymity, or lack thereof. For example, Jacob, a gay, white male in our sample, who had also expressed concern about Tinder's crudeness, was also wary that the app requires users to connect through their Facebook account. However, students also expressed that the lack of anonymity helped to safeguard users from lewd behavior: "So Tinder connects to your Facebook so I feel like when you're on Tinder you're semi-more accountable unless you go through this trouble to make a whole Facebook, which I'm sure people do, which luckily has never been my experience." The ambivalence here is an important one—positioning privacy and security as mutually exclusive concepts. Given Tinder's Facebook requirements, it requires that LGBTQ+ users be "out" to access the dating app; however, the connection to one's Facebook account might also mitigate the threatening or violent consequences of a Tinder hookup. This ambivalence was consistent with our earlier finding that LGTBQ+ students are more wary of losing anonymity through online activity yet believe that anonymity can provide a more secure online environment (Press and Tripodi 2014).

In sum, the idea that meet-ups/hookups bring with them their own potential dangers is explicitly different depending on who you talk with. For students of color and LGBTQ+ Tinder users, the expectation for violence was higher. Both groups we spoke with were wary of dating in a way not expressed by our white respondents. While studies have backed these fears, demonstrating that LGBTQ+ and Black women are more likely to experience sexual violence (West and Johnson 2013), such a disjunction between users is also an important example of media-ready feminism.

For while white, cisgender, heterosexual women in college are also at risk of sexual assault (with some studies finding that one in four college women will experience a form of sexual violence during their undergraduate career), the respondents in our study who fit within this subgroup were less likely to identify that risk and posed the potential to perform an "obligatory blow job" as simply an everyday reality of hookup culture.

While Tinder aims to bend the expectations of popular feminism, providing an opportunity for white, heterosexual, and cisgender users to "play" Tinder, it is clear that it also reaffirms the existing norms of hookup culture that perpetuate sexist behavior. However, when #MeToo aimed to tackle this problem, and shine a light on the everyday sexism that has become so normative, there was a backlash, arguing that accusations of assault had gone "too far." Capturing reactions to this moment is another example of media-ready feminism.

Swipe Right for Ansari

The underlying expectations embedded in Tinder meet-ups, in particular women's limited ability to say "no" after a certain point, were painstakingly detailed in "Grace's" account of her encounter with Aziz Ansari, captured in the online venue *Babe*. Despite Ansari's work with sociologist Eric Klinenberg (2016) on the way in which online dating has complicated modern-day romance, creating an environment where it always seems like someone "better" is out there, neither author acknowledged the role implicit consent plays in this sociotechnical world of dating. Such a lack of awareness by heterosexual, cisgender men is not particularly surprising given Ansari's repeated advances on Grace, whereby her "no" was not acknowledged, and she described an environment where she had implicitly consented upon going to dinner with him. According to her piece in *Babe* (Way 2018a), Grace agreed to meet with Ansari after she was introduced to him at a party. Ostensibly thinking he might be interested in a relationship, Grace met him for a date in the days that followed their first encounter. As the date unfolded it became clear to Grace that Ansari was only interested in a sexual encounter with her (he rushed through dinner and did not ask about her drink preferences). Despite this impression, she decided to accompany him to his apartment that same evening, thinking perhaps it was the public attention that was making him nervous. When she got back to his home, Ansari nevertheless tried to initiate a sexual encounter.

Similar to the accounts of those interviewed in this study, Ansari seemed to feel that Grace's decision to return to his apartment implied "consent" to sexual activity. According to her detailed account, Ansari continued to try to pressure her into sexual contact—as she described: "He [Ansari] probably moved my hand to his dick five to seven times," she said. "He *really* kept doing it after I moved it away." But the main thing was that he wouldn't let *her* move away from him. She compared the path they cut across his apartment to a football play. "It was 30 minutes of me getting up and moving and him following and sticking his fingers down my throat again. It was really repetitive. It felt like a fucking game."

Throughout the course of her short time in the apartment, she says she used verbal and nonverbal cues to indicate how uncomfortable and distressed she was (Way 2018a). In the end, Grace participated in what our respondents described as the "obligatory blow job": "He sat back and pointed to his penis and motioned for me to go down on him. And I did. I think I just felt really pressured. It was literally the most unexpected thing I thought would happen at that moment because I told him I was uncomfortable."

Yet unlike the many women we spoke to regarding hookup culture, Grace seized the momentum of the #MeToo movement to publicize the moment, sharing with the world how she had felt violated by the incident. In response, Ansari has consistently denied any wrongdoing or any awareness that she was not enjoying all aspects of the encounter, and he apologized by text when she informed him of this the next day. Shortly thereafter he issued a public statement denying sexual misconduct (Way 2018b).

The subsequent reactions to Grace's account were widely covered and debated, providing an excellent analysis of media-ready feminist response to Grace's feminist assertions—this time, the response was by the popular media (see Franke [2018] for a full summary of the controversy and its coverage). Accounts differed as to who was identified to be at fault, but major, influential news organs almost uniformly ridiculed Grace's position, deeming it "unworthy" of the #MeToo movement and "not really" sexual assault. With titles such as "The Humiliation of Aziz Ansari" in *The Atlantic* (Flanagan 2018) and "Aziz Ansari Is Guilty. Of Not Being a Mind Reader" in the *New York Times* (Weiss 2018), the coverage invoked Grace's account as evidence of the "dangers" of the #MeToo movement and claimed that the *Babe* story would *hurt* the #MeToo movement. Despite the few articles of support that ran in the *New York Times* (West 2018; Russonello 2018) none of the journalistic commentary discussed the "situational" dimensions that transfer the idea of "consent" into an implicit rather than explicit action.

By taking this position we do not insinuate that consent is something that is "muddy." Either someone is or is not interested in receiving sexual advances and pursuing a sexual encounter. However, it is clear from our data that many women feel that their consent is interpreted as "a given" after a certain point, making them "feel bad" about stopping once they've gotten to what they describe as a point "too far" along to say no again. What this indicates is that active consent is not being given in many sexual encounters, despite university and legal initiatives attempting to mandate an active consent policy.

Moreover, when women say "no" in many sexual situations, are they being heard? This is a question that has clearly been contested in discourse over #MeToo and is directly impacting the way the movement is being valued or criticized. While Grace did not appear to believe that she gave consent to sex simply by entering Ansari's apartment, the fact that she was there seemed to color his and others' interpretation of her actions. He simply could not hear her assertions of "no." Many commentators agreed that this would be reasonable and expected.

We felt that the Aziz Ansari incident engaged several of the gender-specific attributes of hookup culture, and therefore spoke directly to the media-ready feminism aspects of hookup culture *and* of coverage of these incidents in mainstream media. To follow up on these ideas, we therefore conducted (through our peer research team) a series of interviews with college students about the incident. What follows are some of the results of our peer review research on the issue. Ansari's accuser had been widely slammed in both the feminist and mainstream press for being "over the top" in turning what many journalists and commentators read as a "bad date," or typical post-event regret, into a story of assault or harassment. The college-aged women in our sample, however, strongly disagreed with these comments by a wide margin. These are some of their responses, from a group of white, heterosexual, junior (third-year) college women:

> KATHLEEN: Though some may call this a "witch hunt" because every man has most likely acted inappropriately in varying degrees towards women, be it as small as cat-calling or as large as sexual assault, it's important to publicly declare these behaviors as wrong, and not to write them off because there are men committing worse acts or because "boys will be boys."

This needs to result in cultural upheaval. Women's sexual liberation has resulted in sexual constraint because of the dangers of sexual harassment; this has become what we know as the "hookup culture," both emotionally damaging while posing real threat to women's safety. Our society needs to collectively redefine what it means to give consent, to be in a relationship, and how to properly engage with members of the opposite sex in all settings, not just the workplace. Without stories like that of Ansari, his actions and behavior like his are being validated rather than indicted.

KAITLIN: When you let people get away with the less serious stuff, it becomes a slippery slope, a gray area rather than a hard line between ok and not ok. That said, you can't assume false equivalency and condemn Ansari as harshly as Weinstein.

MARIE: We have to change the sexual narrative and the way we think about sex and relationships. Hell, we just have to change the way we all interact.

JESSICA: Everyone has experienced this shit and everyone, men and women, have made these mistakes. It shows that this is systemic. We can't ignore it any longer.

SUSAN: Rather than let everyone off the hook, everyone should be held accountable.

It was clear that the college students in our study could relate to Grace's frustration, and to her discomfort with the series of events that comprised her narrative. They were familiar and almost accustomed to the experience Grace described, of not being in control of the hookup. Not unlike the findings presented at the beginning of this chapter, it is clear that women's desires are less likely to be articulated and, even when they are verbally announced (e.g., "no"), their requests are not heard. Like them, Grace found it simply easier to offer the "obligatory blow job," or its equivalent, rather than trying to stop the encounter entirely. Her narrative—and their concomitant experiences—expose what has become a series of "implied consent" situations that make the issue of "consent" a vital place for more sociological inquiry.

The current sexual assault epidemic on campuses has been addressed with increased attention to the process by which consent is given. Yet these efforts are undercut, we argue, by the presence of "implied consent" in a series of situations, including those that occur in the course of scenarios initiated by the increasingly popular dating apps. Moreover, our research indicates that conversations of consent are purposefully avoided because they "ruin the mood" of the sexual encounter. However, our research also reaffirms how popular feminism affects majority and minority groups differently. We found that while cisgender, heterosexual, white students were grappling with problems of implicit consent, LGBTQ+ students and students of color were more likely to think through processes of consent. These groups, however, are also more marginalized by hookup culture. If heterosexual white undergraduates are largely unaware of how active consent is to be achieved, then it makes sense that so many hookup encounters are mismatched, as white heterosexuals are more likely to participate in this culture—the expectations for women in this subgroup are to finish what they started, but whether these expectations are acceptable or problematic for women is something they rarely articulate.[2] In relationships where a cisgender, heterosexual male is involved, women's ability to initiate and control sexual situations is undercut by the assumption of implicit consent. The popular feminist promise of Tinder is undercut by a media-ready feminist cultural assumption that sexual consent can be implied by context—simply by using a dating app, or by initiating an in-person meeting.

Conclusion

As this book continuously argues, media-ready feminism investigates how opportunities to push beyond popular feminism are often thwarted by the persistence of everyday sexism. What this chapter begins to demonstrate is how media-ready feminism operates across media platforms. While the last few chapters have considered more traditional media products, documenting the reception of television series that grapple with the gendered contradictions of representation and hookup culture, this chapter goes further, considering how the sexist underbelly of hookup culture persists within an app marketed, in true popular feminist fashion, as an empowerment platform. While Tinder and other dating apps promote themselves as platforms to embolden daters, they fail to transcend the everyday sexism characterizing the culture in which they operate. That these apps are often created in a vacuum in Silicon Valley is clearly part of the problem. As research demonstrates, the entrepreneurial culture of start-ups is dominated by white men in positions of privilege (Marwick 2013). However, by understanding how media forms interact and engage with communities (Press and Tripodi 2014), we can examine more closely how apps like Tinder are used within the culture of college life, reaffirming a form of sexism that persists in heterosexual hookups and amplifying the existing racial and sexual inequalities that are also present in hookup culture.

We find that while LGBTQ+ students are more inclined to broach the topic of consent, they are wary of apps in which their anonymity is not protected. While students of color are equally trapped in the double standard of hookup culture, they (primarily Asian men and Black women) are further isolated by the use of Tinder. Rather than feeling "empowered," they are often shut out altogether from "playing Tinder" like their white peers. Not only are these exclusionary practices similar to those observed in hookup culture (e.g., Wade [2017] demonstrates that Black women and Asian men are often left out of the "hookup game" in real life), but Tinder practices also have the potential to open marginalized populations up to the increased possibility of sexual assault, since they are unaware of the underlying expectations of heterosexual hookup culture embedded within apps like Tinder.

For our heterosexual respondents, intimacy is reserved for "talking," which happens rarely during sex, and only seldom afterward, following a significant number of rather nonverbal, non-"intimate" sexual encounters. This is reflected in our data when many respondents noted that talking about sex "ruins the mood" and that very rarely do hookups involve a discussion of sexual expectations and desires. By examining more closely how college students navigate hookup culture and the role Tinder plays in facilitating these kinds of encounters, we describe how the process of tacit consent becomes encoded into the swipe. In sum, Tinder's promise of an empowered, feminist sexual agency is undermined by the way users accede to the everyday sexism characterizing the hookup culture that determines how it is used.

What is clear from our data is that the plethora of expectations users express in connection with Tinder mirror the range of expectations with which young people encounter hookup culture. The recent social media movement known as "#MeToo" has shed some light on the importance of active consent. But, given the overwhelmingly negative reaction in the press to "Grace's" encounter, it is clear that the true feminist reach of the #MeToo movement is also limited.

It seems that popular and legal definitions of sexual assault can only include situations in which active "no's" are articulated, but these popular and legal definitions fail to consider the complicated ways in which many women do not feel comfortable or able to say "no" to begin with. Apps like Tinder, despite their seeming promise, do not help navigate these tenuous situations. While they apparently give users control over those with whom they communicate and hook up, ultimately the apps place white, heterosexual women back in the same place they were originally at the pre-Tinder bar scene: feeling like they've gone "too far" not to go "all the way."

5

Wikipedia

Sign(s) Say Keep Out

Introduction

It is late afternoon, and the sunlight pouring into the windows of the public library begins to dim. Unaware of the waning daylight, volunteers continue to type busily on their laptops. They arrived at the public space that morning with a purpose, donating their entire Saturday to improving one of the world's largest sources of information—Wikipedia. They sit in small groups of three around square tables adjacent to the information desk at a local public library. At the front of the room is a whiteboard with a list of twenty-two names. They are biologists, neuroscientists, anesthesiologists, botanists, and chemists who have made major contributions to the field of science. These are scientists who have invented pharmaceuticals and materials that many of us rely on today. They have published widely, taught at prestigious institutions, and served as presidents of international scientific organizations. Despite their notability, they have limited to no presence on Wikipedia.[1] Every person on the list is a woman.

The volunteers each choose a scientist whose page they will improve or create and place their initials beside the name. They do so as part of an "edit-a-thon," an informal gathering sponsored by the city's local Wikipedia chapter created to increase the number of Wikipedia biographies of notable women scientists. Before the edit-a-thon begins, new editors receive a brief lecture on how to create an account and learn about Wikipedia's editing procedures and notability criteria. Then, with the help of a few seasoned veterans, the volunteers work as a unit to try to decrease what Wikipedians colloquially refer to as the "gender gap."

Started in 2001, Wikipedia has become one of the world's largest sources of information, containing more than thirty-five million articles created by volunteers. Despite its reach and scope, there remains a gap in who edits the site and the type of content that is subsequently covered. As a way of combating this problem, Wikipedia groups and the Wikimedia Foundation have turned to edit-a-thons. We argue that such a solution is a quintessential example of media-ready feminism because it frames the lack of women's biographies on Wikipedia as an individual rather than structural problem and thereby amenable to solution by individual efforts. By framing the problem's solution as one solved by volunteers (many of whom are women), our ethnographic observations reveal that the media-ready feminism of edit-a-thons do not adequately address the underlying inequalities inside Wikipedia's bureaucratic structure. By unpacking how edit-a-thons are organized and executed as well as the ways well-respected editors have to navigate the cultural terrain, we argue that edit-a-thons are not as effective as they could be because they fail to acknowledge the strength of everyday sexism, which continues to limit the effectiveness of edit-a-thons attempting to close Wikipedia's "gender gap."

Wikipedia's "Gender Gap" and the Rise of Edit-a-thons

English-language Wikipedia has over five million articles[2] and hovers between the fourth and sixth most frequented website in the world.[3] Moreover, Google's "answer boxes," colloquially referred to as "rank zero,"[4] often draw from Wikipedia content, thereby furthering the important role Wikipedia plays in curating knowledge in the twenty-first century. The tagline of this knowledge giant is the "free online encyclopedia anyone can edit," and within its first month, unpaid editors all over the world created one thousand articles. To date, Wikipedia contributors (self-identified as "Wikipedians") have created over twenty thousand encyclopedia entries. The large quantity of articles amassed obviously represents a considerable effort. Yet in recent years arguments regarding content equity have begun to surface, as have questions as to how editors' specific biases might be skewing available information. One of the most well-known examples of such a debate hit mainstream media in 2013 when editors decided to relegate "American women novelists" to a subcategory, thereby making "American novelists" an exclusively male space (Filipacchi 2013).

A 2011 study found that a majority of Wikipedia's editors are tech-savvy white men in their thirties, and a 2013 study estimated that male editors make up 87 percent of the community (Wikimedia Foundation 2011; Zara 2013). Researchers have determined that Wikipedia's interface is part of the problem. They argue that because Wikipedia's standard markup language and cultural jargon are not readily accessible to newcomers, women are at a disadvantage because they are more likely to *be* newcomers (Hargittai and Shaw 2015; Jemielniak 2014). Described as a "second-level digital divide" (Hargittai 2002), a technical skills deficit explains why women are less likely to edit Wikipedia.

Many have found a connection between this editorial gender gap and a larger gap with regard to the kind of content that is subsequently added to Wikipedia. As of October 2016, less than 17 percent of English-language Wikipedia's biographies are about women. Articles about women are underdeveloped and underrepresented and Wikipedia's articles "favor the tastes of some over the inclusion of all" (Adams and Brückner 2015, 3, Lam et al. 2011). Another study also found that women's articles are more likely to feature gendered language that indicates the person is a woman. This use of gendered pronouns *exclusively* in female biographies perpetuates the bias that articles of notable people are, by default, about a man unless otherwise stated (Wagner et al. 2015). Articles about women are also less likely to link to men's pages—and less likely to have links generally—than are articles about men. Not linking to other content might seem innocuous, but another study found that edits work like "magnets," attracting more editors to the page (Aaltonen and Seiler 2015). Not linking women's biographies to other content means that women's biographies are less likely to improve over time.

As a way of combating this problem, the Wikimedia Foundation has turned to "edit-a-thons." An edit-a-thon is a meet-up sponsored by Wikipedia chapters. These meet-ups are designed to encourage new people to start editing Wikipedia by partnering them with existing "Wikipedians"—a colloquial term for individuals who are experienced editing Wikipedia. During the edit-a-thon, people meet in a physical location and edit Wikipedia as a group. An edit-a-thon lasts about eight hours with the host providing refreshments, meals, and technical support throughout the day. When edit-a-thons first began, they did not have altruistic motives and were simply partnerships between large institutions looking to increase the visibility of their archives. These kinds of edit-a-thons still exist today—for example, the Guggenheim has hosted two edit-a-thons to increase the coverage of artists on Wikipedia and increase the visibility of their collections.

Over the past few years, the goal of the edit-a-thon has shifted, with more attention and focus on encouraging women and minorities to learn how to edit Wikipedia. In addition to hosting edit-a-thons to help improve the diversity of editors, edit-a-thons are also used to improve content disparities. During women's history month, edit-a-thons devoted to creating articles about women took place around the globe.

Another change is that edit-a-thons have also shifted in geographic location in order to broaden the reach and scope of the initiative. Starting in 2014, Wiki Loves Pride began organizing virtual edit-a-thons where users around the globe could connect to Wikipedia pages and improve LGBTQ content across several projects. These events were focused during June and October as a way to amplify celebrations around lesbian, gay, bisexual, and transgender communities on the ground. In 2015, a similar initiative began to improve coverage of women when groups of prominent editors (mostly women) created an initiative called Women in Red. The goal of the group is to turn "red links" (a signal on Wikipedia that a page does not yet exist) into "blue ones" (i.e., a hyperlinked Wikipedia article). Neither Wiki Loves Pride nor Women in Red has hosted a physical meet-up. Edit-a-thons have become so widespread that there is now a "how-to" guide for how (and why) to run an edit-a-thon.[5]

Nonetheless, not all Wikipedians are convinced by the efficacy of edit-a-thons. While these internal debates on efficacy are important, Tripodi's ethnographic observations and interviews reveal some specific problems with the structure of edit-a-thons. Unpacking these observations within the framework of media-ready feminism, it is clear how edit-a-thons hosted in physical locations with a primarily new-to-Wikipedia editor base are unable to combat the strength of everyday sexism, because they foster an environment where blatant sexist actions remain accepted and unchallenged. In this chapter, we document how the media-ready feminism of edit-a-thons draws attention to wider problems of gender inequality but in a distinctly apolitical way, demonstrating that unless there is a strong network of feminist editors working as a unit, the "free encyclopedia that *anyone can edit*" remains dominated by everyday sexist ideology.

Uninviting Interface

Similar to Hargittai and Shaw's (2015) and Eckert and Steiner's (2013) findings, new users were drawn to edit-a-thons because they found the

Wikipedia interface too daunting to tackle alone. Unlike WordPress or Facebook, which use what computer programmers call a "WYSIWYG" (what you see is what you get) kind of language, Wikipedia uses a text editor that is much less transparent and is similar to HTML programming language. Even during the edit-a-thon and with the help of Wikipedia mentors, new editors expressed clear apprehension in editing, frequently noting that they were unlikely to have figured out how to do this on their own.

Veteran editors readily acknowledged that the text editor was not intuitive, even in their own usage experiences. During one edit-a-thon Judy, a woman with long gray hair and a warm smile, consoles another young woman who is becoming frustrated by the experience. With one arm over the other woman's shoulder, she talks through the difficulties with the new volunteer: "You have to code the article as you're writing it, which is not a skill that most people actually have. It makes it very difficult. You're constantly going 'I have no idea how to do this. Can somebody help me?'" She reassures the young woman that she is there to help, and while she does so Jack, another longtime editor with a white beard and rimless glasses, peers across his laptop. We make eye contact and he confides in me that even with his computer engineering background "Wiki code" took him about a month to learn and to start to feel comfortable. "But for the average new person?," he covers his hand while he points to the young woman getting help from Judy, "It's an additional burden and it's a hurdle to get over."

Early on in the study, the Wikimedia Foundation rolled out a visual editor (akin to WordPress) that those new to Wikipedia can now set as their writing default. Even people who have edited before now have the option to switch over to a visual editor, and in the box there is a disclaimer that "anyone can edit and everything helps." However, changing the default to this user-friendly interface was not easy, and many editors not affiliated with the foundation pushed back on an interface change. Part of this struggle was due to early rollout—when the initial visual editor was launched, it was filled with bugs that frustrated longtime editors. However, the continued resistance to an interface that invites inexperienced editors to contribute is also indicative of the problem of everyday sexism on Wikipedia and is typically not discussed during edit-a-thons. This pushes back against Hargittai and Shaw's (2015) findings that the gender gap is not something that stems from *within* the group. While it is true that women might lack the skills necessary to edit Wikipedia, the community itself seemed less willing to implement changes that could address this problem: we call this blindness to the systematic inequity engendered by the existing system the "everyday sexism" within Wikipedia as a structure.

In accord with this continuing blindness to its structurally engendered sexism, even though the visual editor makes it *easier* for new people to make edits, it does not go very far down the road toward making Wikipedia editing intuitive. Deciding to edit a page means that users must actively click on the "edit" tab at the top right of a Wikipedia article, and if they run into trouble there is not an easily accessible "help" button. Even if someone were to venture into the "talk" tab to post a question or try to collaborate with other editors, the interface design is clunky and difficult to navigate. Wikipedians seem to embrace these challenges embedded in the editing process, with an explicit distance from making Wikipedia an environment where everyday individuals can gather, socialize, edit, and have fun. As Dave, a well-respected Wikipedian with thousands of edits to his credit, described: "Wikipedia is more like Web 1.5. It kinda embraces the crowdsource idea but at the same time it very explicitly, at times, rejects the user-friendly, hyper-social kind of community that you get on places like Facebook, Twitter, and Tumblr." This distinction becomes important when it leads to systematic inequities vis-à-vis gender and race, which have been well documented. It is not trivial.

Some of the Wikipedians that I (Tripodi)[6] interviewed reasoned that the existing design was created to be difficult—and perhaps mastery of it was a way for Wikipedians to demonstrate their loyalty. Since those who have amassed a large number of edits had to diligently learn the software, they believe that others should go through the same process. However, the refusal to move in the direction of better user engagement matters, especially if Wikipedia wishes to improve editorial diversity. When it comes to engaging different kinds of people, interface matters. Lisa, a longtime Wikipedian devoted to racial inequality in the encyclopedia, notes, "There is something about Wikipedia that isn't attracting the same women and children who apparently dominate Facebook, in the sense that they're very present there—whereas the Wikipedia interface is kind of repellent, quite frankly, to that same demographic."

The uninviting and difficult-to-navigate interface is also problematic when it comes to the success of an edit-a-thon. In all of the edit-a-thons observed, the primary platform for publicizing the event was Wikipedia itself, so that the only way individuals could sign up or indicate their interest in the events observed was through Wikipedia.[7] As a result, the majority of those I spoke with at edit-a-thons had learned about the event through a Wikipedian they know. While this "strong tie" (Granovetter 1973) network might help insure that a new editor who signs up for the event actually comes, it also confines the growth of Wikipedian editors to a small, well-defined group. By opening up recruitment to more social media spaces (e.g., Facebook, Instagram, Eventbrite, or even Snapchat), edit-a-thons could harness the power of "weak ties" in the form of social media networks, as well as tap into the structural holes (Burt 1992) currently missing from the relatively homogeneous group of existing, regular Wikipedia editors.

In addition to closing off potential recruits to the event, limiting registration through Wikipedia precludes the ability to track adequately who is planning to attend, as well as verify who did so, because many of the people interested in coming do not know how to edit the Wikipedia interface. In fact, the first few hours of every edit-a-thon I attended was devoted to new editors creating a username and then editing the event page. While adding their username helped to account for how many interested editors showed up, had edit-a-thon organizers utilized a service capable of tracking outsiders' interest in the event (e.g., something like Eventbrite, SurveyMonkey, or Google Forms), organizers would have access to more information that could facilitate follow-up afterward, leading to more widespread editorial participation in the long run, rather than merely bolstering the small groups of insiders that essentially characterizes the platform at present.

When I asked Ian, a white man in his midforties who organized a large number of edit-a-thons, why edit-a-thon organizers used Wikipedia to publicize and register attendees instead of using a service that allows users to register with their personal email address, I was surprised by his answer. A soft-spoken man with rimmed glasses, Ian ran his fingers through his hair as he spoke, describing to me why driving recruitment of edit-a-thons was purposeful. For him, a long-standing Wikipedian, other platforms were superfluous—not only can you receive notifications via Wikipedia, you can privately message on Wikipedia as well. He reasoned that communicating with editors exclusively through Wikipedia provided continuity throughout the community. Yet it did not occur to him that those unfamiliar with navigating the space might appreciate other forms of communication (e.g., a personal email) as a way to gently nudge them back onto the platform. His concept of community was rather exclusive, despite his desire to host edit-a-thons in order to encourage more people to become Wikipedians.

New editors (frequently women) did not share Ian's sentiments regarding the effectiveness of Wikipedia-only notifications for edit-a-thons. In my interviews they described how frustrated they were that they hadn't received any follow-up communication since the edit-a-thon had ended. When I asked if they had been back on Wikipedia to see if they had received messages there, most did not even know this was a possibility enabled by the site—again illustrating that difficulty of accessing information led to a small group of knowledgeable insiders controlling the game. Moreover, none of the new editors I had worked with remembered their passwords, and they were unsure how to reset them. A few were also frustrated with the layout of the edit-a-thon. While working with well-established Wikipedians committed to opening up equity on Wikipedia *seemed* like a good way to teach newcomers, new users often felt inadequate due to their skill deficit. Jared, an older man looking to contribute some of his knowledge of world affairs to the site, described to me how uncomfortable it felt for him to be such a novice. Since he had held a prominent position at the World Bank for several years, he did not think the edit-a-thon fostered a "safe place to demonstrate utter ignorance." In his case, he had gone from a subject matter expert (in life) to someone just starting out (as a Wikipedia editor), and he did not feel there were enough resources available for him to become comfortable with his limited computer-programming skill set.

Sign(s) Say Keep Out

In addition to user interface, new editors also describe a different type of trepidation when it comes to editing Wikipedia. Leah, a young woman with dark glasses and bright lipstick, describes her first time engaging with Wikipedia:

> There's a fear, whether the fear is I'm going to break it, or I'm going to not really know what I'm doing, or I'm going to feel out of my depth with this, or I'm going to feel overwhelmed . . . I'm not even sure where to start. It was mysterious and intimidating and I just didn't know whether it was even appropriate for me to add information on what the standards were. I felt like I was breaking into someone else's club.

Again this last is a reference to the exclusive "feel" of the Wikipedia editing community.

Other editors echoed Leah, noting that Wikipedia has a culture of exclusion. The process of creating a new article is a daunting task, one that requires not only a solid command of *how* to edit Wikipedia, but also a firm understanding of *what* Wikipedia is and *what* it is not. Matt, a young white man in his thirties who is widely respected within the community, describes how new users need to familiarize themselves with policies of Wikipedia before they jump into creating new articles. He notes that while the visual editor might make it easier for someone to create a new Wikipedia page, "it takes a lot of time not only to learn the policies—but also to learn the culture." Wikipedia as a body of knowledge—and, in his words, a "culture"—isn't something one learns overnight. Matt's statement is telling, and highlights two of the central problems I observed regarding edit-a-thons. Considering the deep cultural knowledge required to feel comfortable on the site, it is problematic that many edit-a-thons center around creating new content, rather than fixing existing problems or improving the scope of coverage in articles that already exist about women. Part of this design flaw is baked into attracting new people to the event; most people I spoke with who had come to an edit-a-thon as first-time editors were there to add someone specific who fit with the theme (e.g., "Women in Science").

Although the function of many feminist edit-a-thons is to increase women's editorial participation and representation on Wikipedia, the edit-a-thon organizers rarely acquaint new users with the backlash that has accompanied such events in the past, such as rampant deletionism and possible harassment. Moreover, since many edit-a-thon attendees are new editors to Wikipedia they are also encouraged to create an account before they begin editing. Creating an account is encouraged for two reasons: first, anonymous edits are more likely to be seen as spam by "bots"[8] and targeted for deletion; second, creating new accounts allows the organizers to walk away with a tangible metric to report back to the Wikimedia Foundation.[9] However, little (if any) time during the edit-a-thons observed was devoted to discussing the problems within Wikipedia culture that may result for new users explicitly trying to close the gender gap. As a result, we argue that Wikipedia edit-a-thons are an example of "media-ready feminism." They attempt to accomplish feminist goals of increased participation and representation without acknowledging the ways in which the everyday sexism structurally coded into the organization impedes such progress.

What's in a Name?

Even though you do not need to create an account to edit Wikipedia, one of the first points of business under the "How to run an edit-a-thon" Wikipedia page is to take time to help new editors create an account. Based on my (Tripodi's) observations, this is typically a rushed process aimed at getting individuals to edit as quickly as possible. As a result, many new editors use a derivative of their given names or usernames that links back to other online personae e.g., some would use their Twitter handle). Unfortunately this type of username decision may result in disastrous repercussions, especially for women, who were the overwhelming majority of participants in all the edit-a-thons I observed.

Numerous reports have demonstrated that women are continuously at risk of harassment online (Pew Research Center 2014; Citron 2014; Phillips 2015; Buni and Chemaly 2014). A recent study of data collected by the *Guardian* found that eight of the top ten most abused journalists were women (Gardiner et al. 2016), and another editorial specifically investigating Wikipedia similarly found that users who identified as women were more frequently targeted for harassment (Paling 2015). These stories focus on the atrocities that women face on the internet, classifying harassment as unwanted sexual advances or innuendoes, repeated contact (e.g., stalking someone's Wikipedia user page or revision history), verbal threats of violence, doxing (publishing private information on the internet about a particular individual with malicious intent), revenge porn (a sexually explicit portrayal of one or more persons distributed without their consent via any medium), and simulated rape. As Buni and Chemaly (2014) found, women who are the subject of harassment are often left with few resources to combat the problem, and this treatment of women has led to many leaving the site altogether (Paling 2015).

Such has certainly been the case for Becky, a middle-aged white woman who volunteers her time in arbitration. Many self-described Wikipedians take on this role, and rather than devote time to creating new content, they volunteer their time doing the administration work to keep the community humming. Since not all edits on Wikipedia are readily accepted by the community (we elaborate on this process later), there are a select number of "administrators" who have higher capabilities than editors.[10] Over Skype, I sit with Becky as she has one laptop open arbitrating Wikipedia and another facing her and a view of her living room couch. We talk about how her feminine sounding username has attracted attention in ways that she never would have imagined. Specifically Becky describes that she is outwardly harassed with gender-specific language (bitch, whore, cunt) and feels as though her decisions are more frequently met with agitated responses than are the arbitration decisions made by her male counterparts. "I would say don't use your real name, don't make it easy for people to find you. If [a woman] wants to fly under the radar I would probably advise her to use a gender-neutral name and to just generally avoid [certain places]."[11]

Conversations regarding harassment of women online and how this might translate over Wikipedia are not overtly discussed during edit-a-thons. I did not even learn that username selection might be a problem until I started conducting individual interviews. On three separate occasions women disclosed that they wished they had picked a more discrete name. Jeannie, an older woman who was surprised by the transparency of her Wikipedia volunteerism, first realized how exposed she was when she Googled herself and saw her name "popping up over and over." Immediately after that realization, Jeannie changed her username in order to hide her identity. When I asked her what was behind this reasoning, she described how her gender made her a more likely target. In her words, "I changed it [her username] . . . because I'm a woman, I felt exposed and worried a bit for my personal safety." Judy, a retired woman who spends her free time editing Wikipedia, also wished that she had created a username that was gender neutral. In a Skype interview, she tells me, "If I could do it over again, I wouldn't [use an identifier with my username]. Knowing what I know now, having seen some of the very personal, very pointed attacks that other female editors have experienced, I wouldn't have used anything that could tie it to me." Throughout the interview she shares her screen with me, demonstrating the extent of these attacks. Margaret, a young woman with a quiet voice but a fierce determination, was also the subject of such attacks. It got so bad for her that she "finally changed my username so I could dissociate my username from my real name . . . I was becoming a target." Over the course of our interview, Margaret revealed how she had received messages that threatened physical violence, in addition to a large number of messages from men she did not know asking her to go on dates or for sexually explicit photos. Joan, another woman who works in arbitration like Becky, relayed to me a particularly frightening doxing experience. After rendering a contentious decision to ban an editor from being able to make edits for a month, she received an anonymous message inside her Wikipedia account. The message was a photograph of her daughter's soccer team with a sentence "admiring" her daughter's beautiful smile. Unfortunately these messages were clearly meant to intimidate, and they accomplished this goal. Joan, Margaret, and Becky all slightly modified their actions in response by changing their usernames and avoiding certain spaces to limit harassment.

Not only did the women with feminine-sounding usernames receive unwanted attention and harassment, but a recent study also demonstrated that these names make them more vulnerable to deletions (what Wikipedians colloquially refer to as "reversions") and even to having their account indefinitely blocked (Lam et al. 2011). This is particularly troublesome when one realizes that changing one's username or disassociating from a previous name is more difficult than one might imagine. In order to prevent an individual from editing under multiple accounts—what Wikipedia refers to as "sock puppetry"—English-language Wikipedia has a widely accepted policy that each editor should only have one account. Therefore, even though Margaret and Jeannie changed their usernames, all of the edits associated with their previous names are still accessible in their user history.

While some of the editors Tripodi spoke with described how they had chosen feminine sounding usernames very deliberately, in order to "claim space" on Wikipedia and demonstrate their ability to edit content, this was a decision they made clearly knowing the potential repercussions. If the goal of edit-a-thons is to encourage increased and sustained participation on the site, then it is imperative for new editors to have this information about the potential backlash attendant upon "feminine" names *before* selecting a username. In addition, choice of a username should not be a rushed decision, and the reason why it *is* rushed circles back to the way edit-a-thons recruit attendees to begin with. Were organizers to use alternative methods for recruitment and registration, they could inform those planning on attending that they should come prepared to create a username and could provide brief information on the pros and cons of selecting a username affiliated with one's off-line identity, advice targeted particularly to the issues facing women and minorities.

The cavalier attitude toward picking a username at Wikipedia edit-a-thons is a prime example of the kind of media-ready feminism we describe in this book. When Tripodi asked the organizers directly about username selection they acknowledged that not having a gender-neutral username could be problematic. However, they felt that addressing the subject in a large group of new users would take away from the desired "agency" dimension of username selection, explaining to me that how people chose their username should really be a personal choice. They also told me that username bias was a "charged" issue, and they did not want to misrepresent the problem by influencing how new users selected their names.

Such logic embraces the idea of media-ready feminism. Clearly, the role of feminism is being referenced in the idea of collective action that inspires edit-a-thons, which after all are gathering as a group of like-minded individuals to edit Wikipedia. However, the role of participation is also distinctly *individualized* (username selection is a personal process).[12] Despite this, the edit-a-thon events—at least, the ones studied here—are explicitly political. As described, earlier social justice edit-a-thons surrounding equal representation are extremely different from institutionally sponsored edit-a-thons with the goal of digitizing their archival materials. The former are explicitly rooted in a discourse of equal rights for women and people of color and openly identify as "feminist." For example, one of the largest and most well-respected groups that organizes edit-a-thons does so under the title "Art+Feminism," with the explicit goal of increasing the number of women artists on Wikipedia worldwide.

However, organizers' inability to articulate and draw attention to the possible harassment and harms new editors might experience if they were to select a feminine username is an example of, to channel Betty Friedan's 1963 description of the need for second-wave feminism, the "problem that has no name." Indeed everyday sexism on Wikipedia is as persistent as catcalling on the street. We see it is there, we even hear it occasionally, but the structure of Wikipedia insures that it remains disconnected, in actors' minds, from the larger problem of gendered inequality. Even those editors who have experienced this harassment firsthand are reluctant to recognize it as a widespread problem. By framing username selection as a *personal* choice, one that each user must make on his or her own, we see how media-ready feminism frames a political movement through a neoliberal lens. While a lesson in username selection (in particular, the message to refrain from personal identification) could serve to minimize future editors' negative encounters on Wikipedia, there is literally no language to describe the phenomenon they are witnessing firsthand. The missing step from experience to action—clearly visible in this case—is precisely the moment that we theorize. Particularly in the case of Wikipedia edit-a-thons specifically targeted toward increasing the representation of women and minorities on the site, it would seem logical that harassment often specifically encountered by these groups as a direct result of these efforts would, and should, be addressed. Yet the widespread acceptance of everyday sexism, and the widespread inability to critically acknowledge it, leads to this contradictory situation whereby media designed to empower simultaneously falls short of effectively addressing the hidden dangers of everyday sexism.

In addition to failing to train new editors as to the potential risks attendant upon username selection, the events I attended also did not inform new users that the spaces they were stepping into might be culturally charged and could result in harassment of various types. Two longtime Wikipedians described to me in their interviews how they avoid certain spaces because they know they will face retaliation for their edits. Olivia is a vibrant young woman whose personality is infectious. A self-described feminist, she regularly organizes edit-a-thons on her college campus. A tireless crusader for gender equality, Olivia focuses her time and attention on creating and improving biographies about women. We first met at a Wikipedia conference, but I had followed her blog posts and opinion pieces for some time. Given her obdurate attitude, I was surprised to learn that even she was worried about the consequences of "bringing more women to Wikipedia." As she describes, she's worried "they might stray out of the bubble I've created for myself and find those toxic places. There are just places where I don't go on Wikipedia because they are a shit storm." Leah echoes Olivia's concerns, telling me about how she also avoids "articles that are really, really popular, that have a lot of visibility." Despite the fact that neither of these women strike me as wallflowers, Leah, like Olivia, is hesitant and cautious when editing Wikipedia, choosing to work "in the quiet corners."

Discussion of such toxic pages on Wikipedia (e.g., Gamergate, or abortion) was well known throughout the community of Wikipedians who attended edit-a-thons but surprisingly was rarely discussed explicitly at edit-a-thons with newcomers. The omission of such obviously relevant topics at these edit-a-thons is a prime example of the tendency of media-ready feminism to avoid explicitly political discussion in part based on the implicit assumption that it is unnecessary and irrelevant. The unstated logic goes something like this: we all know there are toxic sexist and racist spaces on the internet, spaces that might engender some unpleasant pushback for individual editors with feminine-sounding names. And we all know that this is wrong. But since we all know this, no action need be taken. Perhaps the implicit assumption is that we are all working together, and the collective effort will be enough to counter whatever unpleasantness occurs.

This strikes us as an odd assumption to make, however, given the extent of the dangers women have encountered in incidents like Gamergate, and given the extent of the discrimination against women's and minorities' notability in Wikipedia entries that is not widely known nor acknowledged. Considering the nature of the edit-a-thons (i.e., social justice missions for improving gender and racial equality online), we would argue it's essential that this kind of information be included in order for new editors to understand what their experience might be—and the extent of the dangers they might encounter—but also to indicate the existence of a support network available should this happen. For example, during Women in Red edit-a-thons, all editors star the pages they are collaboratively working on so that if content created during their edit-a-thons is challenged they can work as a group to make sure the content persists. Unfortunately, smaller in-person edit-a-thons do not have those resources.

As a result of the constant pushback and unpleasant or threatening encounters editors experienced, Wikipedia editors who focused on improving coverage of women and women's interests began an unfortunate strategy of *avoiding* certain spaces as a way of proactively defending themselves from harassment, working in what they described as the "quiet corners." Take Angelica, for example, who focused on improving articles about women in STEM fields. As she described: "I've been very careful to stay out of conversations like that [referring to Gamergate] . . . I see myself as being a *stealth feminist* in that I'm not one of the people who speaks loudly, but in doing so I maintain my ability to talk to people who are really anti-feminist." Olivia, the edit-a-thon organizer we met earlier, is explicitly wary of some places on Wikipedia. She frequently advises new editors to stay away from "feminist areas," encouraging them to write about low-stakes content where "no one will bother you, ever." In some respects Olivia and Angelica have a point. By avoiding topics that solicit a charged response (see the next section on harassment), they are able to circumvent those attacks. The overall impact on Wikipedia, however, is a dampening of the efforts to increase representation *and* a lessening of editing work undertaken by women and minorities.

Unfortunately, smaller in-person edit-a-thons do not have the kind of manpower necessary to provide support and preemptive information. Based on my observations, it is clear that content added during edit-a-thons (in particular biographies about women currently absent from the site) is often flagged as "non-notable" and nominated for deletion shortly after it is created.

"Deletionism" on Wikipedia

The *ability* for a new editor to create a new Wikipedia article (particularly new biographies) takes more than mastering the technical skills to navigate the platform. It also requires understanding the culture of Wikipedia and learning how to create content that won't be challenged as non-notable or non-neutral. According to Wikipedia guidelines, a topic is only presumed notable if it has received significant coverage in reliable sources that are independent of the subject.[13] By establishing how articles should be written and what constitutes notability, Wikipedia was able to also establish itself as a credible source of information. An independent study confirmed that Wikipedia was as credible as its hardbound predecessor—*Encyclopedia Britannica* (Giles 2005).

These credibility standards are maintained in part by meticulous Wikipedians who constantly monitor changes to existing pages or new articles added to the site. As Janet—a longtime Wikipedian who has designed large classroom assignments to incorporate Wikipedia editing as part of a pedagogical model—described, this process for maintaining quality control is essential in order to "debunk the myths out there that Wikipedia is unreliable. We want to demonstrate that it has quality control, so librarians and teachers and professors stop saying don't use it." While this effort at deleting content that Janet describes as "crappy articles done by teenagers" does occur, the scope of nominating content for deletion and categorizing biographies as non-notable can have unintended consequences. In particular, a subset of Wikipedians, self-identified as "deletionists," are motivated by a desire for Wikipedia to focus on what they think of as "significant topics." To do so, they regularly nominate for deletion articles they feel are promotional propaganda, trivia, not of "general interest," too short, lacking in "suitable source material for high quality coverage," or unacceptably poor in quality.[14]

Relying on Wikipedia's "Five Pillars,"[15] deletionists use Wikipedia's own quality-control standards to justify, make sense of, and defend their actions. In this way, deletionists rely on "cultural resources" (DiMaggio 1997; Lamont 1992; Lareau 2003) when nominating an article for deletion, treating the Five Pillars almost as a sociological "toolkit" (Swidler 1986) to navigate new situations and resolve problems. This is particularly interesting since the process by which content is nominated for deletion relies on cultural frameworks that can contradict themselves.

Take, for example, the tension between maintaining a neutral point of view ("NPOV") and establishing notability. Wikipedia's NPOV policy indicates that articles must be written "fairly, proportionately, and as far as possible without editorial bias." For an article to have a NPOV, "all of the significant views that have been published by reliable sources on the topic" must be included.[16] On the other hand, notability is established by a subject or person having "significant coverage" in "reliable sources" that are "independent of the subject."[17] However, concepts like what constitutes significant coverage or a reliable source is subjective (and therefore non-neutral).

As a way of illustrating this point, we could take a closer look at how academic notability is accessed.[18] In order for an academic to be on Wikipedia, they must pass a "professor test." Some of these requirements are straightforward and include holding a named chair at a major university or presiding over a prestigious scholarly society. Other criteria, however, are more opaque and open for interpretation. For example, the person's academic work must make "significant impact in the area of higher education" or "significant impact outside of academia." Not only are these conditions non-neutral, they are also rooted in systemic biases when one considers that women and minorities remain underrepresented in top-tier university jobs, and that knowledge associated with women's or African American studies remains underfunded and undervalued (Feber 1986; Rossiter 1993).

It is also problematic outside of academia when one considers that women and people of color are relatively underrepresented in many fields. For example, at an edit-a-thon I attended focusing on increasing coverage of female artists, Wikipedians acknowledged during the opening presentation the extra work editors have to put in to establish women as notable subjects. Lisa, a Wikipedian devoted to improving racial diversity on Wikipedia, describes how "what constitutes a 'credible source' is itself very charged." In our interview, she tells me that for artists there is an extra layer—they have to have two major exhibitions, at "two *major* museums." We talk for a bit longer regarding what constitutes a "major" museum and she describes why that market is problematic for the historically disenfranchised. In Lisa's own words, "Many women artists or artists of color aren't granted the same affordances when it comes to being featured in a museum." Margaret, another Wikipedia editor, put it a bit more bluntly: "Most art institutions are run by white men and their collection strategies have mostly collected white males." Since women artists and artists of color are often barred from "prominent" art museums, they don't count as a "notable" artists. While they are often able to take their projects to alternative spaces, those are not afforded "mainstream" (white male) validation.

In essence, then, Wikipedia reinforces criteria of notability that are already tainted with sexism and racism—women and minorities' lack of representation is overdetermined. As Judy, mentioned earlier, describes: "There is a gender gap in all of history, not just Wikipedia," meaning that finding secondary sources that cover the accomplishments of influential female scientists is more difficult than finding sources about male scientists. In this way, Wikipedia maintains the dominant position, acting as an institutional force that "makes and remakes" the effective dominant culture, rejecting alternative and oppositional cultural forms (Williams 1973, 10).

By linking traditional forms of accreditation to its criteria for establishing notability, Wikipedia continues to marginalize women and people of color under the same exclusionary practices used in the arts, sciences, history, and journalism (Chambers, Steiner, and Fleming 2004; DiMaggio 1982; Collins 2008; Reagle and Rhue 2011; Smith 1998). Jack elaborated on the systemic bias embedded in what constitutes secondary sources, describing how digital archives also favor white men: "There is an online bias to Wikipedia. If something's digitized or it's online, it's easy to incorporate, but if it's not [online], it makes it harder to incorporate a source. That is a bias against women's history, or minority histories."

This is concerning since sources are less likely to be questioned by Wikipedians if they are readily available online. According to my interviews and conference proceedings, when sources that establish a person's notability are not "linkable," meaning there are fewer other online sources citing this person, the article is more likely to be scrutinized and nominated for deletion because editors are not able to check the validity of a source by reading it for themselves. Therefore, a reliance on digital sources favors some biographies and puts others at a disadvantage.

Jeannie, mentioned earlier, is visibly agitated when we discuss these continuing problems related to gender representation. Her work within the community is heralded as a success in this regard, and when others in the community learned of my research, they often suggested I reach out to her as a point of contact. During our interview she elaborates on this problem: "The policies [regarding deletion on Wikipedia] are important, but are they what we need in 2015 versus 2005? How about notable people who don't have books written about them? How do we access that information? If it exists, but not in a book published by Macmillan—how do we access it?"

Wikipedia creates and defines the rituals, actions, and practices that justify deleting content from the site. Ironically, the site also requires one to write articles in a seemingly "neutral" way (explicitly, guidelines state that articles should be "from a 'neutral' point of view").[19] However, what constitutes "notability" can never be "neutral," because the very concept of notability ultimately protects discriminatory practices by adopting a practical attitude toward exclusion. Nonetheless, the culture of Wikipedia sees NPOV and notability as separate entities and frequently cites notability as a reason for deletion.

When a Wikipedian deems an article "non-notable," the editor nominates the article for deletion. Once nominated, it is moved to the "Articles for Deletion"[20] page where other editors debate whether an article should be kept, deleted, or merged with another article. Nominated articles are up for a review period of at least seven days, although through my observations I learned that sometimes the nomination process could go longer if there is a substantial debate and a decision-maker feels more time for discussion is needed. Articles nominated for deletion can be closed quickly if they constitute a clear case of self-promotion or vandalism. In our interview, Matt explained how decisions in the "Articles for Deletion" space are rendered. He is actually an expert on these matters since he spent years "lurking" on "Articles for Deletion" before rendering any decisions himself. He tells me of the process. First, "an administrator[21] who is not involved [with neither the original nomination nor the subsequent discussions] will evaluate what has been said in the discussion, and they will look at arguments and weigh them against the policies, notability being the main one . . . [they will ask] have they made a strong and persuasive argument, and is that consistent with our policies?"

In theory, all articles that have been nominated for deletion have been nominated in good faith. Before something is nominated, it is assumed that the editor clicked on the sources available to assess the quality of the content as well as searched elsewhere to determine if the sources are inadequate. Matt elaborated on this process in detail. Before you tag something as non-notable or nominate it for deletion, an editor is "supposed to put in a quick search to see what the sources say about a topic." This quick search is typically done via Google and is easy to do. Matt elaborates, "There is a set of criteria that you should follow where basically you should make a good-faith effort to search and see if the topic has some coverage in independent and reliable sources."

Ken, a slender man with large eyes and a bigger smile, describes how Wikipedians rarely deviate from this effort. Routinization determines that these standards are high, in his account, because it makes it so that content nominated is done so in an objective way. "Wikipedians are institutionalized," Ken reasons, "they are like robots. What they're looking for are two sources. I don't think it's ever happened that somebody's article has been deleted if they had two sources that featured their subject. Just needs two sentences." He pauses to reflect, then lifts up two long fingers: "Two sentences, two citations." Ken was essentially blind to the operation of discrimination in Wikipedia editing. He denied what could be in plain sight for an active editor. While it seems that decisions rendered are clear-cut, the aforementioned text notes that how that notability is quickly assessed, typically via Google, is rooted in historical problems of underrepresentation. Not only is notability a mechanism for blocking content, it is clear that content created about women during edit-a-thons is often subject to many assaults on its notability after the fact, and that most of these assaults ignore the fact that two or more citations are present. For example, after an "Art+Feminism" event held at a university in Canada in 2016, ten articles were nominated for deletion after the event was over, despite each featuring more than two citations supporting the notability of their subjects.

When I asked Matt about these discrepancies he relayed to me his own observations and extensive time volunteering as an administrator in "Articles for Deletion," noting that women seem to be unfairly targeted—especially women's biographies:

> Just in my experience of going through AfD (Articles for Deletion) on certain topics, I think it is the case—whether it is intentional or not—that topics that deal with women generally or biographies in specific that are more scrutinized when compared against a similar kind of biography for men. I think the discussions on women[22]—they can be, but not always are, just longer, there are more people saying things about them and kinda weighing in on the discussion, so they take longer

to parse through because more things have been said. I think there are things both in the nomination and the discussion itself that reflect this higher level of scrutiny relative to biographies on men. I think when we're looking at the question of are these sources reliable or not, there is more analysis of that question for articles on women than compared to men. So if someone has created an article and there are a bunch of sources on it already, I don't think an editor is as likely to thoroughly look at those sources for reliability compared to an article about a woman. And my evidence, based on my experience in articles for deletion, is that I see more time dedicated to that kind of discussion than when I see biographies of men that are brought to attention.

It's interesting that Matt describes this discrepancy in such detail, yet seems to find it unproblematic and somehow obvious—an example of the kind of "everyday sexism" we describe as so pervasive. It simply "is," and remains unquestioned.

Some of the editorial decisions that repeatedly target women as non-notable might have to do as well with how sources pertaining to women are assessed. This came up when Judy, who is regularly involved with Women in Red edit-a-thons, described a particular instance of deletion:

I don't think they [people who revert or delete articles] have any idea how to evaluate sources. People don't know how to access information especially when it comes to women. We had a guy last month who questioned why a scientist had some documents that listed her name as Jane Doe, but later documents carried her name as Jane M. Smith. This seems like a totally normal woman naming thing to me. Her name was probably Jane Marie Doe and she started publishing, but then got married so then she called herself Jane Doe Smith. He's like 'I don't understand this. It makes no sense to me." I'm like "If you don't even understand the naming conventions that women use, how can you possibly assess whether a file should be deleted or not?" He was like "It doesn't make any sense. If they were professional, they wouldn't change their name." He didn't think the sources added up because he didn't understand naming conventions associated with women.

These comments ignored the fact that despite the growing number of professional women who do not change their names with marriage, the vast majority of women (over 92 percent) still do change their names. Obviously this would encompass quite a large percentage of professional women (Suter and Oswald 2008).

However, my data also demonstrate that, in some instances, targeting for deletion may be more nefarious. Margaret, another passionate editor who regularly hosts edit-a-thons, describes how an article about a feminist activist that she wrote was nominated for deletion for being "non-notable," despite the national press coverage regarding this particular woman's involvement in feminist protests. She recalls of the situation, "My friend had a photo of her from a protest and I wrote her Wikipedia article because of her press notability. The article was subsequently flagged after a few hours and pushed into 'articles for deletion' AFD. There were [sic] a strain of arguments that basically said we can't [sic] add her yet because we can't tell if she's going to be historically notable, so we can't add her yet." While some might argue that the merits of an activist could be questioned as notable, this pattern was seen in a variety of biographies, for example, as in a biography of a woman who pioneered a specific technology.[23] Her page was nominated for deletion shortly after longtime editor Brenna created it. She had to dig deeper into archived newspapers in order to demonstrate her notability but, in Brenna's own words, the process was frustrating, demonstrating that *"you have to work twice as hard to prove that* the content [about women] is valuable and is worthy of being in."

Brenna's observation—that editors had to work "twice as hard" to prove the notability of female subjects—is not exclusive to biographies of living people. As my research on the "Articles for Deletion" page reveals, even Wikipedia pages about characters in television shows that are more popular among a female audience *also* seem to be disproportionally targeted for deletion. Take, for example, the page about Serena van der Woodsen—a character from the book and television series *Gossip Girl*. Despite the fact that this page was created over a decade ago (July 15, 2005) it maintains a relatively high level of page-view traffic. If you look at the "Page View Statistics" under the "View History" tab, Serena van der Woodsen averages about 653 views/day.[24]

Despite the regular traffic Serena van der Woodsen's page receives, it has been nominated for deletion *twice* since its creation (once in August of 2008 and again in April 2016). In both instances, the editors nominating Serena van der Woodsen's page used the rationale that the character was "non-notable" and did not deserve a standalone page, despite the page having significant coverage, in reliable sources. While both nominations ultimately ended in a decision to "keep" Serena van der Woodsen's page active, this is just another example of how Wikipedians interested in improving the gender gap with regard to content have to work "twice as hard" to keep content from disappearing from the site.

Combating problems with notability as well as continuous challenges for inclusion, it is also clear that race and gender intersect with how biographies are reviewed and nominated for deletion. Tripodi is currently working on another project using scraped data from Wikipedia's "Articles for Deletion" page and finds that people who are not white or cisgender face an uphill battle in order to demonstrate that they are "worthy" of a Wikipedia page. Drawing on preliminary analysis of this data, Tripodi finds that of the women whose biographies were nominated for deletion but ultimately kept, more than half were described in their articles as a person of color (e.g., "Black" or "Hispanic"). Preliminary data indicate that Black women tended to be denied notability regardless of the fact that they met Ken's notability standards (two sources independent of the subject). As these data demonstrate, the discrimination happening on Wikipedia exemplifies Crenshaw's (1989) central argument of how Black women are impossible subjects—too similar to be different, to different to be the same. Despite these women's contributions to myriad fields, their pages were denied visibility because editors were unfamiliar with their achievements and not making a "good faith" assumption for inclusion.

More troubling still is that Tripodi's data indicate a pattern regarding the targeting of edit-a-thons. Since Wikipedia is a completely transparent platform, one can trace when articles were created. Using my scraped dataset, I also found that many articles were nominated for deletion *on the same day* they were created, indicating they were created as part of an edit-a-thon. For example, "Sojourner Street"[25] had immense periodical coverage detailing the integral role she played in the commemoration of female African American writers. Street founded two museums focused on African American literature, wrote a book on the history of Black women authors in the United States, ran two boutique bookshops, and wrote her own novels. Not only did her museums memorialize the contributions of some of the most prominent African American authors, but Street also used the space to give free courses in writing, English, mathematics, and African American history. Shortly after her death in 2007, Street's daughter donated her collection of over seven hundred novels, three hundred manuscripts, and sixty boxes of archived material to the Smithsonian National Museum of African American History and Culture. When she died, the *Washington Post* ran an obituary on Street, detailing her accomplishments and crediting her as a prominent figure in memorializing African American history.

Despite the significance of Street's contributions, she did not have a Wikipedia page until eight years after her death. While not particularly prolific, the editor who began Street's page was knowledgeable of her legacy, and she was deliberate in her actions, using seven credible sources. Using basic information, Street's life became instantaneously available on Wikipedia. Simultaneously, another editor moved the draft page to the "Articles for Creation" submission page, citing this was the "preferred location for an Articles for Creation submission." Not only was Street's article *rejected* for submission despite the fact that the article included more than two citations from reliable sources, it is clear that Street's Wikipedia page was created during an edit-a-thon designed to increase the number of biographies about notable minority women and to train minority editors. It is also clear that the creator of Street's Wikipedia page was a new editor and because she used a real-name identifier; a quick Google search reveals that she is a woman.[26]

While this analysis is only in its preliminary stages, it is very clear that more work must be done to consider the various ways in which gender, race, and sexuality impact one's ability to have adequate representation on Wikipedia. Not only are Wikipedia's notability criteria problematic, it is also clear that biographies about women and people of color are being targeted after they are created. Based on my evidence, it also seems as though the edit-a-thon itself has become a target to challenge biographies for their "notability."

Conclusion

In the end, not all is lost when it comes to the potential for gender and racial equality on Wikipedia. Edit-a-thons can and have been used to make substantial inroads into gender inequality on the site. During Tripodi's yearlong ethnography, Women in Red made steady improvements to the number of biographies about women on English-language Wikipedia from 15 percent to 16.48 percent (as of September 18, 2016). The Wikimedia Foundation is also working to eradicate the problem of gendered harassment on Wikipedia and is continuously providing rapid grants for researchers devoted to this problem. A few devoted Wikipedians have also joined forces with Wikimedia to create a Gender Task Force committed to understanding the prevalence of harassment and finding solutions that can eradicate the problem. At the same time, edit-a-thons continue to try to create a "safe space" for new editors to feel comfortable contributing to the site and are aimed at improving the number of biographies about women still missing from Wikipedia. For example, Art+Feminism hosted a series of concurrent edit-a-thons during the month of March to maximize awareness of the problem during Women's History Month.

Yet the strength and persistence of everyday sexism continue to make it difficult for Wikipedians who organize the edit-a-thons to acknowledge how their own standards for "notability" are not neutral. Moreover, the idea that women and minorities who do meet this limited inclusion criteria are subject to intensified scrutiny appears to be widely unchallenged. When Tripodi directly addressed this at conferences and in her interviews, many people felt like the problem was people becoming "too attached" to content they created, or that they had simply written the article in a "non-neutral" tone, thereby justifying the articles for deletion. By rebuking discriminatory concerns as "matters of clashing personality" (Hochschild 1979, xxi) rather than examining the societal contradictions embedded in the fact that Wikipedia's notability criteria were created in a male-dominated environment, Wikipedia prevents the legitimate investigation into whether women and people of color are being disproportionately targeted for exclusion. Such an example of everyday sexism on Wikipedia is troubling given its influence and growing importance in our information culture. As a result, we can see why edit-a-thons are thought of as a perfect solution: in the age of media-ready feminism, a type of taken-for-granted sexism exists and is systematically reproduced. The efforts it would take to amend the structure enabling these mechanisms are extreme and difficult and to date have not been incorporated effectively into the operation of Wikipedia, which remains a major source of the repository of knowledge in our culture.

Conclusion

A World Beyond Media-Ready Feminism

The treatment of feminism in media of different forms has shifted dramatically over time. The various forms feminism takes sometimes reflect the cultural moment—the perpetuation of popular feminist logic is in part due to the way media have appropriated this perspective. Yet media can also push the boundaries, exposing audiences to ideas they may not be familiar with and advancing public acceptance of concepts once considered taboo. This book provides examples of times when media work to portray a transformative feminism alongside the popular feminism that predominates in their representations. Shows like the wildly popular *Game of Thrones* and even classics like *Desperate Housewives* or low-budget series like *Jersey Shore* often reiterated a banal sense of feminism devoid of collective politicism. *Game of Thrones* and *Jersey Shore* were also complicit in blending both a neoliberal logic alongside popular misogyny (Banet-Weiser 2018). At the same time, episodes within these long-running series (many of them upwards of eight years) also pushed the boundaries, touching on classic and authentic ideas of gender equality, and challenging a culture that falls short. At these moments, television shed light on the perils women face in society and addressed issues related to sexuality, power, and career ambitions. Yet everyday sexism remains an integral part of everyday life and is consistently reproduced in our cultural institutions and social life.

"The media" in the new environment are no longer bound to traditional forms of production that discretely separate producers from consumers. Yet newer participatory spaces like Wikipedia are entrenched in patriarchal, pervasive systems of inequality—in the extreme case of Wikipedia, in a citation system that reifies existing definitions of what constitutes knowledge. At the same time, the institution of Wikipedia is working, in a way however flawed and incomplete, to improve the representation of women and minorities whose achievements would otherwise remain culturally invisible. Popular apps like Tinder and Bumble are giving more sexual agency to women, albeit also within a broader environment where women still feel like "obligatory blow jobs" are necessary. In short—media can reflect the cultural milieu, but at times the mirror cracks, opening a space for representations to play around with those distortions.

This book focuses on these "magnified moments" (Hochschild 1994, 4) of breakthrough feminist media representations and their reception, and in doing so it sheds light on the social construction of feminism and the persistent reproduction of everyday sexism. Drawing on audience ethnography, our books adds another layer of complexity to the conversation, enabling us to examine how representations of feminism are actually received and made meaningful for media audience members. By tracing the ways in which audiences interact with various forms of media, this book has introduced the concept of "media-ready feminism." Media-ready feminism captures the interactive processes by which individuals and groups make meanings from the media, particularly enabling description of audiences' ambivalence toward media content that transgresses our cultural moment in building on the foundation of powerful feminist theorists of culture. Banet-Weiser's "popular feminism" (2018), Favaro and Gill's "glossy feminism" (2018), and Rottenberg's "neoliberal feminism" (2018) are all seminal for understanding the cultural milieu in which we currently live. This work has been generative for us and we have sought to build on it in this book. To do so we have turned to audience study, to unpack how media attempts to transcend and respond to current feminist thought and to capture the ways in which audiences make sense of these media moments. Understanding how audiences engage with media depictions that attempt to challenge popular feminist logic also sheds light on the pervasiveness of everyday sexism, which when unchallenged insures the reproduction of patriarchy (Ortner 2014).

Though feminism has been in the forefront of media coverage and representation of late, as in the case of the #MeToo movement, to date we know little about how audiences engage with these moments of extreme media feminism. To what extent are audiences "ready" to engage in the kind of feminism media offer? Are the kinds of meanings embedded in feminist media coverage actually visible and sentient? Most importantly, in an era of participatory media products, do media, when serving as a tool for advancing public knowledge of feminism, open audiences up to dangers in ways they might not fully conceptualize? If audiences are missing the language by which they can critique and make sense out of what they are witnessing, and receiving, we then miss out on the opportunity to push the boundaries of gender equality into the twenty-first century. Moreover, by continuing to frame feminism in a way that elevates the needs and experiences of white, cisgender, heterosexual, women, media often fail to understand how the essence of twenty-first-century feminist theory mandates more inclusivity vis-à-vis race, class, gender definitions, and sexual orientation. As long as a white, middle-class perspective remains hegemonic even in media's breakthrough feminist moments, media's revolutionary reach will be limited, leaving out as it does those outside the top of the social hierarchy.

To make our case, we applied a case study approach to examine the ways audiences engage with and make meaning from a variety of media formats and contents. First, we considered the ways in which examples of premium access television, reality television, and broadcast television pushed feminism in different and sometimes new and strong directions, yet were often received more tepidly than the texts seemed to merit.

Our research on *Game of Thrones* illustrated media-ready feminist responses to what some have argued is the most feminist television show in recent memory, and others have argued is the most misogynist. We use conflicting responses to this thick and contradictory text to explore current iterations of popular feminism in the media and to introduce our working concept of "media-ready feminist" reception. Media-ready feminism illustrates how audiences push back on the potential of popular feminism, insuring that its critique of sexism does not engage the structural-level changes needed to accomplish far-reaching feminist reforms. Viewer reactions to *Game of Thrones* mirror the text—a representation of strong female characters fraught with ambivalence. While breakthrough feminist moments in recent media may appear to introduce at the textual level structural challenges to patriarchy and sexism, examining reception of these moments exposes the difficulties audiences have in accepting popular feminism in its most extreme iterations. And in fact, *Game of Thrones'* misogyny can be seen to undercut its feminism, a perspective that has been recognized in both feminist and mainstream media criticism of the show. While audiences in Johnson's (forthcoming) interviews recognize easily both the feminist and the misogynist layers of its text, their discussions and debates over the feminist nature of the unusual women characters introduced in the show allow us to probe the contours of popular feminism, illustrating its potential and its limitations. From one perspective, *Game of Thrones* is a perfect iteration of popular feminism: its female characters, though powerful, are all highly sexualized to an extreme for cable television shows. From another, it is a show that breaks through the limits of popular feminism in showing us strong leading women who eschew traditional femininity and can be described as queer. From yet another, this show is paradoxically exceedingly misogynist in showing us a level of sexual violence that is, again, extreme, even for cable television shows. Perhaps this multilayered text, where feminism is concerned, is the new form of popular feminism. Viewers' attempts to grapple with the show's misogyny indicate that they are savvy about everyday sexism and extreme misogyny. But their consistent tendency to temper the extreme power of some of *Game of Thrones*' most salient women illustrates the complexity of media-ready feminism. Even audiences paying to watch a show that both challenges and reinforces female subjugation tend to oversimplify the strong female leads into "good" or "bad," and tend to dismiss the extreme sexual violence as just part of the show's "entertainment" value, or even justify it as an illustration of historical reality.

Jersey Shore offered a window into how audiences today consider the problematic nature of the heterosexual gendered "double standard." At one level the show could not be more retrograde and stereotyped in its portrayal of both sexuality and class, yet it was one of the most popular shows of the millennium. The guido ethnicity was in a complicated way defined in class-specific terms. Characters were seen for the most part as not pursuing higher education and as not being very serious about preparation for their careers. In a caricature of working-class culture, the pleasures of the moment were paramount. Sex was a frequent topic of discussion on the show, and nights of partying that might lead to sexual activity were a common preoccupation. Unlike other popular shows on MTV, the show rarely questioned heterosexuality and contained no ongoing queer characters, although there were media treatments of *Jersey Shore* that commented on the appeal of its male characters to the gay community (Moylan 2010).

So we found it surprising and worthy of note when one of the least-liked characters on the show, Angelina, argued for the gendered equality of sexual opportunity in one episode. We decided to use this episode in our reception study, concentrating on its discussions of the "double standard," which Angelina critiqued and which other cast members defended. When Angelina appeared to have sex with two different men on two consecutive nights, cast members drew from the values of the double standard to castigate her for being a "too" sexually active woman. They applied derogatory terms commonly used to shame sexually active women—the word "slut," for example—to describe her behavior. Angelina drew from the lexicon of feminism to defend her sexual freedom and to denounce the practice of using different standards to evaluate men's and women's sexual behavior. We use this example, and viewers' reactions to it, to illuminate the broader debate about the acceptance and critique of the terms of popular feminism as well as the racial and class-based limits of sexual expression. Viewers, many of whom were fans of the show, pulled back from Angelina's assertion of sexual independence, even when identifying as feminists themselves. When pushed, they acknowledged the existence of the "double standard," which still exerted power over their lives and activities despite the presence of a popular feminism that denies it. Moreover, reception of the chapter unpacks how women of color on college campuses, and first-generation college students from working-class families, are less likely to engage in hookups both because of the layers of sexual inequality (Wade 2017) as well as the risk of jeopardizing their social standing in ways white, middle-class women are not forced to consider.

On *Desperate Housewives* viewers were able to follow the leading housewife characters as they grappled with the attempt to combine work and family in an unsentimental text attuned to the problems of working mothers. We were particularly struck by the storyline of one of the housewives, Lynette, shown interviewing for a high-powered advertising job as she attempted to reenter the labor force, baby in tow due to the incompetence of her babysitter husband. The interview process was shown in detail, replete with a male boss oblivious to the baby's presence and a hostile, unsympathetic female administrator who watched in horror as Lynette diapered her baby during her pitch. Lynette nevertheless triumphed. Her image offered us a breakthrough feminist character attuned to the injustices of a working world stacked against high-achieving women who were also mothers. Yet this image was limited by its embodiment of racial and social-class privilege: Lynette was a white, highly educated character, in competition for a prestigious and well-paid professional position.

Viewer responses to this text fell short of recognizing the truly radical aspect of Lynette's character. As characterizes reception of most media representations of the issue, viewers individualized rather than offering a systemic critique of the many problems women face in this regard. Despite the fact that many women we spoke with had grappled with these issues in a world unsympathetic and unsuited to the problems of working mothers, younger women found Lynette too nagging or bossy, in contrast with older women who resonated quite differently with her story. We learned in this chapter that age makes a big difference when understanding the complexities of feminism.

Older white audience members recognize the near-universal difficulties women experience when combining work and family in our society, and those who have experienced them personally are often angry about the way their work lives have been penalized by family obligations and activities. Yet most reverted to personalistic discussions of how individuals they knew had managed or failed to manage the issue, without invoking feminism's more structural discussions of the need for flextime in workplaces; affordable, quality daycare; more universal paid family leave; and general acceptance of women who choose to both work and care for their families.

We learned also that race and social class are key components to consider when examining dominant representations and experiences of work-family balance and its complexities. Women of color or women who were first-generation college students did not expect to ever stay at home with their children—some even juggled children and full-time jobs during their college experience. So the very complexity of what Lynette was facing was outside of their particular worldview. Although one African American mom very tellingly attempted to clue her daughter in to the complexities of work-family balance, none of the white daughters in our sample seemed to have had such an intense discussion with their own moms. Perhaps women in less privileged groups did not feel they had the luxury of facing the kind of unrestricted choice that more privileged white women envisioned in their future. The invisibility of the limits of choice functions as a privilege. In general, we argue, audience members stop short of moving to the next level of recognizing the structural changes necessary to eliminate this almost unconquerable conflict and of demanding that these changes be made. Decades of feminist research concerning women's work-family conflict and what might be necessary to overcome it remain culturally opaque and inaccessible, even to women for whom this conflict occupies a central place in their own experiences and psyches.

For the most part, critical analysis of feminist media and the role popular feminism plays in audience reception is limited to traditional modes of consumption (television, advertising, etc.). By considering the important role participatory media play in the feminist landscape, this book also complicates the idea that new media provide a voice for the historically disenfranchised. Rather than consider "the media" in isolation, chapters 4 and 5 unpack the way in which participation in media production as well as reception have become integrated into social life (Tripodi 2017) and the role media-ready feminism plays when audiences are both creators and consumers. In chapter 4, "Swipe Right for Consent," we considered the paradoxical uses and impact of a dating app designed to empower its users. While Tinder and other dating apps appear to be a step forward in the move toward feminist empowerment, the way they are used ends up putting women and other users in positions where the passive consent of their "swipes" can be mistaken for a more active consent to sexual activity. As a result, women who use dating apps often find themselves in compromised positions and feel unable to say "no," even when they would prefer to. For this reason, dating apps may initially appear empowering but substitute implied for actual consent to sexual activity. Debates over Tinder have shaded into other discussions as exemplified by the highly publicized Aziz Ansari dating encounter, in which an unnamed participant claims to have denied consent to sexual activity multiple times during the encounter but found her protests ignored. Our research indicates that our Tinder data touch on a much larger set of issues surrounding dating and the effectiveness of the mode by which participants actively give consent to sexual activity in a variety of settings. The way Tinder is used indicates that a new form of consent—implicit consent—dominates the use of this dating app. And in an era that has encouraged a new focus on consent that is actively, vocally offered as the way to combat instances of harassment and assault, the implicit consent we see in Tinder use is problematic and dangerous.

Another of our findings regarding Tinder involves the way the structure of the app reproduces existing hierarchies of sexuality and race. whites are privileged in the "hierarchy" of sexual choices that characterize the way users select partners on the app, something others have noted and which our research also illustrates. In addition as others have noted, an assumption of normative sexuality underlies the way partners are presented by the app's structure—in fact, LGBTQ communities had previously developed apps specific to their communities. Both of these factors, we would argue, contribute to the way the Tinder app facilitates a culture that downplays active consent, subjecting it to a series of embedded heteronormative, white supremacist and sexist assumptions, by those involved in in-person encounters.

In chapter 5, "Wikipedia: Sign(s) Say Keep Out," we discussed the challenges women face when trying to edit Wikipedia. Driven by a feminist model of collective political engagement, we described how the process of "edit-a-thons" has formed in order to combat the gender inequality on the site. At the same time, we note the ways in which many who devote their time and energy to gender inequality are wary of framing themselves as "feminist" and instead opt for "quiet corners" in order to avoid harassment. In an effort to protect new editors, long-standing Wikipedians who have experienced harassment firsthand fail to communicate strategies to women who enter into the space; however, that reluctance perpetuates the likelihood of everyday sexism persisting. By undermining the clearly feminist agenda of their work to avoid harassment, these fear-induced behaviors consequently opened up the possibility for the harassment cycle to continue. Specifically, we described how the selection process by which new editors (frequently women) choose their usernames is rarely discussed as a response to the persistent sexism on the site. One possible strategy that could be considered to disrupt this cycle is to consider ways this sexism could be directly addressed, by explicitly invoking feminist theory. While this might hamper the recruitment of new editors, it would also afford women the strategies they will need when they encounter harassment. Specifically, a portion of edit-a-thons must address safety considerations when choosing a username. While some hosts caution against the use of identifiers that link back to one's real name, this is framed as an issue of privacy rather than as an open discussion of sexism. Education regarding the site's charged spaces could also be an important step forward, and this could be accomplished both within and outside an edit-a-thon environment. For example, when contentious pages are locked by administrators to avoid editorial disputes, no disclaimer is given. Perhaps a hover box detailing the reasons for locking a page (e.g., vandalism or sexism) could be included in the future. Wikipedia could also consider training for existing editors in order to address the feelings of exclusion explicitly experienced by many women editors. At Wikimania, conferences panels are being held to discuss these policies, but Wikipedia could also mandate a yearly online training in which people are made aware of Wikipedia's norms and engagement policies. While this process might alienate longtime Wikipedians, it would also work to alleviate the stress women in particular feel when beginning to edit and make the Wikipedia community feel more welcoming to women.

The Way Forward: Toward a More Inclusive Future

The goals of this book are twofold. First, we sought to describe the ways in which media often challenge popular feminist logics. By examining media forms across platforms, these cases outline multiple examples of media getting at the crux of feminism—thinking about how gender equality transcends the boundaries of work, home, and pleasure and creeps into systems of knowledge and power. By addressing these issues, media work to provoke their audiences—seeking to have us grapple with issues we might not have otherwise considered. But is the logic of popular feminism too ingrained in our society for us to effectively confront and combat the deeply embedded nature of everyday sexism? Therein lies the challenge of the media-ready feminist reception pattern we have documented here. For while media products can push the boundaries, if audiences are unable or unwilling to address the broader structural problems limiting feminist change, the narrative will not be engaged in a meaningful way.

In addition, often the feminist meanings encoded into media products remain profoundly biased toward the privileged. The "double standard" and even "work-life balance" are, arguably, concepts unevenly felt by those who hold more power and status in society. Thinking about how to balance career and family, or considering sexual liberation, are indeed important but also fail to engage with problems that other women may feel are more pressing (e.g., income inequality, lack of affordable child care / medical care, domestic violence, access to education, heterosexist and cisgendered societal assumptions, etc.).

However, we live in an age of participatory media. Not all hope is lost. We have the ability to create new narratives, ones that push the boundaries in more than one direction. But if we want those messages to make a difference, we must incorporate cognizance of the larger process of their reception. As Stuart Hall taught us decades ago, audiences make meaning in context-specific ways. For media-ready feminism to matter, the future feminist agenda must begin to be more inclusive of those whose needs are not currently being seen. Moreover, media must work to address the everyday nature of a continuing and pervasive sexism that is so ubiquitous that many fail to even notice the frequency with which women are subjected to it. This sexism is often inextricably bound with white supremacist, middle-classist, heterosexist, and cisgendered forms of hegemony that extend the domination of sexism to these groups as well. Making all forms of sexism visible will allow us to craft a language enabling us to confront and combat the real problems women and others affected by it face and, in doing so, to push the boundaries of media representations further in a genuinely feminist, liberatory direction.

Notes

Introduction

1. See Blum and Mickey (2019) for an excellent history of the sexual harassment movement focusing on the activist group WOASH (Women Organized Against Sexual Harassment) of which Andrea Press, coauthor of this volume, was a founding member.

2. Banet-Weiser, Gill, and Rottenberg (2019) discuss the similar reappropriation of feminism in Banet-Weiser's "popular feminism" and Rottenberg's "neoliberal feminism," in contrast to its repudiation in Gill's "postfeminist sensibility."

3. Rottenberg elaborates how problematic are all attempts to define the boundaries of what a definition of actual feminism might look like (Zeisler [2016] quoted in Rottenberg [2018, 167]). We are not claiming that media-ready feminism characterizes *all* representations and presentations of feminism in the media. Of course there are explicitly "feminist" media such as the publications *Bitch* or *Jezebel*, which are influenced in part by media-ready feminism but are able to largely transcend it given their fringe status. Our argument pertains to a pervasive discourse that is adopted across mainstream and popular media platforms. Any of these platforms may contain niche markets that appeal to the central nodes of feminism. What we are saying is that the larger and more visible conception of what constitutes feminism—across a variety of media platforms—is "media-ready." This means it both encompasses popular feminism, with all of its limitations, while *at times* containing the seeds of a more revolutionary perspective.

4. For a broader discussion of Gramsci's theory of hegemony, see Adamson (2014) and of course Gramsci (2011). Laclau and Mouffe (2014) also provide an interesting discussion of the way hegemony operates in advanced capitalist cultures.

5. See https://www.guttmacher.org/fact-sheet/induced-abortion-united-states?gclid=Cj0KCQjwov3nBRDFARIsANgsdoHNKNBkfmP7CXQbjOpI-iO-7

FwoU0maMiAFm2DwWNyzOMIIILmc0TQaAu8zEALw_wcB for statistics underscoring that over time one in four US women will have had abortions.

Chapter 1. Considering the Limits of Extreme Misogyny: Game of Thrones as Feminist?

1. This chapter is based on a reanalysis of data gathered by Sarah Johnson under Andrea Press's supervision for her master's thesis, "Hybridizing Feminism in and through Popular Culture," in the Department of Sociology, University of Virginia (completed May 2017), and it also draws from her manuscript "Hybridizing Feminism: *Game of Thrones* as a Site of Discourse Construction," which is currently under review.

2. Dany's salience may have receded by the end of the series, at which point her story takes a turn and she experiences a tragic downfall, succumbing to the influence of her power-hungry family. Our interviews might have yielded different responses to her character if they had been conducted after the series ended.

Chapter 2. Prudes, Sluts, and Sex: The Classing of Female Sexuality in Media-Ready Feminism

1. See Caporimo (2018), Lord (2016), and Liebowitz (2015) for fuller discussions of the definition of demisexuality.

2. In an earlier work Press argues that the Marilyn Monroe persona was actually more complex than the word "trashy" connotes, given the beguiling innocence that was combined with overt sexuality in this star persona; however, her filmic roles were almost entirely working-class or poor women, in distinction to the more upscale Hitchcock blondes. Sexuality is often classed in Hollywood cinema of the classical period (Press and Rosen 2017).

3. See Spoto (2009) for a discussion of how Hitchcock constructed the prototypical "Hitchcock blonde" and how he fell in love with his own creations.

4. We are indebted to Laurie Ouellette for pointing out their increasing tendency to "play" guido-guidette.

5. A confessional is used in most reality television shows to give private insight into how individuals characters think about a situation. It is typically used to give individual commentary on a storyline as it unfolds during the show. See https://en.wikipedia.org/wiki/Confessional_(reality_television).

6. The idea that women feel pressured into having sex once they reach a certain threshold is also explored in our chapter "Swipe Right for Consent," in which we detail the ways in which media-ready feminism fails to engage with the societal pressures women face to say yes in certain situations. As many have now documented, sometimes saying yes is just easier than saying no.

7. Farvid and Braun (2016) and Farvid, Braun, and Rowney (2017) offer further research that helps unpack and articulate these particular dilemmas facing young women in the era of hookup culture.

8. Armstrong, England, and Fogarty (2010) and Armstrong, Hamilton, and England (2010) document some of these changes.

9. Scharff (2019) presents new data pertaining to the United Kingdom and Europe demonstrating that only a minority of women identify with feminism, despite assertions that popular feminism has taken over media representations. These data raise the question of how influential popular feminism has been on women's identifications and attitudes despite its ubiquity in current media.

10. In the spring of 2017 we trained a class of twenty-four undergraduates to investigate the culture of sexual consent on a variety of local college campuses. Our data on this issue consists of over 110 individual interviews, over fifteen focus group interviews, and hours of ethnographic observation of campus sexual cultures.

11. While Farvid interviewed women who do embrace more sexual freedom than those in our sample, we find that many heterosexual women were not willing to admit that they engage in casual sexual activity, which was a prerequisite of participation in her samples (Farvid and Braun 2016; Farvid, Braun, and Rowney 2017). Braun and Farvid (2014) find also that women fear being termed "sluts." In support of our findings, Farvid and Braun (2016) also find that women discuss a "hierarchy" of sexual activity, where the allegedly minority position—demisexuality, sex with emotional connection—retains the highest status.

12. See Walker (1992) for an explication of the "third wave." See also Coppock and Richter (1995), Hall and Rodriguez (2003), and Walby (2011) for in-depth discussions of the "third wave" in relation to postfeminism.

Chapter 3. Balancing Work and Family: What "Choice" Conceals

1. See the Bureau of Labor Statistics 2016, https://www.bls.gov/TUS/CHARTS/HOUSEHOLD.HTM.

2. It is important to note that both shows did have a diverse cast but center white cast members. For example, in *Workin' Moms* the lead role is played by Kate, a white, cisgender, heterosexual woman. There are some moms in the broader group who are people of color and Frankie, a supporting character, portrays life as a lesbian mother.

3. Ironically, Felicity Huffman has become notorious in real life for paying a consultant to actually falsify her children's college admissions portfolios. She has pled guilty to felony fraud charges, served fourteen days in jail, and paid a $30,000 fine. Apparently the demands and pressures of being a working celebrity mom were intensive even for this successful, white, glamorous actress and drove her to illegal actions (Wilson 2019).

4. ABC Media Net, Press Release on Tuesday, September 27, 2005, https://web.archive.org/web/20090601190247/http://abcmedianet.com/web/dnr/dispDNR.aspx?id=092705_03, accessed July 23, 2019.

5. We are grateful to Michelle A. Massé, our series editor at State University of New York Press, for reaffirming the notion that this issue remains vital to the interests of feminist scholars.

6. See Press and Tripodi's piece on this in *Slate*, http://www.slate.com/blogs/xx_factor/2014/06/05/sexism_on_college_campuses_what_we_found_lurking_on_college_acb_at_a_large.html, and in the *Chronicle of Higher Education*, http://chronicle.com/blogs/conversation/2014/07/02/the-new-misogyny/.

7. See Rampell (2012) on the "mommy penalty." See also Hoobler and colleagues (2009). See also Toff (2009), and Nussbaum (2010).

8. Sheryl Sandberg has started a campaign to turn the label "bossy" from a pejorative term, often used against her childhood self, into a positive description of women with a penchant for leadership. See http://www.theguardian.com/commentisfree/2014/mar/11/bossy-banned-boost-girls-self-esteem-facebook-sheryl-sandberg-beyonce.

9. See "Job Switching," season 2, episode 1 of the *I Love Lucy Show*, a prime text from television's golden age of situation comedy. See Press (2009) for a more complete discussion of this and related issues in the representations of television's golden age.

10. See Hartman (2017), Glover (2018), and Konrad and Yang (2012).

Chapter 4. Swipe Right for Consent: Hookup Culture, Tinder, and Structural Sexism

1. Https://www.gotinder.com/community-guidelines?locale=en.

2. Studies show that nonnormative sexual preferences often follow a more active consent process (Tripodi 2017). However, our data set shed light on how those actively pursuing virginity were also more likely to articulate consent clearly and frequently. Interestingly, our data indicate that abstinence is only powerful for heterosexual women, that heterosexual and homosexual men felt much more pressure to "want" to engage in hooking up, and that because of this saying "no" was often pushed back upon. Given these preliminary findings, we wish to conduct more research on abstinence groups within colleges.

Chapter 5. Wikipedia: Sign(s) Say Keep Out

1. The data collected and subsequent analysis are specific to English-language Wikipedia.

2. Articles are constantly added and deleted. For the most up-to-date article count, visit Wikipedia directly.

3. Https://searchenginewatch.com/2017/05/11/google-answer-box-strategy-the-dos-and-donts/.

4. Https://searchenginewatch.com/2017/05/11/google-answer-box-strategy-the-dos-and-donts/.

5. Https://en.wikipedia.org/wiki/Wikipedia:How_to_run_an_edit-a-thon.

6. The research for this chapter was conducted by Francesca Tripodi and is part of her PhD dissertation in the Department of Sociology at the University of Virginia. We use the pronoun "I," therefore, when referring to the research itself, which she conducted and analyzed.

7. For an example of what an edit-a-thon event page looks like, see https://en.wikipedia.org/wiki/Wikipedia:Meetup/LA/ArtAndFeminism_2016/LACMA.

8. More than half of Wikipedia's edits are made by "bots"—a software application that runs automated tasks that are relatively simple and structurally repetitive. For those interested in learning more about the role of bots and content moderation, see work by Stuart Geiger at http://stuartgeiger.com/articles/.

9. Many edit-a-thon organizers receive a small amount of funding from the Wikimedia Foundation to host edit-a-thons. Those who do must report back to the foundation on the success of the event. Having a metric like registering ten new Wikipedia editors allows the organization to track new users and also see if they make future edits after the edit-a-thon is over.

10. To become an administrator you must first be nominated or nominate yourself for the position. Then over the course of about a week, current administrators and editors review your editing history and your answers to three main questions that Matt (in his interview) summarized as: 1) Why do you want to be an administrator? 2) What are your best contributions as an editor? 3) How have you dealt with conflict? However, the administrator to close the discussion must make a decision that is consistent with existing discussion—doing otherwise would be considered inappropriate and grounds for removing administrative privileges.

11. She also offered to help me "hide" my original account and make a new one. However, we reasoned that given the public nature of my eventual publications, harassment would likely ensue regardless of my handle.

12. Many feminist and nonfeminist scholars, writing currently about neoliberalism, have made this point that the necessity for collective action is rarely recognized in popular writing and thinking about political issues. Most recently Alex Press (2017) argued this vis-à-vis the issue of sexual harassment, but see also Banet-Weiser and Portwood-Stacer (2017).

13. Https://en.wikipedia.org/wiki/Wikipedia:Notability.

14. Https://en.wikipedia.org/wiki/Deletionism_and_inclusionism_in_Wikipedia.

15. Wikipedia's "rules" are conceptualized within the community as pillars. Broadly speaking these include: 1) Wikipedia is an encyclopedia and not a place for original research, advertising, personal opinions, and so on; 2) Wikipedia articles must be written in a neutral point of view; 3) Wikipedia content is free, so you should not put content up that infringes on copyright; 4) There is a code of

conduct and one should assume that people are acting in good faith; 5) There are no firm rules and perfection is not required. For a more in-depth understanding of these pillars, visit https://en.wikipedia.org/wiki/Help:Five_pillars.

16. Https://en.wikipedia.org/wiki/Wikipedia:Neutral_point_of_view.
17. Https://en.wikipedia.org/wiki/Wikipedia:Notability.
18. Https://en.wikipedia.org/wiki/Wikipedia:Notability_(academics).
19. Https://en.wikipedia.org/wiki/Wikipedia:Five_pillars.
20. Https://en.wikipedia.org/wiki/Wikipedia:Articles_for_deletion.

21. In actuality, anyone can render a decision as to whether an article should be deleted, kept, or merged. However, if a non-administrator closes the case it is labeled as "non-administrator." While anyone can render a decision only an administrator can reverse that decisions. For example, if a page is deleted only an administrator can "un-delete" the page.

22. This is in reference to the earlier process of how a decision is made on an article nominated for deletion.

23. As a reminder, Wikipedia is a completely transparent website. In an effort to protect the confidentiality of those interviewed, I try to remove as many identifiers as possible.

24. The statistics of page views over a ten-day period represents the period of June 13, 2016, to June 22, 2016.

25. The authors have altered both the username as well as the description regarding this woman's contributions to US history to protect confidentiality. Since Wikipedia is an entirely transparent platform, we did this to protect both the user who created the page as well as the user who rendered decisions on her page.

26. These assertion are made though date matching. Street's revision history notes her page was created on the same day as an edit-a-thon designed to increase coverage of African American women on Wikipedia. This event page listed "Sojourner Street" as a potential subjection for creation. Moreover, one can see the username of the person who created Street's page is a variation of the last name of a woman who signed up for the edit-a-thon taking place that day, providing further evidence that Street's page was created in conjunction with an edit-a-thon. When I Googled the name of the person who signed up for the event, her social media accounts and blog posts indicate that she identifies as a Black woman—meaning the incident in question also impacted the gender and racial imbalance of Wikipedia's editors because she has not edited under this username since this event took place.

Bibliography

Aaltonen, Aleksi, and Stephan Seiler. 2015. "Cumulative Growth in User-Generated Content Production: Evidence from Wikipedia." *Management Science* 62(7): 2054–2069.

ABC Media Net. 2005. Daily Press Release, Tuesday, September 27, 2005. http://abcmedianet.com/web/dnr/dispDNR.aspx?id=092705_03.

Adams, Julia, and Hannah Brückner. 2015. "Wikipedia, Sociology, and the Promise and Pitfalls of Big Data." *Big Data and Society* 2(2). https://doi.org/10.1177%2F2053951715614332.

Adams, Julia, Hannah Brückner, and Cambria Naslund. 2019. "Who Counts as a Notable Sociologist on Wikipedia? Gender, Race, and the 'Professor Test.'" *Socius* 5: 1–14.

Adamson, Walter L. 2014. *Hegemony and Revolution: Antonio Gramsci's Political and Social Theory*. New York: Echo Point Books and Media.

Ahlm, Jody. 2017. "Respectable Promiscuity: Digital Cruising in an Era of Queer Liberalism." *Sexualities* 20(3): 364–379.

Alcon, Amy. 2015. "Science Says *Lean In* Is Filled with Flawed Advice, Likely to Hurt Women." *Observer*, 2015. http://observer.com/2015/05/science-says-lean-in-is-filled-with-flawed-advice-likely-to-hurt-women. May 15, 2015. Accessed September 11, 2017.

Alexander, Michelle. 2016. "Why Hillary Clinton Doesn't Deserve the Black Vote." *Atlantic*, February 29, 2016. https://www.thenation.com/article/hillary-clinton-does-not-deserve-black-peoples-votes/. Accessed August 30, 2017.

American Academy of Pediatrics. 2010. Policy Statement: Sexuality, Contraception, and the Media. *Pediatrics*. http://pediatrics.aappublications.org/content/126/3/576. Accessed May 29, 2013.

Andersen, Margaret L. 2014. *Thinking about Women: Sociological Perspectives on Sex and Gender*. 10th ed. New York: Pearson.

Andrews, Helena. 2007. "Rhymes with 'Shashmortion.'" *Politico*, June 6, 2007. https://www.politico.com/story/2007/06/rhymes-with-shmashmortion-004367. Accessed December 20, 2018.

Andrews, Travis M. 2018. "The 'Roe v. Wade' Movie Has an All-Star Conservative Cast and a Bone to Pick with the Media." *Washington Post*, July 16, 2018. https://www.washingtonpost.com/lifestyle/style/the-roe-v-wade-movie-has-an-all-star-conservative-cast-and-a-bone-to-pick-with-the-media/2018/07/16/bb4ab352-8912-11e8-85ae-511bc1146b0b_story.html?utm_term=.5e780e955778. Accessed August 17, 2018.

Ansari, Aziz, and Eric Klinenberg. 2016. *Modern Romance*. New York: Penguin.

Agarwal, Pragya. 2018. "Not Very Likeable: Here Is How Bias Is Affecting Women Leaders." *Forbes*, October 23, 2018. https://www.forbes.com/sites/pragyaagarwaleurope/2018/10/23/not-very-likeable-here-is-how-bias-is-affecting-women-leaders/#32e1830f295f. Accessed December 19, 2018.

Armstrong, Elizabeth A., and Laura Hamilton. 2015. *Paying for the Party: How College Maintains Inequality*. Cambridge, MA: Harvard University Press.

Armstrong, Elizabeth A., Paula England, and A. C. K. Fogarty. 2010. "Orgasm in College Hookups and Relationships." In *Families as They Really Are*, edited by B. J. Risman, 362–377. New York: Norton.

Armstrong, Elizabeth A., Laura Hamilton, and Paula England. 2010. "Is Hooking Up Bad for Young Women?" *Contexts* 9(3): 22–27.

Armstrong, E. A., L. Hamilton, and B. Sweeney. 2006. "Sexual Assault on Campus: A Multi-Level, Integrative Approach to Party Rape." *Social Problems* 53(4): 483–499.

Arruzza, Cinzia, Tithi Battacharya, and Nancy Fraser. 2019. *Feminism for the 99%: A Manifesto*. London: Verso.

Arthur, Kate. 2013. "9 Ways *Game of Thrones* Is Actually Feminist." *Buzzfeed*, April 17. http://www.buzzfeed.com/kateaurthur/9-ways-game-of-thrones-is-actually-feminist#.it28Y9AMO. Accessed August 6, 2020.

Arthurs, Jane. 2003. "*Sex and the City* and Consumer Culture: Remediating Postfeminist Drama." *Feminist Media Studies* 3(1): 83–98.

Associated Press (AP). 1985. "An Episode of *Cagney* Under Fire on Abortion." *New York Times*, November 6, 1985, C26. https://www.nytimes.com/1985/11/06/arts/an-episode-of-cagney-under-fire-on-abortion.html. Accessed July 28, 2018.

Auerbach, David. 2014. "Gaming Journalism Is Over." *Slate*, September 4, 2014. http://www.slate.com/articles/technology/bitwise/2014/09/gamergate_explodes_gaming_journalists_declare_the_gamers_are_over_but_they.html. Accessed July 17, 2015.

Avishai, Orit, Lynne Gerber, and Jennifer Randles. 2012. "The Feminist Ethnographer's Dilemma: Reconciling Progressive Research Agendas with Fieldwork Realities." *Journal of Contemporary Ethnography* 42(4): 394–426.

Balancing Jane. 2015. "I'm a Feminist, and I Still Watch Game of Thrones." *Balancing Jane*, May 19, 2015. http://www.balancingjane.com/2015/05/im-feminist-and-i-still-watch-game-of.html.

Banet-Weiser, Sarah. 2018. *Empowered: Popular Feminism and Popular Misogyny.* Durham: Duke University Press.
Banet-Weiser, Sarah, Rosalind Gill, and Catherine Rottenberg. 2019. "Postfeminism, Popular Feminism, and Neoliberal Feminism? Sarah Banet-Weiser, Rosalind Gill, and Catherine Rottenberg in Conversation." *Feminist Theory* 21(1): 3–24.
Banet-Weiser, Sarah, and Laura Portwood-Stacer. 2017. "The Traffic in Feminism." *Feminist Media Studies* 17(5): 884–888.
Banner, Lois. 2008. "The Creature from the Black Lagoon: Marilyn Monroe and Whiteness." *Cinema Journal* 47(4): 4–29.
Banyard, Kat. 2010. *The Equality Illusion.* London: Faber.
Bates, Laura. 2016. *Everyday Sexism.* London: St. Martin's Griffin.
Baumgardner, J., and A. Richards. 2010. *Manifesta: Young Women, Feminism, and the Future.* 10th anniversary ed. New York: Farrar, Straus & Giroux.
Beale, Lewis. 1992. "Maude's Abortion Fades into History: The TV Networks Can Ill Afford to Make Such a Choice Today." *Chicago Tribune*, November 13, 1992. http://articles.chicagotribune.com/1992-11-13/features/9204130017_1_mothers-as-donna-reed-messy-family-life-maude-findlay/2. Accessed July 25, 2018.
Beck, Ulrich, and Elizabeth Beck-Gernsheim. 2002. *Individualization.* Thousand Oaks: Sage.
Beckert, Jens, and Milan Zafirovski, eds. 2011. *The International Encyclopedia of Economic Sociology.* New York: Routledge.
Behlmer, Rudy, ed. 2018. *Memo from Darryl F. Zanuck.* New York: Grove Press.
Belkin, Lisa. 2003. "The Opt-Out Revolution." *New York Times*, October 26, 2003. https://www.nytimes.com/2003/10/26/magazine/the-opt-out-revolution.html. Accessed April 23, 2019.
Bennetts, Leslie. 2008. "Heigl's Anatomy." *Vanity Fair*, January 2008. https://www.vanityfair.com/news/2008/01/heigl200801. Accessed August 7, 2018.
Beres, Melanie A., and Pantea Farvid. 2010. "Sexual Ethics and Young Women's Accounts of Heterosexual Casual Sex." *Sexualities* 13(3): 377–393.
Bharath, Sreedhar, T., M. P. Narayanan, and H. Nejat-Seyhun. 2009. "Are Women Executives Disadvantaged?" March 9, 2009. Ross School of Business Paper No. 1128. http://papers.ssrn.com/so13/papers.cfm?abstract_id=1276064. Accessed September 14, 2012.
Billson, Anne. 2005. *Buffy the Vampire Slayer.* London: BFI.
Bixby, Scott. 2015. "*Game of Thrones* Is Back—And More Feminist than Ever Before." *Mic*, April 10, 2015. http://mic.com/articles/115172/game-of-thrones-is-back-and-more-feminist-than-ever-before#.eAHiTYlLd. Accessed August 7, 2020.
Blackwell, Courtney, Jeremy Birnholtz, and Charles Abbott. 2015. "Seeing and Being Seen: Co-situation and Impression Formation Using Grindr, a Location Aware Gay Dating App." *New Media and Society* 17(7): 1117–1136.
Blake, Meredith. 2017. "From Dramas Like *Scandal*, to Documentaries Like *Abortion: Stories Women Tell*, the Hot Button Topic Is Evolving on TV." *Los*

Angeles Times, March 31, 2017. http://www.latimes.com/entertainment/tv/la-ca-st-abortion-on-television-20170331-story.html#.

Blau, Francine D., and Lawrence M. Kahn. 2007. "The Gender Pay Gap." *Economists' Voice* 4(4): Article 5.

Blum, Linda, and Ethel Mickey. 2019. "Women Organized Against Sexual Harassment: Protesting Sexual Violence on Campus, Then and Now." In *The Routledge Handbook of Contemporary Feminism*, edited by Tasha Oren and Andrea L. Press, 245–268. London: Routledge.

Bobo, Jacqueline. 1995. *Black Women as Cultural Readers*. New York: Columbia University Press.

The Body Pacifist. 2014. "A Feminist Blogger Always Pays Her Debts—Victories and Failures of *Game of Thrones*." WordPress, July 26, 2014. https://thebodypacifist.wordpress.com/2014/07/26/a-feminist-blogger-always-pays-her-debts-victories-and-failures-of-game-of-thrones/.

Bogle, Donald. 2001. *Toms, Coons, Mulattoes, Mammies, and Bucks: An Interpretive History of Blacks in American Films*. 4th ed. New York: Continuum.

Bogle, Donald, and John Singleton. 2019. *Hollywood Black: The Stars, the Films, the Filmmakers*. Los Angeles: Running Press Adult.

Bolton, Michele Kremen. 2010. *The Third Shift: Managing Hard Choices in Our Careers, Homes, and Lives as Women*. New York: Jossey-Bass.

Bonilla-Silva, Eduardo. 2010. *Racism without Racists: Color-Blind Racism and the Persistence of Racial Inequality in America*. 3rd ed. New York: Rowman & Littlefield.

Bordo, Susan. 1993. *Unbearable Weight: Feminism, Western Culture, and the Body*. Berkeley: University of California Press.

Bordo, Susan. 2009. "Not Just 'a White Girl's Thing': The Changing Face of Food and Body Image Problems." In *Critical Feminist Approaches to Eating Disorders*, edited by Helen Malson and Maree Burns, 46–60. New York: Routledge.

Bordo, Susan. 2017. *The Destruction of Hillary Clinton*. New York: Melville House.

Bourdieu, Pierre. 1977. *Outline of a Theory of Practice*. Translated by Richard Nice. Cambridge: Cambridge University Press.

Bourdieu, Pierre. 1984. *Distinction: A Social Critique of the Judgement of Taste*. Translated by Richard Nice. Cambridge, MA: Harvard University Press.

Bourdieu, Pierre. 2000. *Pascalian Meditations*. Translated by Richard Nice. Stanford: Stanford University Press.

Bovey, Shelley. 1994. *The Forbidden Body: Being Fat Is Not a Sin*. San Francisco: Harper.

boyd, danah. 2007. *Social Network Sites: Public, Private, or What?* https://www.danah.org/papers/KnowledgeTree.pdf.

Boyer, Katie. 2013. "Don't Let the Genre Fool You—Game of Thrones Is Full of Feminist Surprises." *About-Face*, June 7, 2013. https://www.about-face.org/

dont-let-the-genre-fool-you-game-of-thrones-is-full-of-feminist-surprises/. Accessed August 6, 2020.

Bradley, Laura. 2016. "How *Jane the Virgin* Crafted the Perfect Abortion Story Line." *Vanity Fair*, October 24, 2016. https://www.vanityfair.com/hollywood/2016/10/jane-the-virgin-abortion-interview-jennie-snyder-urman. Accessed August 14, 2018.

Braun, Virginia, and Pantea Farvid. 2014. "The 'Sassy Woman; and the 'Performing Man': Heterosexual Casual Sex Advice and the (Re)Constitution of Gendered Subjectivities." *Feminist Media Studies* 14(1): 118–134.

Bravo, Ellen. 2012. http://www.facebook.com/FamilyValuesAtWork.

Brown, Anna, and Eileen Patten. 2017. "The Narrowing, but Persistent, Gender Gap in Pay." April 3, 2017. Pew Research Center Report. http://www.pewresearch.org/fact-tank/2017/04/03/gender-pay-gap-facts/. Accessed April 6, 2017.

Brugnoli-Ensin, Mia. 2014. "The Feminist Paradoxes of *Game of Thrones*." *Her Campus*, May 3, 2014. http://www.hercampus.com/school/u-mass-amherst/feminist-paradoxes-game-thrones. Accessed August 6, 2020.

Bruni, Frank. 2012. "One-Way Wantonness." *New York Times*, March 13, 2012. www.nytimes.com/2012/03/13/opinion/bruni-limbaugh-and-one-way-wantonness.html. Accessed May 29, 2013.

Brunsdon, Charlotte. 2000. *The Feminist, the Housewife, and the Soap Opera*. Oxford: Oxford University Press.

Brunsdon, Charlotte. 2005. "Feminisms, Postfeminism, Martha, Martha, and Nigella." *Cinema Journal* 44(2): 110–116.

Bucholtz, Shawn, and Jed Kolko. 2018. "American Really Is a Nation of Suburbs." *Citylab*, November 14, 2018. https://www.citylab.com/life/2018/11/data-most-american-neighborhoods-suburban/575602/. Accessed July 18, 2019.

Buck, Jerry. 1989. "Jessica's Rescue Highest Rated Show for Past Week." *News-Telegraph, Sulphur Springs, Texas*, May 28, 1989. https://texashistory.unt.edu/ark:/67531/metapth824198/m1/24/. Accessed July 25, 2018.

Bureau of Labor Statistics. 2016. American Time Use Survey. U.S. Department of Labor. https://www.bls.gov/TUS/CHARTS/HOUSEHOLD.HTM. Accessed November 7, 2017.

Burt, Ronald S. 1992. *Structural Holes: The Social Structure of Competition*. Cambridge, MA: Harvard University Press.

Butler, Judith. 2011a. *Bodies That Matter: On the Discursive Limits of Sex*. London: Taylor & Francis.

Butler, Judith. 2011b. *Gender Trouble: Feminism and the Subversion of Identity*. New York: Routledge.

Cancian, Francesca M. 1986. "The Feminization of Love." *Signs* 11(4): 692–709.

Cancian, Francesca M. 1990. *Love in America: Gender and Self-Development*. Cambridge: Cambridge University Press.

Caporimo, Alison. 2018. "Am I Demisexual?" *Seventeen*, October 2, 2018. https://www.seventeen.com/love/a21999166/demisexual-meaning-definition-signs/. Accessed September 4, 2019.

Cavalcante, Andre, Andrea L. Press, and Katherine Sender, eds. 2017. *Feminist Audience Research*. Feminist Media Studies special issue 17(1).

Cerrato, Javier, and Eva Cifre. 2018. "Gender Inequality in Household Chores and Work-Family Balance." *Frontiers in Psychology* 9: 1330. doi:10.3389/fpsyg.2018.01330.

Cerulo, Karen. 2000. "The Rest of the Story: The Sociocultural Patterns of Story Elaboration." *Poetics* 28(1): 28–45.

Chambers, D., L. Steiner, and C. Fleming. 2004. *Women and Journalism*. New York: Routledge.

Champagne, Anthony. 2001. "Interest Groups and Judicial Elections." *Loyola of Los Angeles Law Review* 34(4): 1391–1410. https://heinonline.org/HOL/P?h=hein.journals/1la34&i=1438. Accessed November 29, 2018.

Cheng, William. 2016. "The Long Sexist History of Shrill Women." *Time*, March 23, 2016. http://time.com/4268325/history-calling-women-shrill/. Accessed April 7, 2017.

Chernin, Kim. 1982. *The Obsession: Reflections on the Tyranny of Slenderness*. New York: Harper Colophon Books.

Cills, Hazel. 2017. "Everyone's Trying to Make a Movie about Jane, the Illegal Abortion Collective from the 1970s." *Jezebel*, July 26, 2017. https://jezebel.com/everyones-trying-to-make-a-movie-about-jane-the-illega-1797279836. Accessed August 17, 2018.

Citron, Danielle Keats. 2014. *Hate Crimes in Cyberspace*. Cambridge, MA: Harvard University Press.

Coleman, M. Nicole, Akila A. Reynolds, and Autena Torbati. 2019. "The Relation of Black Oriented Reality Television Consumption and Perceived Realism to the Endorsement of Stereotypes of Black Women." *Psychology of Popular Media Culture*, January 28, 2019. http://dx.doi.org/10.1037/ppm0000223. Accessed August 19, 2019.

Collins, Caitlyn. 2019. *Making Motherhood Work: How Women Manage Careers and Caregiving*. Princeton: Princeton University Press.

Collins, Patricia Hill. 2008. *Black Feminist Thought: Knowledge, Consciousness, and the Politics of Empowerment*. New York: Routledge.

Collins, Patricia Hill, and Sirma Bilge. 2016. *Intersectionality*. London: Polity.

Condit, Celeste Michelle. 1989. "The Rhetorical Limits of Polysemy." *Critical Studies in Mass Communication* 6(2): 103–122.

Coontz, Stephanie. 1997. *The Way We Really Are: Coming to Terms with America's Changing Families*. New York: Basic Books.

Coontz, Stephanie. 2013. "Why Gender Equity Stalled." *New York Times*, October 26, 2013. http://www.nytimes.com/2013/02/17/opinion/sunday/why-gender-equality-stalled.html?pagewanted=all. Accessed August 6, 2020.

Coontz, Stephanie. 2016. *The Way We Never Were: American Families and the Nostalgia Trap*. New York: Basic Books.
Cooper, Marianne. 2013. "For Women Leaders, Likeability and Success Go Hand in Hand." *Harvard Business Review*, April 30, 2013. https://hbr.org/2013/04/for-women-leaders-likability-a. Accessed December 19, 2018.
Coppock, Vicki, Deena Haydon, and Ingrid Richter. 1995. *The Illusions of "Post-feminism": New Women, Old Myths*. London: Taylor & Francis.
Cottom, Tressie McMillan. 2016. "Trickle-Down Feminism Revisited: "Having It All" Is Not a Feminist Theory of Change." *Dissent*, April 21, 2016. https://www.dissentmagazine.org/blog/anne-marie-slaughter-trickle-down-feminism-unfinished-business-review. Accessed August 2, 2019.
Couldry, Nick. 2011. "Class and Contemporary Forms of 'Reality' Production or, Hidden Injuries of Class." In *Reality Television and Class*, edited by H. Wood and B. Skeggs, 33–44. London: Palgrave Macmillan.
Crenshaw, Kimberlé. 1989. "Demarginalizing the Intersection of Race and Sex: A Black Feminist Critique of Antidiscrimination Doctrine, Feminist Theory and Antiracist Politics." *University of Chicago Legal Forum* 1989(1): Article 8. http://chicagounbound.uchicago.edu/uclf/vol1989/iss1/8. Accessed August 8, 2020.
Crenshaw, Kimberlé, Heil Gotanda, Gary Peller, and Kendall Thomas, eds. 1996. *Critical Race Theory*. New York: New Press.
Custen, George F. 1997. *Twentieth Century's Fox: Darryl F. Zanuck and the Culture of Hollywood*. New York: Basic Books.
D'Acci, Julie. 1984. *Defining Women: The Case of Television and Cagney and Lacey*. Chapel Hill: University of North Carolina Press.
Dandridge, Dorothy, and Earl Conrad. 2000. *Everything and Nothing: The Dorothy Dandridge Tragedy*. New York: Harper.
Day, Kary, and Tammy Keys. 2009. "Anorexia/Bulimia as Resistance and Conformity in Pro-Ana and Pro-Mia Virtual Conversations." In *Critical Feminist Approaches to Eating Disorders*, edited by Helen Malson and Maree Burns, 87–96. New York: Routledge.
Davis, Angela. 1983. *Women, Race, and Class*. New York: Vintage.
De Benedictis, Sara, Shani Orgad, and Catherine Rottenberg. 2019. "@MeToo, Popular Feminism, and the News: A Content Analysis of UK Newspaper Coverage." *European Journal of Cultural Studies* 22(5–6): 718–738.
De Moraes, L. 2012. "*Jersey Shore* Will End This Season." *Washington Post*, August 30, 2012. https://www.washingtonpost.com/blogs/tv-column/post/jersey-shore-will-end-after-this-season/2012/08/30/8a0d44ae-f2bd-11e1-adc6-87dfa8eff430_blog.html. Accessed August 7, 2020.
Debold, Elizabeth. 2012. "Too Many Shades of Grey." *Huffington Post*. http://www.huffingtonpost.com/elizabeth-debold/50-shades-of-grey_b_1459689.html. Accessed August 7, 2020.
Deery, June, and Andrea L. Press. 2017. *Media and Class: TV, Film, and Digital Culture*. London: Routledge.

DelVecchio, Monica. 2012. "Anti-Feminist Ideals in Fifty Shades of Grey." *Her Circle: A Magazine of Women's Creative Arts and Activism*, May 2, 2012. http://www.hercircleezine.com/2012/05/02/anti-feminist-ideals-in-fifty-shades-of-grey/. Accessed August 7, 2020.

Denis, Ann. 2008. "Intersectional Analysis: A Contribution of Feminism to Sociology." *International Sociology* 23(5): 677–694.

Dicker, Rory, and Alison Piepmeier, eds. 2003. *Catching a Wave: Reclaiming Feminism for the 21st Century*. Boston: Northeastern University Press.

DiGregario, Luciano. 2006. "*Buffy the Vampire Slayer*." *Screen Education* 42: 90–93.

DiMaggio, Paul. 1982. "Cultural Entrepreneurship in Nineteenth-Century Boston: The Creation of an Organizational Base for High Culture in America." *Media, Culture, and Society* 4: 33–50.

DiMaggio, Paul. 1997. "Culture and Cognition." *Annual Review of Sociology* 23(1): 263–287.

Dishman, Lydia. 2019. "Here's Evidence That the Gendered Wage Gap and Glass Ceiling Are Real." *Fast Company*, April 17, 2019. https://www.fastcompany.com/90335734/heres-evidence-that-the-glass-ceiling-and-gender-wage-gap-are-real. Accessed August 1, 2019.

Ditum, Sarah. 2015. "It's Time to Stop Defending the Rape Scenes in *Game of Thrones*." *New Statesman*, May 19, 2015. http://www.newstatesman.com/culture/2015/05/it-s-time-stop-defending-rape-scenes-game-thrones. Accessed August 7, 2020.

Docketerman, Eliana. 2014. "*Game of Thrones*: More Feminist than You Think." *Time*, June 14, 2014. http://time.com/2865626/game-of-thrones-more-feminist-than-you-think/.

Docketerman, Eliana. 2015. "*Game of Thrones*' Woman Problem Is about More than Sexual Assault." *Time*, June 11, 2015. http://time.com/3917236/game-of-thrones-woman-problem-feminism/.

Douglas, Susan J., and Meredith Michaels. 2004. *The Mommy Myth: The Idealization of Motherhood and How It Has Undermined Women*. New York: Free Press.

Douglas, Susan J. 2010. *Enlightened Sexism: The Seductive Message That Feminism's Work Is Done*. New York: Times Books.

Dow, Bonnie. 1996. *Prime-Time Feminism*. Philadelphia: University of Pennsylvania Press.

Dow, Dawn Marie. 2019. *Mothering While Black: Boundaries and Burdens of Middle-Class Parenthood*. Berkeley: University of California Press.

Duggan, Maeve. 2014. "Online Harassment." *Pew Research Center*. https://www.pewresearch.org/internet/2014/10/22/online-harassment/. Accessed August 17, 2020.

Dworkin, Andrea. 1981. *Pornography: Men Possessing Women*. New York: Perigee Books.

Dworkin, Andrea, and Catherine A. MacKinnon. 1988. *Pornography and Civil Rights: A New Day for Women's Equality*. Minneapolis: Organizing Against Pornography.

Eagly, A. H., R. D. Ashmore, M. G. Makhijani, and L. C. Longo. 1991. "What Is beautiful Is Good, but . . . : A Meta-Analytic Review of Research on the Physical Attractiveness Stereotype." *Psychological Bulletin* 110: 109–128.
Eckert, Stine, and Linda Steiner. 2013. "Wikipedia's Gender Gap." In *Media Disparity: A Gender Battleground*, edited by C. L. Armstrong, 87–98. Lanham: Lexington Books.
Ehrenreich, Barbara. 1983. *The Hearts of Men: American Dreams and the Flight from Commitment*. New York: Anchor.
Elfity. 2013. "Shocker (Not): Women Like *Game of Thrones*." *Persephone Magazine*, June 7, 2013. http://persephonemagazine.com/2013/06/shocker-not-women-like-game-of-thrones/. Accessed August 7, 2020.
Eliasoph, Nina. 1998. *Avoiding Politics: How Americans Produce Apathy in Everyday Life*. Cambridge: Cambridge University Press.
Eppolito, Sophia. 2017. "Here's What Matt Damon Said about #MeToo and the Backlash That Followed." *Boston Globe*, December 19, 2017. https://www.bostonglobe.com/arts/2017/12/19/here-what-matt-damon-said-about-metoo-and-backlash-that-followed/PNOjcVddMV9rQ13eqsDm4I/story.html. Accessed December 19, 2018.
Fairclough, K. 2008. "Fame Is a Losing Game." *Genders* 48: 1–13.
Falotico, Corifal. 2014. "10 Reasons Why Arya Stark Is the Baddest Bitch in Westeros." *Feminist Feline*, June 20, 2014. http://www.thefeministfeline.com/10-reasons-why-arya-stark-is-the-baddest-bitch-in-westeros/.
Faludi, Susan. 1996. *Backlash: The Undeclared War Against American Women*. New York: Crown.
Faludi, Susan. 1999. *Stiffed: The Betrayal of the American Man*. New York: Perennial Books.
Fandoms and Feminism. 2013. "Cersei Lannister Is Not a Feminist, but Is Still Interesting from a Feminist Perspective." *Tumblr*, April 27, 2013. http://fandomsandfeminism.tumblr.com/post/49056490672/cersei-lannister-is-not-a-feminist-but-is-still.
Farvid, Pantea, and Virginia Braun. 2016. "Unpacking the 'Pleasures' and 'Pains' of Heterosexual Casual Sex: Beyond Singular Understandings." *Journal of Sex Research* 54(1): 1–18.
Farvid, Pantea, Virginia Braun, and Casey Rowney. 2017. " 'No Girl Wants to Be Called a Slut!': Women, Heterosexual Casual Sex and the Sexual Double Standard." *Journal of Gender Studies* 26(5): 544–560.
Fausto-Sterling, Anne. 2012. *Sex/Gender: Biology in a Social World*. London: Routledge.
Favaro, Laura, and Rosalind Gill. 2018. "Feminism Rebranded: Women's Magazines Online and the Return of the F-word." *Revista Dígitos* 4: 37–66.
Fenton, Natalie. 2016. *Digital Political Radical*. London: Polity.
Ferber, Marianne A. 1986. "Citations: Are They an Objective Measure of Scholarly Merit?" *Signs: Journal of Women in Culture and Society* 11(2): 381–389.

Filipacchi, Amanda. 2013. "Wikipedia's Sexism Toward Female Novelists." *New York Times* Opinion. https://www.nytimes.com/2013/04/28/opinion/sunday/wikipedias-sexism-toward-female-novelists.html. Accessed July 3, 2020.

Flaherty, Colleen. 2016. "Bias Against Female Instructors." *Inside Higher Ed*, January 11. https://www.insidehighered.com/news/2016/01/11/new-analysis-offers-more-evidence-against-student-evaluations-teaching#.WOJ3UwDwUdc.mailto. Accessed April 3, 2017.

Flanagan, Caitlin. 2018. "The Humiliation of Aziz Ansari." *Atlantic*, January 14. https://www.theatlantic.com/entertainment/archive/2018/01/the-humiliation-of-aziz-ansari/550541/. Accessed July 23, 2018.

Franke, Caroline. 2018. "The Controversy Around Babe.net's Aziz Ansari Story, Explained." January 17, 2018. https://www.vox.com/culture/2018/1/17/16897440/aziz-ansari-allegations-babe-me-too. Accessed July 23, 2018.

Fraser, Nancy. 2009. "Feminism, Capitalism, and the Cunning of History." *New Left Review* 56: 97–117.

Fraser, Nancy. 2016. "Contradictions of Capitalism and Care." *New Left Review* 100: 99–117.

Freeman, Hadley. 2014. "Even If 'Bossy' Could Be Banned, There Are Far Better Ways to Boost Girls' Self-Esteem." *Guardian*, March 11, 2014. http://www.theguardian.com/commentisfree/2014/mar/11/bossy-banned-boost-girls-self-esteem-facebook-sheryl-sandberg-beyonce. Accessed July 28, 2014.

Friedan, Betty. 1963. *The Feminine Mystique*. New York: Norton.

Friedan, Betty. 1998 [1981]. *The Second Stage*. Cambridge, MA: Harvard University Press.

Gamson, Joshua. 2017. *Modern Families: Stories of Extraordinary Journeys to Kinship*. New York: New York University Press.

Gandy, Imani. 2014. "Black Women Are Already Leaning-In." *Rewire News*, September 18, 2014. https://rewire.news/article/2014/09/18/black-women-already-leaning/. Accessed August 2, 2019.

Gardiner, B., M. Mansfield, I. Anderson, J. Holder, D. Louter, and M. Ulmanu. 2016. The Dark Side of *Guardian* Comments." *Guardian*. https://www.theguardian.com/technology/2016/apr/12/the-dark-side-of-guardian-comments. Accessed September 29, 2016.

Gerhard, Jane F. 2001. *Desiring Revolution: Second-Wave Feminism and the Rewriting of American Sexual Thought*. New York: Columbia University Press.

Gerson, Kathleen. 1985. *Hard Choices: How Women Decide about Work, Career, and Motherhood*. Berkeley: University of California Press.

Gerson, Kathleen. 1993. *No Man's Land: Men's Changing Commitments to Family and Work*. New York: Basic Books.

Gerson, Kathleen. 2009. "Changing Lives, Resistant Institutions: A New Generation Negotiates Gender, Work and Family Change." *Sociological Forum* 24(4): 735–753.

Gerson, Kathleen. 2011. *The Unfinished Revolution: Coming of Age in a New Era of Gender, Work and Family*. New York: Oxford University Press.
Giles, J. 2005. "Special Report: Internet Encyclopedias Go Head to Head." *Nature* 438: 900–901.
Gill, Rosalind. 2003. "From Sexual Objectification to Sexual Subjectification: The Resexualization of Women's Bodies in the Media." *Feminist Media Studies* 3(1): 100–105.
Gill, Rosalind. 2007. 'Postfeminist Media Culture: Elements of a Sensibility,' *European Journal of Cultural Studies*, 10: 147–66.
Gill, Rosalind, and E. Herdieckerhoff. 2006. "Rewriting the Romance: New Femininities in Chick Lit?" *Feminist Media Studies* 6(4): 487–504.
Gill, Rosalind, and Scharff, Christina, eds. 2011. *New Femininities: Postfeminism, Neoliberalism and Subjectivity*. Basingstoke: Palgrave Macmillan.
Gill, Rosalind, and Katie Toms. 2019. "Trending Now: Feminism, Postfeminism, Sexism, and Misogyny." In *Journalism, Gender, and Power*, edited by Cynthia Carter, Linda Steiner, and Stuart Allen, 97–112. New York: Routledge.
Gilligan, Carol. 1982. *In a Different Voice: Psychological Theory and Women's Development*. Cambridge, MA: Harvard University Press.
Gillis, Stacy, Gillian Howie, and Rebecca Munford, eds. 2004. *Third-Wave Feminism: A Critical Exploration*. Basingstoke: Palgrave Macmillan.
Gitlin, Todd. 1978. "Media Sociology: The Dominant Paradigm." *Theory and Society* 6(2): 205–253.
Glover, Emily. 2018. "Yes, It Really Is Harder Now for Families to Get By on a Single Income." *Motherly*. https://www.mother.ly/news/youre-not-imagining-it-its-harder-for-families-to-make-do-on-single-incomes. Accessed December 26, 2018.
Glucksmann, M. A. 2005. "Shifting Boundaries and Interconnections: Extending the *Total Social Organization of Labour*." In *A New Sociology of Work?*, edited by J. Parry, R. Taylor, L. Pettinger, and M. Glucksmann. Oxford: Blackwell.
Glucksmann, Miriam A. 2009. "Call Configurations: Varieties of Call Centre and Divisions of Labour." *Work, Employment and Society* 18(4): 795–811.
Goffman, Erving. 1959. *The Presentation of Self in Everyday Life*. New York: Anchor.
Goldberg, Abbie E. 2013. "'Doing' and 'Undoing' Gender: The Meaning and Division of Housework among Same-Sex Couples." *Journal of Marriage and Family Theory and Review* 5: 85–104.
Goldberg, Michele. 2015. "Feminist Writers Are So Besieged by Online Abuse That Some Have Begun to Retire." *Washington Post*, February 20, 2015. http://www.washingtonpost.com/opinions/online-feminists-increasingly-ask-are-the-psychic-costs-too-much-to-bear/2015/02/19/3dc4ca6c-b7dd-11e4-a200-c008a01a6692_story.html. Accessed July 17, 2015.
Goldman, Robert. 1992. *Reading Ads Socially*. London: Routledge.

Goodman, Ellen. 2008. "In Movies, She Keeps the Baby." *Washington Post Writers Group*, January 3, 2008.

Grady, Constance. 2016. "How *Jane the Virgin* and *Crazy Ex-Girlfriend*'s Understated Abortion Plots Show the Value of Choice." *Voxx*, November 15, 2016. https://www.vox.com/culture/2016/11/15/13627692/jane-the-virgin-crazy-ex-girlfriend-abortion-choice. Accessed August 14, 2018.

Gramsci, Antonio. 2011. *Prison Notebooks*. vols. 1–3. Translated by Joseph Buttigieg. New York: Columbia University Press.

Granovetter, Mark S. 1973. "The Strength of Weak Ties." *American Journal of Sociology* 78(6): 1360–1380.

Gray, Billie. 2010. "*Jersey Shore* Men: Accidental Gay Icons." *Guest of a Guest*. http://guestofaguest.com/media/-shore-men-accidental-gay-icons. Accessed October 16, 2017.

Gray, Herman S. 1995. *Watching Race and the Struggle for "Blackness."* Minneapolis: University Minnesota Press.

Gray, Herman S. 2005. *Cultural Moves: African Americans and the Politics of Representation*. Berkeley: University of California Press.

Grindstaff, Laura. 2002. *The Money Shot: Trash, Class, and the Making of TV Talk Shows*. Chicago: University of Chicago Press.

Grindstaff, Laura. 2011. From *Jerry Springer* to *Jersey Shore*: The Cultural Politics of Class in/on US Reality Programming." In *Reality Television and Class*, edited by H. Wood and B. Skeggs, 197–209. London: Palgrave Macmillan.

Grindstaff, Laura, and Andrea L. Press. 2014. "Too Little but Not Too Late: Sociological Contributions to Feminist Media Studies." In *Media Sociology: A Reappraisal*, edited by Silvio Waisbord, 151–167. London: Polity.

Guttmacher Institute. 2018. "Requirements for Ultrasound: State Laws and Policies." https://www.guttmacher.org/state-policy/explore/requirements-ultrasound. Accessed December 20, 2018.

Guttmacher Institute. 2019. "United States Abortion." https://www.guttmacher.org/united-states/abortion. Accessed June 9, 2019.

Halberstam, Judith. 1998. *Female Masculinity*. Chapel Hill: Duke University Press.

Halberstam, Judith. 2011. *The Queer Art of Failure*. Chapel Hill: Duke University Press.

Hall, Elaine J., and Marnie Salupo Rodriguez. 2003. "The Myth of Postfeminism." *Gender and Society* 17(3): 878–902.

Hall, Jane. 1985. "Cagney and Lacey Creators Barbara Corday and Barney Rosenzweig Mix Cops, Controversy and Marriage." *People*, November 25, 1985. https://people.com/archive/cagney-lacey-creators-barbara-corday-and-barney-rosenzweig-mix-cops-controversy-and-marriage-vol-24-no-22/. Accessed July 25, 2018.

Halliwell, Katie. 2016. "The 11 Most Honest Portrayals of Abortion on TV." *Indie wire*, June 28, 2016. https://www.indiewire.com/2016/06/abortion-tv-portrayal-scandal-girls-friday-night-lights-1201700144/. Accessed August 16, 2018.
Haralovich, Mary Beth. 1989. "Sitcoms and Suburbia: Positioning the 1950s Homemaker." *Quarterly Review of Film and Television* 11(1): 61–83.
Haralovich, Mary Beth, and Andrea L. Press, eds. 2018. *The New Feminist Television Studies: Queries into Postfeminist Television*. Moldova: Lambert Academic.
Hargittai, Eszter. 2002. "Second-Level Digital Divide: Differences in People's Online Skills." *First Monday* 7(4): http://firstmonday.org/article/view/942/864.
Hargittai, Eszter, and Aaron Shaw. 2015. "Mind the Skills Gap: The Role of Internet Know-How and Gender in Differentiated Contributions to Wikipedia." *Information, Communication and Society* 18(4): 424–442.
Harris, Aisha. 2018. "She Founded Me Too. Now She Wants to Move Past the Trauma." *New York Times*, October 15, 2018. https://www.nytimes.com/2018/10/15/arts/tarana-burke-metoo-anniversary.html. Accessed December 21, 2018.
Hartman, Mitchell. 2017. "How Women Raised the Median Family Income." April 11, 2017. https://www.marketplace.org/2017/04/11/economy/ive-always-wondered-family-income-women-and-work. Accessed December 26, 2018.
Haskell, Molly. 1974. *From Reverence to Rape: The Treatment of Women in the Movies*. New York: Holt, Rinehart and Winston.
Haslam, Alexander S., and Michelle K. Ryan. 2008. "The Road to the Glass Cliff: Differences in the Perceived Suitability of Men and Women for Leadership Positions in Succeeding and Failing Organizations." *Leadership Quarterly* 19(5): 530–546.
Hays, Sharon. 1998. *The Cultural Contradictions of Motherhood*. New Haven: Yale University Press.
Hemmings, Clare. 2005. "Invoking Affect: Cultural Theory and the Ontological Turn." *Cultural Studies* 19(5): 548–567.
Hemmings, Clare. 2009. "Telling Feminist Stories." *Feminist Theory* 6(2): 115–139.
Herman, Alison. 2013. "The *Game of Thrones* Universe Is Violent and Sexist—And That's Not a Bad Thing." *Favorwire*, July 31, 2013. http://flavorwire.com/406994/the-game-of-thrones-universe-is-violent-and-sexist-and-thats-not-a-bad-thing.
Herzog, Herta. 1943. "What Do We Really Know about Daytime Serial Listeners." *Radio Research* (1942): 3–33.
Hewlett, Sylvia Ann, and Norma Vite-Leon. 2001. *High-Achieving Women*. New York: National Parenting Association.
Hickman, Jessica. 2015. "George R. R. Martin Has Feminist Reason Behind *Game of Thrones*' Rape." *She Knows*, June 3, 2015. http://www.sheknows.

com/entertainment/articles/1085574/george-rr-martin-has-feminist-reason-behind-game-of-thrones-rape.
Hochschild, Arlie. 1979. *The Managed Heart: The Commercialization of Human Feeling*. Berkeley: University of California Press.
Hochschild, Arlie. 1989. *The Second Shift: Working Families and the Revolution at Home*. Revised edition. New York: Penguin Books.
Hochschild, Arlie. 1994. "The Commercial Spirit of Intimate Life and the Abduction of Feminism: Signs from Women's Advice Books." *Theory, Culture and Society* 11(2): 1–24. https://doi.org/10.1177/026327694011002001.
Hochschild, Arlie. 2003. *The Commercialization of Intimate Life*. Berkeley: University of California Press.
Hochschild, Arlie, with Anne Machung. 2012. *The Second Shift*. New York: Penguin.
Hogeland, Lisa Maria. 2001. "Against Generational Thinking, or Some Things That 'Third-Wave' Feminism Isn't." *Women's Studies in Communication* 24(1): 107.
Hoobler, Jenny M., Sandy J. Wayne, and Grace Lemmon. 2009. "Boss' Perception of Family-Work Conflict and Women's Promotability: Glass-Ceiling Effects." *Academy of Management Journal* 52(5): 939–957.
hooks, bell. 2006. *Outlaw Culture: Resisting Representations*. New York: Routledge.
Hopper, Becky. 2015. "Why Feminist Critics of *Game of Thrones* Are Wrong." *Huffington Post*, February 6, 2015. http://www.huffingtonpost.co.uk/becky-hopper/game-of-thrones_b_7486226.html.
Horkheimer, Max. 2002. *Critical Theory: Selected Essays*. Translated by Matthew J. O'Connell and others. New York: Continuum.
Horkheimer, Max, and Theodor W. Adorno. 2002. *Dialectic of Enlightenment*. Translated by Edmund Jephcott. New York: Continuum.
Houvouras, Shannon, and J. Scott Carter. 2008. "The F Word: College Students' Definitions of a Feminist." *Sociological Forum* 23(2): 234–256.
Hudson, John. 2010. "Gay Teen Suicide Sparks Debate Over Cyber Bullying." *Atlantic Wire*. http://www.theatlanticwire.com/national/2010/10/gay-teen-suicide-sparks-debate-over-cyber-bullying/22829/.
Hunter, A. 2012. "Dr. Drew: *50 Shades of Grey* Pathological, Poorly Written." *WTOP*, May 22, 2012. www.wtop.com/267/2874733/Dr-Drew-50-Shades-of-Grey-pathological-poorly-written. Accessed May 29, 2013.
Jackson, Sarah. 2019. "New Image Emerges of Felicity Huffman in Prison." *NBC News*, October 20, 2019. https://www.nbcnews.com/news/us-news/new-image-emerges-felicity-huffman-prison-n1069171. Accessed November 4, 2019.
Jacobs, Lea. 1995. *The Wages of Sin: Censorship and the Fallen Woman Film 1928–1942*. Berkeley: University of California Press.
Jacobs, Matthew. 2017. "10 Years Later, the First Season of *Desperate Housewives* Is Still a Television Touchstone." *Huffington Post*, May 12, 2012. http://www.huffingtonpost.com/2014/10/03/desperate-housewives-season-1-anniversary_n_5793322.html. Accessed July 19, 2015.

Jefferson, Whitney. 2012. "Snooki and JWoww Claim That Mike 'The Situation' Sorrentino Is Gay." *Huffington Post*, February 8, 2012. https://www.buzzfeed.com/whitneyjefferson/snooki-and-jwoww-claim-that-mike-the-situations?utm_term=.by6OLkdVb#.qbVVMBE0g. Accessed September 27, 2017.

Jemielniak, Dariusz. 2014. *Common Knowledge? An Ethnography of Wikipedia*. 1st ed. Stanford: Stanford University Press.

Jermyn, Deborah. 2009. *Sex and the City*. Detroit: Wayne State University Press.

Jessica. 2007. "Now That Her Paycheck Has Cleared, Katherine Heigl Calls *Knocked Up* 'a Little Sexist.'" https://jezebel.com/329085/now-that-her-paycheck-has-cleared-katherine-heigl-calls-knocked-up-sexist. Accessed August 7, 2018.

Johnson-Palomaki, Sarah R. 2017. "Hybridizing Feminism in and through Popular Culture." Paper presented at the American Sociological Association Annual Meeting, Montreal.

Johnson-Palomaki, Sarah R. Forthcoming. "Hybridizing Feminism: *Game of Thrones* Reception and Feminist Discourse Construction." Manuscript in preparation.

Johnson, Stephanie K., and David R. Hekman. 2016. "Women and Minorities Are Penalized for Pushing Workplace Diversity." *Harvard Business Review*, March 23, 2016. https://hbr.org/2016/03/women-and-minorities-are-penalized-for-promoting-diversity. Accessed April 7, 2017.

Kamenetz, Anya. 2016. "Why Female Professors Get Lower Ratings." *National Public Radio*, January 25, 2016. http://www.npr.org/sections/ed/2016/01/25/463846130/why-women-professors-get-lower-ratings. Accessed April 6, 2017.

Kearney, Mary Celeste. 2006. *Girls Make Media*. London: Routledge.

Kessler, Jim. 2005. "The Demographics of Abortion: The Great Divide between Abortion Rhetoric and Reality." Third Way Issue Brief, August 30, 2005. http://content.thirdway.org/publications/17/Third_Way_Policy_Memo_-_The_Demographics_of_Abortion.pdf. Accessed November 27, 2018.

Keyham, Rochelle. 2013. "Daenerys Targaryen: Feminism for the Iron Throne." *HBO Watch*, May 29, 2013. http://hbowatch.com/danaerys-targaryen-feminism-for-the-iron-throne/.

Khazan, Olga. 2017. "Why Do Women Bully Each Other at Work?" *Atlantic*, September 2017. https://www.theatlantic.com/magazine/archive/2017/09/the-queen-bee-in-the-corner-office/534213/. Accessed December 17, 2018.

Kimmel, Michael. 1996. *Manhood in America: A Cultural History*. New York: Free Press.

Kimmel, Michael. 2009. *Guyland: The Perilous World Where Boys Become Men*. New York: Harper.

Kimmel, Michael, and Gloria Steinem. 2014. "'Yes' Is Better than 'No.'" *New York Times* September 4, 2014. https://www.nytimes.com/2014/09/05/opinion/michael-kimmel-and-gloria-steinem-on-consensual-sex-on-campus.html. Accessed September 18, 2018.

King, Jason. 2017. *Faith with Benefits: Hookup Culture on Catholic Campuses.* New York: Oxford.

Kingston, Maxine Hong. 2015. *The Woman Warrior.* New York: Picador.

Kitzinger, Jean. 2004. *Framing Abuse: Media Influence and Public Understanding of Sexual Violence Against Children.* London: Pluto Press.

Klein, Amanda Ann. 2014. "Abject Femininity and Compulsory Masculinity on *Jersey Shore.*" In *Reality Gendervision: Sexuality and Gender on Transatlantic Reality Television*, edited by Brenda Weber, 350–400. Bloomington: Indiana University Press.

Kliff, Sarah. 2018. "A Stunning Chart Shows the True Cause of the Gendered Wage Gap: The Gendered Wage Gap Is Really a Childcare Penalty." *Voxx*, February 19, 2018. https://www.vox.com/2018/2/19/17018380/gender-wage-gap-childcare-penalty. Accessed December 10, 2018.

Koedt, Ann. 1970. *The Myth of the Vaginal Orgasm.* Somerville: New England Free Press.

Kolko, Jed. 2015. "How Suburban Are Big American Cities?" *FiveThirtyEight*, May 21, 2015. https://fivethirtyeight.com/features/how-suburban-are-big-american-cities/. Accessed December 17, 2018.

Konneker, Zoie. 2019. "*Workin' Moms* Disappoints in Third Season." September 18, 2019. http://nique.net/entertainment/2019/09/18/workin-moms-disappoints-in-third-season/. Accessed September 19, 2019.

Konnikova, Maria. 2014. "Lean Out: The Dangers for Women Who Negotiate." *New Yorker*, June 10, 2014. https://www.newyorker.com/science/maria-konnikova/lean-out-the-dangers-for-women-who-negotiate. Accessed September 11, 2017.

Konrad, Alison M., and Yang Yang. 2012. "Is Using Work-Life Interface Benefits a Career-Limiting Move? An Examination of Women, Men, Lone Parents, and Parents with Partners." *Journal of Organizational Behavior* 33: 1095–1193.

Kramer, Andrea S., and Alton B. Harris. 2019a. *It's Not You, It's the Workplace: Women's Conflict at Work and the Bias That Built It.* London: Nicholas Brealey, John Murray Press.

Kramer, Andrea S., and Alton B. Harris. 2019b. "Women 'Don't Ask' Is a Myth: Two Gender Equality Experts Say Women Aren't Getting Ahead, and It's Because of How Workplaces Are Set Up." *Business Insider*. August 27, 2019. https://www.businessinsider.com/women-advance-less-because-how-workplace-culture-is-set-up-2019-8. Accessed December 21, 2019.

Kristeva, Julia. 1982. *Powers of Horror: An Essay on Abjection.* Translated by Leon S. Roudiez. New York: Columbia University Press.

Kumar, Priya. 2015. "New Mothers Have a Third Shift—on Facebook." *Time*, March 25, 2015. https://time.com/3758085/third-shift-social-media/. Accessed November 4, 2019.

Kurp, Josh. 2016. "Katherine Heigl Thinks It Was 'Dumb' of Her to Call *Knocked Up* 'a Little Sexist.'" *UpRoxx*, April 20, 2016. https://uproxx.com/movies/katherine-heigl-knocked-up-sexist/. Accessed August 7, 2018.

Kurtulus, Fidan Ana, and Donald Tomaskovic-Devey. 2012. "Do Female Top Managers Help Women to Advance? A Panel Study Using EEO-1 Records." *Annals of the American Academy of Political and Social Science* 639(1): 173–197. doi:10.1177/0002716211418445. Accessed January 28, 2019.

Laclau, Ernesto, and Chantal Mouffe. 2014. *Hegemony and Socialist Strategy: Towards a Radical Democratic Politics*. 2nd ed. London: Verso.

Laghate, Gaurav. 2018. "Television Remains the Choice of the Masses Even in Digital Times." *Economic Times* July 23, 2018. https://economictimes.indiatimes.com/industry/media/entertainment/television-remains-the-choice-of-the-masses-even-in-digital-times/articleshow/65097493.cms?from=mdr.

Lakoff, Robin Tolmach. 2017. *Context Counts: Papers on Language, Gender, and Power*. Edited by Laurel Sutton. Oxford: Oxford University Press.

Lam, Shyong (Tony) K., Anuradha Uduwage, Zhenhua Dong, Shilad Sen, David R. Musicant, Loren Terveen, and John Riedl. 2011. "WP: Clubhouse: An Exploration of Wikipedia's Gender Imbalance." In *Proceedings of the 7th International Symposium on Wikis and Open Collaboration*, 1–10. New York: ACM.

Lamont, Michele. 1992. *Money, Morals, and Manners*. Chicago: University of Chicago Press.

Laureau, Annette. 2003. *Unequal Childhoods: Class, Race, and Family Life*. Berkeley: University of California Press.

Laurie, Liz. 2015. "The Most Feminist (Television) Show on Earth." *Clyde Fitch Report*, July 24, 2015. http://www.clydefitchreport.com/2015/07/feminism-women-television/.

Lenhart, Amanda. 2015. "Teens, Social Media, and Technology: Overview 2015." http://www.pewinternet.org/2015/04/09/teens-social-media-technology-2015/. Accessed September 14, 2016.

Leopold, Thomas, Jan Skopek, and Florian Schulz. 2018. "Gender Convergence in Household Time: A Life Course and Cohort Perspective." *Sociological Science* 5: 281–303.

Lerner, Cliff. 2017a. *Explosive Growth*. New York: Clifford Ventures.

Lerner, Cliff. 2017b. "5 Genius Things Tinder Did to Achieve Explosive Growth." *Entrepreneur Handbook*, November 30, 2017. https://entrepreneurshandbook.co/5-genius-things-tinder-did-to-achieve-explosive-growth-36c840e061d3. Accessed September 28, 2018.

Lerner, Gerda. 1986. *The Creation of Patriarchy*. vol. 1. Oxford: Oxford Paperbacks.

Levkoff, Logan. 2011. "Logan Levkoff on *The Today Show—Fifty Shades of Grey*." *You Tube*. www.youtube.com/watch?v=TwOF_tor4q4. Accessed May 29, 2013.

Liebowitz, Cara. 2015. "Let Them Eat Cake: On Being Demisexual." *Everyday Sexism*. https://everydayfeminism.com/2015/02/let-them-eat-cake-on-being-demisexual/. Accessed September 4, 2019.

Lithwick, Dahlia. 2018. "Christine Blasey Ford's Timing Isn't Suspect." *Slate*, September 17, 2018. https://slate.com/news-and-politics/2018/09/christine-blasey-ford-brett-kavanaugh-accusation-timing.html. Accessed December 21, 2018.

Livingstone, Sonia. 2009. "On the Mediation of Everything." *Journal of Communication* 59: 1–18.

Lord, Emma. 2016. "What Does Demi-Sexual Mean? Here Are 6 Signs That You Might Identify as Demi-Sexual." *Bustle*, April 18, 2016. https://www.bustle.com/articles/155277-what-does-demisexual-mean-here-are-6-signs-that-you-may-identify-as-demisexual. Accessed September 4, 2019.

Lotz, Amanda D. 2006. *Redesigning Women: Television After the Network Era*. Urbana: University of Illinois Press.

Luo, Wei, Julia Adams, and Hannah Brückner. 2018. "The Ladies Vanish?" *Comparative Sociology* 17(5): 519–556.

Luther, Catherine A., Carolyn Ringer Lepre, and Naeemah Clark. 2018. *Diversity in U.S. Mass Media*. London: John Wiley and Sons.

MacDonald, Gina F., and Andrew F. MacDonald, ed. 2003. *Jane Austen on Screen*. Cambridge: Cambridge University Press.

Madani, Kimia. 2015. "Amazing Girl Power Moments from *Game of Thrones*." *Livingly*, July 28, 2015. http://www.livingly.com/Livingly+Girl+Power/articles/t4rg9vxnGEM/Amazing+Girl+Power+Moments+Game+Thrones.

Malson, Helen, and Maree Burns, eds. 2009. *Critical Feminist Approaches to Eating Disorders*. New York: Routledge.

Maltby, Kate. 2015. "Why Feminists Like Me Are Addicted to *Game of Thrones*." *Spectator*, June 16, 2015. http://blogs.new.spectator.co.uk/2015/06/why-feminists-like-me-are-addicted-to-game-of-thrones/.

Mann, Judy. 1985. "*Cagney and Lacey*, and Abortion." *Washington Post*, November 15.

Marcotte, Amanda. 2015. "All (Hopefully) of the Bad Arguments about Rape on *Game of Thrones* Debunked." *Raw Story*, May 20, 2015. https://www.rawstory.com/2015/05/all-hopefully-of-the-bad-arguments-about-rape-on-game-of-thrones-debunked/.

Marcotte, Amanda. 2015. "Cersei's Walk of Shame and *Game of Thrones*' Evolution on Sexual Violence." *Slate*, June 15, 2015. http://www.slate.com/blogs/xx_factor/2015/06/15/game_of_thrones_has_been_criticized_for_its_portrayal_of_sexual_violence.html.

Marwick, Alice. 2013. *Status Update: Celebrity, Publicity, and Branding in the Social Media Age*. New Haven: Yale University Press.

Marwick, Alice E, and danah boyd. 2011. "To See and Be Seen: Celebrity Practice on Twitter." *Convergence* 17(2): 139–158.

Maya. 2012. "What Katie Roiphe Gets Wrong about *Fifty Shades of Grey* and Fantasies of Sexual Submission." *Feministing*. http.//feministing.com/2012/04/16/what-katie-roiphe-gets-wrong-about-fifty-shades-of-grey-and-fantasies-of-sexual-submission/.
McCabe, Janet. 2005. "What's in a Label? The Relationship between Feminist Self-Identification and 'Feminist' Attitudes among U.S. Women and Men." *Gender and Society* 19 (4): 480–505.
McCabe, Janet, and Kim Akass. 2006. *Reading Desperate Housewives: Beyond the White Picket Fence*. London: I. B. Tauris.
McCann, Allison. 2017. "The Last Clinics: Seven States Have Only One Remaining Abortion Clinic." *Vice News*. https://news.vice.com/en_us/article/paz4bv/last-clinics-seven-states-one-abortion-clinic-left.
McKinnon, Catharine. 1991. *Toward a Feminist Theory of the State*. Cambridge, MA: Harvard University Press.
McNary, Dave. 2018. "Michele Williams to Star in Underground Abortion Movie *This Is Jane*." *Variety*, May 22, 2018. https://variety.com/2018/film/news/michelle-williams-abortion-movie-this-is-jane-1202819184/. Accessed August 17, 2018.
McNulty, Anne Welsh. 2018. "Don't Underestimate the Power of Women Supporting Themselves at Work." *Harvard Business Review*, September 3, 2018. https://hbr.org/2018/09/dont-underestimate-the-power-of-women-supporting-each-other-at-work. Accessed December 17, 2018.
McNutt, Myles. 2012. "Game of Thrones—'The Night Lands' and Sexposition." *Cultural Learnings*, April 8, 2012. https://cultural-learnings.com/2012/04/08/game-of-thrones-the-night-lands-and-sexposition/.
McRobbie, Angela 2000. "Feminism and the Third Way." *Feminist Review* 64: 97–112.
McRobbie, Angela 2004. "Postfeminism and Popular Culture." *Feminist Media Studies* 4(3): 255–264.
McRobbie, Angela 2007. "Top Girls? Young Women and the Post-Feminist Sexual Contract." *Cultural Studies* 21(4–5): 718–737.
McRobbie, Angela 2008. "Pornographic Permutations." *Communication Review* 11(3): 111.
McRobbie, Angela 2009a. *The Aftermath of Feminism: Gender, Culture and Social Change*. Los Angeles: Sage.
McRobbie, Angela 2009b. "A Response to Susie Orbach: On Generation and Femininity." *Studies in Gender and Sexuality* 9: 239–245.
McRobbie, Angela 2013. "Feminism, the Family, and the New Mediated Maternalism." *New Formations: A Journal of Culture/Theory/Politics* 80–81: 119–137.
Mead, Rebecca. 2014. "Profiles: Jennifer Weiner's Quest for Literary Respect." *New Yorker*, January 13, 2014. https://www.newyorker.com/magazine/2014/01/13/written-off. Accessed August 28, 2017.
Meadows, Sam. 2013. "5 Characters That Prove *Game of Thrones* Is a Feminist Show." *WhatCulture*, October 22, 2013. http://whatculture.com/tv/5-characters-prove-game-thrones-feminist-show.

Mernissi, Fatema. 2002. "Size 6: The Western Women's Harem." In *Scheherazade Goes West: Different Cultures, Different Harems*, 70–75. New York: Simon and Schuster.

Miller, Claire Cain. 2015a. "More than Their Mothers: Young Women Plan Career Pauses." *New York Times*, July 22, 2015. http://www.nytimes.com/2015/07/23/upshot/more-than-their-mothers-young-women-plan-career-pauses.html?mwrsm=Email&_r=0&abt=0002&abg=0. Accessed July 26, 2015.

Miller, Claire Cain. 2015b. "Millennial Men Aren't the Dads They Thought They'd Be." *New York Times*, July 30, 2015. http://mobile.nytimes.com/2015/07/31/upshot/millennial-men-find-work-and-family-hard-to-balance.html?emc=edit_tnt_20150730&nlid=37868544&tntemail0=y&_r=0&referrer=. Accessed July 30, 2015.

Miller, Claire Cain. 2019. "Why Women, but Not Men, Are Judged for a Messy House." *New York Times*, June 11, 2019. https://www.nytimes.com/2019/06/11/upshot/why-women-but-not-men-are-judged-for-a-messy-house.html. Accessed August 2, 2019.

Mizrahi, Ramit. 2004. "'Hostility to the Presence of Women': Why Women Undermine Each Other in the Workplace and the Consequences for Title VII." *Yale Law Journal* 113(7): 1579–1621. JSTOR, www.jstor.org/stable/4135774. Accessed January 28, 2019.

Moore, Antonio. 2017. "America's Financial Divide: The Racial Breakdown of U.S. Wealth in Black and White." *Huffington Post*, December 6, 2017. https://www.huffpost.com/entry/americas-financial-divide_b_7013330. Accessed November 4, 2019.

Morgan, Betsy L. 1996. "Putting the Feminism into Feminism Scales: Introduction of a Liberal Feminist Attitude and Ideology Scale (LFAIS)." *Sex Roles* 34(5–6): 359–390.

Moylan, Brian. 2010. "Yes, the *Jersey Shore* Boys Are Queer as Can Be." *Gawker*, June 23, 2010. https://gawker.com/5570771/yes-the-jersey-shore-boys-are-queer-as-can-be#targetText=MTV%20guidos%20Ronnie%2C%20The%20Situation,of%20the%20Village%20Voice%20shirtless. Accessed October 13, 2019.

Mulcahy, Kevin, Jr. 2011. "The Complete List: 25 Biggest Blunders in Daytime Soap Opera History." *We Love Soaps*, September 2011. https://www.welovesoaps.net/2011/09/25blunders.html. Accessed July 25, 2018.

Mulvey, Laura. 1978. "Visual Pleasure and Narrative Cinema." *Screen* 16(3): 6–18.

Murphy, Meghan. 2013. "Just Because You Like It, Doesn't Make It Feminist: On *Game of Thrones*' Imagined Feminism." *Feminist Current*, April 26, 2013. http://www.feministcurrent.com/2013/04/26/just-because-you-like-it-doesnt-make-it-feminist/.

Nelson, Eileen McClure. 2018. "I Know Why Christine Blasey Ford Didn't Come Forward Earlier. I Didn't, Either." *Washington Post*, September 21, 2018.

https://www.washingtonpost.com/outlook/i-know-why-christine-blasey-ford-didnt-come-forward-earlier-i-didnt-either/2018/09/21/4f9921ea-bd0e-11e8-b7d2-0773aa1e33da_story.html?utm_term=.1958e9297145. Accessed December 21, 2018.

Neumark-Sztainer, Diane, Jillian Croll, Mary Story, Peter J. Hannan, Simone A. French, and Cheryl Perry. 2002. "Ethnic/Racial Differences in Weight-Related Concerns and Behaviors among Adolescent Girls and Boys: Findings from Project EAT." *Journal of Psychosomatic Research* 53(5): 963–974.

Newburger, Emma. 2018. "Most Americans Believe Women Should be Equal at Work, but Attitudes about Their Roles at Home Are More Complicated." *CNBC Make It*, December 13, 2018. https://www.cnbc.com/2018/12/13/americans-value-gender-equality-at-work-more-than-at-home.html. Accessed December 21, 2018.

Newman, Michael Z., and Elana Levine. 2011. *Legitimating Television: Media Convergence and Cultural Status*. New York: Routledge.

Nussbaum, Emily. 2010. "Is Anyone Still Watching *Desperate Housewives*? Talk to Me." *Vulture*, November 2, 2010. https://www.vulture.com/2010/11/nussbaum_is_anyone_still_watch.html. Accessed July 18, 2019.

Olsen, Richard K., and Julie W. Morgan. 2010. "Desperate for Redemption: *Desperate Housewives* as Redemptive Media." *Journal of Popular Culture* 43(2): 330–347.

Orbach, Susie. 1978. *Fat Is a Feminist Issue*. New York: Berkeley Books.

Orbach, Susie. 2009. "Chinks in the Merged Attachment: Generational Bequests to Contemporary Teenage Girls." *Studies in Gender and Sexuality* 9: 215–232.

Oren, Tasha. 2003. "Domesticated Dads and Double-Shift Moms: Real Life and Ideal Life in 1950s Domestic Comedy." *Cercles* 8: 78–90.

Oren, Tasha, and Andrea L. Press, eds. 2019. *The Handbook of Contemporary Feminism*. New York: Routledge.

Orgad, Shani. 2019. *Heading Home: Motherhood, Work, and the Failed Promise of Equality*. New York: Columbia University Press.

Ortner, Sherry. 2014. "Too Soon for Post-Feminism: The Ongoing Life of Patriarchy in Neo-Liberal America." *History and Anthropology* 25(4): 530–549.

Ouellette, Laurie, ed. 2014. *A Companion to Reality Television*. London: Wiley-Blackwell.

Ouellette, Laurie, and James Hay. 2008. *Better Living through Reality TV: Television and Post-Welfare Citizenship*. Oxford: Wiley-Blackwell.

Owens, Rebekah. 2013. *A Fantasy of Female Subjugation*. F-Word, December 27, 2013. https://www.thefword.org.uk/2013/12/game_of_thrones_subjugation/.

Pailhé, Ariane, Anne Solaz, and Clara Champagne. 2014. "Gender Disparities in Housework over the Long Run: A Comparative Analysis of France, the Netherlands, the United Kingdom, and the United States." http://epc2014.princeton.edu/papers/140543. Accessed August 7, 2017.

Palermo, Elizabeth. 2013. "Women Are Better Multitaskers than Men, Study Finds." *Huffington Post*. http://www.huffingtonpost.com/2013/10/29/women-better-than-men-multitasking-study-finds_n_4175470.html. Accessed July 25, 2015.

Paling, Emma. 2015. "Wikipedia's Hostility to Women." *Atlantic*. https://www.theatlantic.com/technology/archive/2015/10/how-wikipedia-is-hostile-to-women/411619/. Accessed July 25, 2019.

Palmer, Landon. 2013. "A Brief (Almost Silent) History of Abortion in the Movies." *Film School Rejects*, July 9, 2013. https://filmschoolrejects.com/a-brief-almost-silent-history-of-abortion-in-the-movies-7e2b7ce99e5e/. Accessed August 4, 2018.

Palmer, Roxanne. 2013. "Medieval Misogyny: *Game of Thrones* and Gratuitous Female Nudity." *IB Times*, June 2, 2013. http://www.ibtimes.com/fighting-words/medieval-misogyny-game-thrones-gratuitous-female-nudity-1287075.

Pantozzi, Jill. 2015. "We Will No Longer Be Promoting HBO's *Game of Thrones*." *Mary Sue*, May 18, 2015. http://www.themarysue.com/we-will-no-longer-be-promoting-hbos-game-of-thrones/.

Pao, Ellen. 2015. "Former Reddit CEO Ellen Pao: The Trolls Are Winning the Battle for the Internet." *Washington Post*, July 16, 2015. http://www.washingtonpost.com/opinions/we-cannot-let-the-internet-trolls-win/2015/07/16/91b1a2d2-2b17-11e5-bd33-395c05608059_story.html. Accessed July 17, 2015.

Parker, Kim. 2015. "Women More than Men Adjust Their Careers for Family Life." http://www.pewresearch.org/fact-tank/2015/10/01/women-more-than-men-adjust-their-careers-for-family-life/. Accessed August 7, 2017.

Parker, Kim, and Wendy Wang. 2013. "Americans' Time at Paid Work, Housework, Child Care, 1965–2011." http://www.pewsocialtrends.org/2013/03/14/chapter-5-americans-time-at-paid-work-housework-child-care-1965-to-2011/. Accessed August 8, 2017.

Payne, Rhiannon, and Alex Henderson. n.d. "Girls of Thrones: Strong Female Characters in a Sexist Fantasy World." *Feminspire*. http://feminspire.com/girls-of-thrones-strong-female-characters-in-a-sexist-fantasy-world/. Accessed December 10, 2015.

Peltola, Pia, Melissa A. Milkie, and Stanley Presser. 2004. "The 'Feminist' Mystique: Feminist Identity in Three Generations of Women." *Gender and Society* 18(1): 122–144.

Perez, G. 2012. "Fifty Shades of Feminist Criticism." *WordPress*. http://fiftyshadesfeminist.wordpress.com/.

Pew Research Center on Opinion and Public Life. 2018. "Public Opinion on Abortion." October 15, 2018. http://www.pewforum.org/fact-sheet/public-opinion-on-abortion/. Accessed November 27, 2018.

Phillips, Whitney. 2015. *This Is Why We Can't Have Nice Things: Mapping the Relationship between Online Trolling and Mainstream Culture*. Cambridge: MIT Press.

Phipps, Alison. 2009. "Rape and Respectability: Ideas about Sexual Violence and Social Class." *Sociology* 43(4): 667–683.
Pollitt, Katha. 2008. "Maternity Fashions, Junior Size." *Nation*, January 21.
Pollitt, Katha. 2012. "Women Who Love Republicans Who Hate Them." *Nation*, August 29, 2012. http://www.thenation.com/article/169630/women-who-love-republicans-who-hate-them#.
Portable. n.d. "*Game of Thrones*: (Another) Feminist Critique on the Khaleesi." *Portable.* http://portable.tv/culture/post/game-of-thrones-another-feminist-critique-on-the-khaleesi/ Page 1 of 3. Accessed December 10, 2015.
Potter, W. James. 1986. "Perceived Reality and the Cultivation Hypothesis." *Journal of Broadcasting and Electronic Media* 30: 159–174.
Press, Andrea L. 1991. *Women Watching Television: Gender, Class and Generation in the American Television Experience.* Philadelphia: University of Pennsylvania Press.
Press, Andrea L. 2009. "Gender and Family in Television's Golden Age and Beyond." *Annals of the American Academy of Political and Social Science* 625(1): 139–150.
Press, Andrea L. 2012a. "The Price of Motherhood: Feminism and Cultural Bias." *Communication, Culture and Critique* 5: 119–124.
Press, Andrea L. 2012b. "Sex, Gender, and the 2012 Struggle over the Presidency of the University of Virginia." *Yale Journal of Sociology* 9: 161–183.
Press, Andrea L. 2012c. "What Would Jefferson Do?" *Contexts* 11(4): 55–57. http://ctx.sagepub.com.proxy.its.virginia.edu/content/11/4/55.full.
Press, Andrea L. 2014. "Fractured Feminism: Articulations of Feminism, Sex and Class by Reality TV Viewers." In *A Companion to Reality Television*, edited by Laurie Ouellette, 208–227. London: Blackwell.
Press, Andrea L. 2021. *Cinema and Feminism: A Quick Immersion.* Barcelona: Tibidabo.
Press, Andrea L., and Elizabeth R. Cole. 1999. *Speaking of Abortion: Television and Authority in the Lives of Women.* Chicago: University of Chicago Press.
Press, Andrea L., and Tamar Liebes. 2003. "Feminism and Hollywood: Whatever Happened to the Golden Age?" In *Contesting Media Power*, edited by Nick Couldry and James Curran, 1–31. Boulder: Rowman & Littlefield.
Press, Andrea L., and Tamar Liebes. 2004. "Feminism and Hollywood: Why the Backlash?" *Media Report to Women* 31–32: 14.
Press, Andrea L., and Sonia Livingstone. 2006. "Taking Audience Research into the Age of New Media: Old Problems and New Challenges." In *Cultural Studies and Methodological Issues*, edited by Mimi White, James Schwoch, and Dilip Goankar, 175–200. London: Basil Blackwell.
Press, Andrea L., and Marjorie Rosen. 2017. "Sex, Class, and Trash: Money, Status and Classed "Dreams" in Classical Hollywood Cinema." In *Media and Class: TV, Film, and Digital Culture*, edited by June Deery and Andrea L. Press, 68–83. London: Routledge.

Press, Andrea L., and Francesca B. Tripodi. 2014. "Feminism in a Postfeminist World: Who's Hot—and Why We Care—on the Collegiate 'Anonymous Confession Board.'" In *The Routledge Companion to Media and Gender*, edited by Cindy Carter, Lisa McLaughlin, and Linda Steiner, 543–553. New York: Routledge.

Press, Andrea L., and Bruce A. Williams. 2010. *The New Media Environment*. Oxford: Wiley-Blackwell.

Press, Alex. 2017. "The Union Option." *Jacobin*. https://www.jacobinmag.com/2017/10/harvey-weinstein-sexual-harassment-women-union. Accessed October 9, 2017.

Quora Forum. n.d. "Is *Game of Thrones* Misogynist, Feminist, or Somewhere in Between?" https://www.quora.com/Is-Game-of-Thrones-misogynist-feminist-or-somewhere-in-between.

Rampell, Catherine. 2012. "The 'Mommy Penalty' Around the World." *New York Times*. http://economix.blogs.nytimes.com/2012/12/17/the-mommy-penalty-around-the-world/?_r=0. Accessed July 25, 2015.

Rapping, Elayne. 1989. "Prime Time for Pro-Choice Film." *Guardian*, May 17.

Reagle, Joseph, and Lauren Rhue. 2011. "Gender Bias in Wikipedia and Britannica." *International Journal of Communication* 5: 1138–1158.

Reger, Jo, ed. 2005. *Different Wavelengths: Studies of the Contemporary Women's Movement*. New York: Taylor & Francis.

Reints, Renae. 2019. "These Are the States That Passed 'Heartbeat' Bills." *Fortune*, May 31, 2019. http://fortune.com/2019/05/31/states-that-passed-heartbeat-bill/. Accessed June 6, 2019.

Return of Kings. 2014. "How Feminism Is Ruining Game of Thrones." *Return of Kings*, July 8, 2014. http://www.returnofkings.com/38518/how-feminism-is-ruining-game-of-thrones.

Ridgeway, Cecilia L. 2011. *Framed by Gender: How Gender Inequality Persists in the Modern World*. New York: Oxford University Press.

Ringrose, Jessica, and Valerie Walkerdine. 2008. "Regulating the Abject: The TV Make-Over as Site of Neo-Liberal Reinvention Towards Bourgeois Femininity." *Feminist Media Studies* 8(3): 227–246.

Ritzer, George, and J. Michael Ryan. 2017. *The Blackwell Encyclopedia of Sociology Online*. London: Wiley Blackwell.

Rivero, Kamila. 2019. "How Many *Real Housewives* Series Are There Now?" *Showbiz CheatSheet*, January 28, 2019. https://www.cheatsheet.com/entertainment/how-many-real-housewives-series-are-there-now.html/. Accessed July 18, 2019.

Rivers, Caryl, and Rosalind C. Barnett. 2013. *The New Soft War on Women*. New York: Penguin.

Robinson, Joanna. 2015. "*Game of Thrones* Absolutely Did Not Need to Go There with Sansa Stark." *Vanity Fair*, May 17, 2015. https://www.vanityfair.com/hollywood/2015/05/game-of-thrones-rape-sansa-stark.

Rohlinger, Deana A. 2014. *Abortion Politics, Mass Media, and Social Movements in America*. Cambridge: Cambridge University Press.

Roiphe, Katie. 2012. "Spanking Goes Mainstream." *Daily Beast*. http://www.thedaily beast.com/newsweek/2012/04/15/working-women-s-fantasies.html.

Romano, Nick. 2015. "6 Reasons *Game of Thrones*' Sansa Stark Is One of the Most Powerful Characters on TV." *Bustle*, May 28, 2015. http://www.bustle.com/articles/86366-6-reasons-game-of-thrones-sansa-stark-is-one-of-the-most-powerful-characters-on-tv.

Rosen, Marjorie. 1974. *Popcorn Venus, or How the Movies Have Made Women Smaller than Life*. New York: Avon.

Rosen, Ruth. 2006. *The World Split Open: How the Modern Women's Movement Changed America*. New York: Penguin.

Rossi, Alice S. 1973. *The Feminist Papers*. New York: Columbia University Press.

Rossiter, Margaret W. 1993. "The Matthew Matilda Effect in Science." *Social Studies of Science* 23(2): 325–341.

Rottenberg, Catherine. 2014. "The Rise of Neoliberal Feminism." *Cultural Studies* 28(3): 418–437.

Rottenberg, Catherine. 2018. *The Rise of Neoliberal Feminism*. Oxford: Oxford University Press.

Rubin, Gayle. 1993. "Thinking Sex." In *The Lesbian and Gay Studies Reader*, edited by Henry Abelove, Michele Aina Barale, and David Halperin, 3–44. New York: Routledge.

Rubin, Gayle. 1997 [1971]. "The Traffic in Women: Notes on the 'Political Economy' of Sex." In *The Second Wave: A Reader in Feminist Theory*, edited by L. Nicholson, 27–62. New York: Routledge.

Rubin, Lillian. 1976. *Worlds of Pain: Life in the Working-Class Family*. New York: Basic Books.

Rudder, Christian. 2015. *Dataclysm: Love, Sex, Race, and Identity: What Our Online Lives Tells Us about Our Offline Selves*. New York: Broadway Books.

Russo, Vito. 1995. *The Celluloid Closet: Homosexuality in the Movies*. New York: Quality Paperback Book Club Press.

Russonello, Giovanni. 2018. "Samantha Bee Weighs in on the Claims Against Aziz Ansari." *New York Times*, January 18, 2018. https://www.nytimes.com/2018/01/18/arts/television/samantha-bee-aziz-ansari.html. Accessed July 23, 2018.

Ryan, Barbara, ed. 2001. *Identity Politics in the Women's Movement*. New York: New York University Press.

Samin, Suzanne. 2015. "Last Night's Episode of *Game of Thrones* Was More Proof of the Show's Disturbingly Un-Feminist Path." *XO Jane*, May 18, 2015. http://www.xojane.com/issues/sansa-stark-marital-rape.

Sandberg, Sheryl. 2013. *Lean In: Women, Work, and the Will to Lead*. New York: Knopf.

Sandberg, Sheryl, and Adam Grant. 2017. *Option B: Facing Adversity, Building Resilience, and Finding Joy*. New York: Knopf.

Sarkar, Aeshna. 2015. "Does Loving *Game of Thrones* Make Me a Bad Feminist?" *Odyssey*, June 30. http://theodysseyonline.com/tulane/loving-game-of-thrones-bad-feminist/114325.

Savage, Charlie. 2018. "Leaked Kavanaugh Documents Discuss Abortion and Affirmative Action." *New York Times*, September 6, 2018. https://www.nytimes.com/2018/09/06/us/politics/kavanaugh-leaked-documents.html. Accessed December 20, 2018.

Schank, Hana, and Elizabeth Wallace. 2016. "Having It All and Hating It." *Atlantic*, December 19, 2016. https://www.theatlantic.com/business/archive/2016/12/having-it-all/488636/. Accessed December 10, 2018.

Scharff, Christina. 2012. *Repudiating Feminism: Young Women in a Neoliberal World*. London: Ashgate.

Scharff, Christina. 2018. "Why So Many Young Women Don't Call Themselves Feminist." *BBC News*, February 6, 2019. https://www.bbc.com/news/uk-politics-47006912. Accessed September 9, 2019.

Schiebinger, Londa, and Shannon K. Gilmartin. 2010. "Housework Is an Academic Issue." http://www.aaup.org/article/housework-academic-issue#.Uuvj7_vOTsZ.

Sepinwall, Alan. 2012. "PrimeTime Soap Broke Various Rules, Turned into Huge Phenomenon." *HitFix*, May 12, 2012. www.huffingtonpost.com/2014/10/03/desperate-housewives-season-1-anniversary_n_5793322.html. Accessed July 19, 2015.

Shannon-Karasik, Caroline. 2019. "Here's How Much Felicity Huffman Allegedly Paid to Get Her Daughter in to School." *InStyle*, March 12, 2019. https://www.instyle.com/celebrity/felicity-huffman-net-worth. Accessed November 4, 2019.

Sharbutt, Jay. 1973. "Maude Abortion Furor in Repeat." *Pittsburgh Post-Gazette*, August 22, 1973. https://news.google.com/newspapers?id=AUsNAAAAIBAJ&sjid=Dm0DAAAAIBAJ&dq=maude%20abortion&pg=3411%2C2835386. Accessed July 25, 2018.

Shaw, Aaron, and Eszter Hargittai. 2018. "The Pipeline of Online Participation Inequalities: The Case of Wikipedia Editing." *Journal of Communication* 68(1): 143–168. https://doi.org/10.1093/joc/jqx003.

Shtende, Niv. 2014. "*Game of Thrones*: Sexist or Feminist?" *Haaretz*, June 17, 2014. http://www.haaretz.com/israel-news/culture/television/1.599421.

Siede, Caroline. 2015. "The Naked Hypocrisy of *Game of Thrones*' Nudity." *Boing Boing*, May 12, 2015. http://boingboing.net/2015/05/12/the-naked-hypocrisy-of-game-of.html.

Skeggs, Beverley. 1997. *Formations of Class and Gender: Becoming Respectable*. Los Angeles: Sage.

Skeggs, Beverley, and Helen Wood. 2012. *Reacting to Reality Television: Performance, Audience and Value*. London: Routledge.

Slaughter, Anne Marie. 2012. "Why Women Still Can't Have It All." *Atlantic*, July/August. https://www.theatlantic.com/magazine/archive/2012/07/why-women-still-cant-have-it-all/309020/. Accessed August 19, 2020.

Slaughter, Anne Marie. 2015. *Unfinished Business: Women, Men, Work, Family*. London: Oneworld.

Smith, Bonnie G. 1998. *The Gender of History: Men, Women, and Historical Practice*. Cambridge, MA: Harvard University Press.

Smith, Dorothy. 1989. *The Everyday World as Problematic: A Feminist Sociology*. Boston: Northeastern University Press.

Smith-Shomade, Beretta E., ed. 2013. *Watching While Black: Centering the Television of Black Audiences*. New Brunswick: Rutgers University Press.

Smolak, Linda. 2011. "Body Image Development in Childhood." In *Body Image: A Handbook of Science, Practice and Prevention*, 2nd ed., edited by T. Cash and L. Smolak. New York: Guildford.

Spar, Deborah. 2013. *Wonder Women: Sex, Power, and the Quest for Perfection*. New York: Farrar, Straus and Giroux.

Spigel, Lynn. 1992. *Make Room for TV: Television and the Family Ideal in Postwar America*. Chicago: University of Chicago Press.

Spoto, Donald. 2009. *Spellbound by Beauty: Alfred Hitchcock and His Leading Ladies*. New York: Three Rivers Press.

Staal, Lesley. 2011. *Reading Women: How the Great Books of Feminism Changed My Life*. New York: Public Affairs.

Stacey, Judith A. 2011. *Unhitched*. New York: New York University Press.

Stein, Arlene. 1997. *Sex and Sensibility: Stories of a Lesbian Generation*. Berkeley: University of California Press.

Stewart, Abigail J., Jayati Lal, and Kristin McGuire. "Expanding the Archives of Global Feminisms: Narratives of Feminism and Activism." *Signs* 36(4): 889–914.

Stice, Eric. 2002. "Risk and Maintenance Factors for Eating Pathology: A Meta-Analytic Review." *Psychological Bulletin* 128: 825–848.

Stone, Elsie. March 27, 2015. "Liking *Game of Thrones* Does Not Make You a Bad Feminist." *Catalogue*, March 27, 2015. https://www.cataloguemagazine.com.au/feature/liking-game-of-thrones-does-not-make-you-a-bad-feminist.

Strasburger, Victor. 2010. "Sexuality, Contraception, and the Media." *Pediatrics* 126(3). http://pediatrics.aappublications.org/content/126/3/576. Accessed October 6, 2017.

Suter, Elizabeth Ann, and Ramona Fay Oswald. 2008. "Do Lesbians Change Their Last Names in the Context of a Committed Relationship?" *Journal of Lesbian Studies* 7(2): 71–83.

Swidler, Ann. 1986. "Culture in Action: Symbols and Strategies." *American Sociological Review* 51: 273–286.

TAASA. 2014. "*Game of Thrones*: How Much of My Politics Will I Suspend for a TV Show? May 8, 2014. http://taasa.org/soapbox/blog/game-of-thrones-how-much-of-my-politics-will-i-suspend-for-a-tv-show/.

Tasker, Yvonne, and Diane Negra, eds. 2007. *Interrogating Postfeminism: Gender and the Politics of Popular Culture*. Durham: Duke University Press.

Taylor, Ella. 1991. *Prime-Time Families*. Berkeley: University of California Press.

Thomas, Keith. 1959. "The Double Standard." *Journal of the History of Ideas* 20(2): 195–216.

Tinder. "A Guide to Tinder." https://www.help.tinder.com/hc/en-us/categories/115000755686-A-Guide-To-Tinder. Accessed September 19, 2018.

Toff, Benjamin. 2009. "Housewives Dominant." *New York Times*, May 18, 2009. https://www.nytimes.com/2009/05/19/arts/television/19arts-HOUSEWIVESDO_BRF.html?searchResultPosition=3. Accessed July 18, 2019.

Token Feminist. 2015. "This Is Why I Don't Watch *Game of Thrones*." *Token Feminist*, May 19, 2015. http://tokenfeminist.com/this-is-why-i-dont-watch-game-of-thrones/.

Travers, Peter. 2014. "*Obvious Child*." *Rolling Stone*, June 5, 2014. https://www.rollingstone.com/movies/movie-reviews/obvious-child-119947/. Accessed August 17, 2018.

Tripodi, Francesca B. 2017a. "Fifty Shades of Consent." *Feminist Media Studies* 17(1): 93–107.

Tripodi, Francesca B. 2017b. "The Silenced Minority: How Integrated Audiences Limit Participation across Platforms." PhD dissertation, University of Virginia Department of Sociology.

Tripodi, Francesca B. 2019. "Escaping the 'Invincible Mom' Trap." *Medium*. https://forge.medium.com/escaping-the-invincible-mom-trap-1791cc3e1da.

Tromble, Rebekah, and Dirk Hovy. 2016. "These 6 Charts Show How Much Sexism Hillary Clinton Faces on Twitter." *Washington Post*, February 24, 2016.

Truong, Ashley. 2015. "Redefining Strong: What Game of Thrones Can Teach Us about Being an Empowered Woman." *Everyday Feminism*, April 11, 2015. http://everydayfeminism.com/2015/04/women-game-of-thrones/.

Tuchman, Gaye S., Arlene Kaplan Daniels, and James Walker Benét, eds. 1978. *Hearth and Home: Images of Women in the Mass Media*. New York: Oxford University Press.

Turban, Jack. 2018. "We Need to Talk about How Grindr Is Affecting Gay Men's Mental Health." *Vox*, April 4, 2018. https://www.vox.com/science-and-health/2018/4/4/17177058/grindr-gay-men-mental-health-psychiatrist.

Tyree, Tia. 2011. "African American Stereotypes in Reality Television." *Howard Journal of Communications* 22(4): 394–413. doi:10.1080/10646175.2011.617217.

Tziallas, Evangelo. 2015. "Gamified Eroticism: Gay Male 'Social Networking' Applications and Self-Pornography." *Sexuality and Culture* 19: 759–775.

Vance, Carole S., ed. 1993. *Pleasure and Danger: Exploring Female Sexuality*. 2nd ed. Oakland: Pandora Press.

Vanderkam, Laura. 2016. "Revisiting *The Second Shift* 27 Years Later." *Second Shift*, January 14, 2016. https://www.fastcompany.com/3055391/revisiting-the-second-shift-27-years-later. Accessed July 18, 2019.

Van Dijck, Jose, Thomas Poell, Martijn de Waal. 2018. *The Platform Society: Public Values in a Connective World*. London: Oxford University Press.

Wade, Lisa. 2016. "The Invisible Workload That Drags Women Down." *Time*, December 29, 2016. http://time.com/money/4561314/women-work-home-gender-gap/. Accessed December 21, 2018.

Wade, Lisa 2017. *American Hookup: the New Culture of Sex on Campus*. New York: W. W. Norton.

Wade, T. D., A. Keski-Rahkonen, and J. Hudson. 2011. "Epidemiology of Eating Disorders." In *Textbook in Psychiatric Epidemiology*, 3rd ed., edited by M. Tuang and M. Tohen, 343–360. New York: Wiley.

Wagner, Claudia, David Garcia, Mohsen Jadidi, and Markus Strohmaier. 2015. "It's a Man's Wikipedia? Assessing Gender Inequality in an Online Encyclopedia." *Proceedings of the North International AAAI Conference on Web and Social Media*. https://pdfs.semanticscholar.org/05e1/0638aab94ca0d46ddde8083ff69859a0401e.pdf.

Walby, Sylvia. 2011. *The Future of Feminism*. Cambridge: Polity.

Walker, Rebecca. 1992. "Becoming the Third Wave." *Ms.*, January/February, 39–41.

Walker, Rebecca. 1995. *To Be Real: Telling the Truth and Changing the Face of Feminism*. New York: Anchor Press.

Walkerdine, Valerie. 2003. "Reclassifying Upward Mobility: Femininity and the Neo-Liberal Subject." *Gender and Education* 15(3): 237–248.

Walkerdine, Valerie. 2011. "Shame on You: Intergenerational Trauma and Working-Class Femininity on Reality Television." In *Reality Television and Class*, edited by H. Wood and B. Skeggs, 225–236. London: Palgrave Macmillan.

Waller, Nikki. 2013. "Lean In, Read On: 21 Perspectives on Sheryl Sandberg's Book." *Wall Street Journal*, March 8, 2013. https://blogs.wsj.com/atwork/2013/03/08/lean-in-read-on-21-perspectives-on-sheryl-sandbergs-book/. Accessed August 28, 2017.

Walters, Suzanna Danuta. 2010. "Lost in Translation: Feminist Media Studies in the New Millennium." In *The Handbook of Cultural Sociology*, edited by J. R. Hall, L. Grindstaff, and M. C. Lo, 87–96. New York: Routledge.

Walters, Suzanna Danuta. 2014. *The Tolerance Trap*. New York: New York University Press.

Way, Katie. 2018a. "I Went on a Date with Aziz Ansari. It Turned into the Worst Nightmare of My Life." *Babe*, January 13, 2018. https://babe.net/2018/01/13/aziz-ansari-28355. Accessed July 23, 2018.

Way, Katie. 2018b. "Aziz Ansari Issues Statement Denying Sexual Misconduct." *Babe*, January 15, 2018. https://babe.net/2018/01/15/aziz-ansari-statement-28407. Accessed July 23, 2018.

Webb, Jonathan. 2017. "The Glass Ceiling Still Keeps Top Jobs for the Boys: Women Earn 75% of Men's Salary." *Forbes*, January 30, 2019. https://www.forbes.com/sites/jwebb/2017/01/30/glass-ceiling-still-keeps-top-jobs-for-the-boys-women-earn-75-of-mens-salary/#667327e22bb2. Accessed August 1, 2019.

Weber, Brenda R. 2009. *Makeover TV: Selfhood, Citizenship, and Celebrity*. Durham: Duke University Press.

Weiss, Bari. 2018. "Aziz Ansari Is Guilty. Of Not Being a Mind Reader." *New York Times*, January 14, 2018. https://www.nytimes.com/2018/01/15/opinion/aziz-ansari-babe-sexual-harassment.html. Accessed July 23, 2018.

West, Carolyn M., and Kalimah Johnson. 2013. "Sexual Violence in the Lives of African American Women." National Online Resource Center on Violence Against Women. file:///Users/alp5n/Dropbox/COURSES/Sexual%20Violence%20in%20the%20Lives%20of%20African%20American%20Women%202013_stamped.pdf. Accessed October 13, 2019.

West, Lindy. 2018. "Aziz, We Tried to Warn You." *New York Times*, January 17, 2018. https://www.nytimes.com/2018/01/17/opinion/aziz-ansari-metoo-sex.html. Accessed July 23, 2018.

Western, Bruce, and Christopher Wildeman. 2009. "The Black Family and Mass Incarceration." *Annals of the American Academy of Political and Social Science* 621: 221–242.

Whitcomb, Dan. 2009. "*Golden Girls* Star Bea Arthur Dies at 86." *Reuters*, April 26, 2009. https://news.google.com/newspapers?id=AUsNAAAAIBAJ&sjid=Dm0DAAAAIBAJ&dq=maude%20abortion&pg=3411%2C2835386. Accessed July 25, 2018.

White, Marney A., J. R. Kohlmaler, Paula J. Varnado-Sullivan, and Donald A. Williamson. 2003. "Racial/Ethnic Differences in Weight Concerns: Protective and Risk Factors for the Development of eating Disorders and Obesity Among Adolescent Females." *Eating and Weight Disorders* 8(1): 20–25.

Wikimedia Foundation. 2011. "Wikipedia Editors Study: Results From the Editor Survey, April 2011." July 1, 2019. https://upload.wikimedia.org/wikipedia/commons/7/76/Editor_Survey_Report_-_April_2011.pdf. Accessed July 3, 2020.

Wilcox, Rhonda V., and David Lavery, eds. 2002. *What's at Stake in "Buffy the Vampire Slayer"?* New York: Rowman & Littlefield.

Wilk, Max. 1999. *The Golden Age of Television: Notes from the Survivors*. Silver Springs: Silver Springs Books.

Williams, Bruce A., and Andrea L. Press. 2016. "'Your Turn, Girl': The (Im)possibility of African American Anti-Heroines in *The Wire*." In *Women Behaving Badly: Anti-Heroines in Crime and Prison Drama*, edited by Milly Buonanno, 237–253. London: Intellect.

Williams, Bruce A., and Andrea L. Press. 2017. "Women of *The Wire*." *Anàlisi: Quaderns de Comunicaió Cultura* 56. https://analisi.cat/article/view/n56-williams-press.

Williams, Joan C. 2010. *Reshaping the Work-Family Debate: Why Men and Class Matter*. Cambridge, MA: Harvard University Press.
Williams, Joan C., and Rachel Dempsey. 2018. *What Works for Women at Work: Four Patterns Working Women Need to Know*. New York: New York University Press.
Williams, Raymond. 1973. "Base and Superstructure in Marxist Cultural Theory." *New Left Review* 1(82): 3–16.
Wilson, Leah, ed. 2006. *Welcome to Wisteria Lane: On America's Favorite "Desperate Housewives."* Dallas: BenBella Books.
Wilson, Samantha. 2019. "Felicity Huffman Releases Statement after Being Sentenced to 14 Days in Prison in College Scandal." *Hollywood Life*, September 13, 2019. https://hollywoodlife.com/2019/09/13/felicity-huffman-sentenced-14-days-prison-college-admissions-scandal/. Accessed September 21, 2019.
Wiltz, Teresa. 2015. "Racial and Ethnic Disparities Persist in Teen Pregnancy Rates." PEW Stateline Article. https://www.pewtrusts.org/en/research-and-analysis/blogs/stateline/2015/3/03/racial-and-ethnic-disparities-persist-in-teen-pregnancy-rates. Accessed December 16, 2018.
Wimmer, Roger D., and Joseph R. Dominick. 2013. *Mass Media Research*. 10th ed. New York: Wadsworth.
Wind, Rebecca. 2017. "U.S. Abortion Rate Continues to Decline, Hits Historic Low." Guttmacher Institute Press Release, January 17, 2017. https://www.guttmacher.org/news-release/2017/us-abortion-rate-continues-decline-hits-historic-low. Accessed November 12, 2018.
Wofford, Taylor. 2014. "Is GamerGate about Media Ethics or Harassing Women? Harassment, the Data Shows." *Newsweek*, October 25. http://www.newsweek.com/gamergate-about-media-ethics-or-harassing-women-harassment-data-show-279736. Accessed July 17, 2015.
Wood, Helen. 2011. *Talking with Television: Women, Talk Shows, and Modern Self-Reflexivity*. Urbana: University of Illinois Press.
Wood, Helen. 2017. "The Politics of Hyperbole on Geordie Shore: Class, Gender, Youth, and Excess." *European Journal of Cultural Studies* 20(1): 39–55.
Wood, Helen, and Beverley Skeggs, eds. 2011. *Reality Television and Class*. London: Palgrave Macmillan.
Wright, E. O. 1993. *Classes, Crisis and the State*. London: Verso.
Wu, Brianna. 2014. "Rape and Death Threats Are Terrorizing Female Gamers. Why Haven't Men in Tech Spoken Out?" *Washington Post*, October 20, 2014. http://www.washingtonpost.com/posteverything/wp/2014/10/20/rape-and-death-threats-are-terrorizing-female-gamers-why-havent-men-in-tech-spoken-out/. Accessed July 17, 2015.
Wuinonez, Ariana. 2014. Jaime Lannister Is a Feminist: Why the *Game of Thrones* Rape Scene Matters." *Hypable*, April 25, 2014. http://www.hypable.com/why-game-of-thrones-rape-matters/.

Yancy, George. 2018. "IAmSexist." *New York Times*, Opinion Section, October 24.
Yoder, Katie. 2015. "TV Shows Laud Opening of 'Funny' Pro-Abortion Film *Grandma*." *MRC NewsBusters*, August 21, 2015. https://www.newsbusters.org/blogs/culture/katie-yoder/2015/08/21/tv-shows-laud-opening-funny-pro-abortion-film-grandma. Accessed August 16, 2018.
Yoder, Katie. 2017. "New Movies to 'Beautifully Depict' Illegal Abortion Network." *MRC NewsBusters*, July 31, 2017. https://www.newsbusters.org/blogs/culture/katie-yoder/2017/07/31/new-movies-beautifully-depict-illegal-abortion-network. Accessed July 25, 2018.
Zara, Christopher. 2013. "Wikipedia's Gender Gap Persists: Why Don't More Women Contribute to the Online Encyclopedia." *International Business Time*. http://www.ibtimes.com/wikipedias-gender-gap-persists-why-dont-more-women-contribute-online-encyclopedia-1390565.
Zeisler, Andi. 2013. "Does It Matter Whether *Game of Thrones* Is Feminist?" *Bitch Media*, June 7, 2013. https://bitchmedia.org/post/does-it-matter-whether-game-of-thrones-is-feminist.
Zeisler, Andi. 2016. *We Were Feminists Once: From Riot Grrrl to Cover Girl®, the Buying and Selling of a Political Movement*. Philadelphia: Public Affairs.
Zurbriggen, Eileen L., and Elizabeth M. Morgan. 2006. "Who Wants to Marry a Millionaire? Reality Dating Television Programs, Attitudes toward Sex, and Sexual Behaviors." *Sex Roles* 54(1–2): 1–17.

Index

abortion
  media-ready feminism illustration in postings on, 7, 8, 9, *10*, 11
  rape debate around, 9, *10*, 11
  statistics, 11
African American women
  dating apps for LGBTQ+, 116–117
  hookup culture for, 105, 111, 116–117, 125
  motherhood obstacles for, 99
  sexuality stereotypes for, 47
  Tinder discrimination and, 111
  Wikipedia discrimination and, 149–150, 168n26
  work-family balance experiences of, 16, 78, 80, 86, 92–96, 99, 158
  workplace discrimination for, 93
Ansari, Aziz
  #MeToo movement and reactions to sexual misconduct allegations against, 18, 121–122, 125–126
  sexual misconduct accusations against, details of, 120–121
  sexual pressure and consent issues around incident with, 103, 109, 120–123, 159
Asian women, 41, 47–48, 111, 118, 125
assertive women, 84–86, 97–98, 158, 166n8

audience. *See* media audiences; *specific shows*

Babe, 103, 109, 120, 121–122
Balancing Jane, 29–30
Banet-Weiser, Sarah, 4, 19, 57, 154, 163n2
bisexuality. *See* LGBTQ+ community; sexual identity and orientation
Bitch Media, 21, 28, 32, 44
#BlackLivesMatter, 11
BoingBoing, 25
"bossy" labeling, 84, 86, 97–98, 158, 166n8
breakthrough feminism
  Desperate Housewives moments of, 80, 98
  domesticating reception of moments of, 9, 11, 14
  Game of Thrones moments of and contradictions with, 23, 25, 31, 33, 34–35, 39, 42
  media-ready feminism relation to moments of, 4, 12, 15, 16, 154
  #MeToo movement aspects of, 3
  popular feminism impacting moments of, 12, 14, 153
  sexual freedom and, 15
  social change opportunity and, 12, 72

breakthrough feminism *(continued)*
   white affluent perspectives limiting, 155
Bruni, Frank, 45–46
Bumble, 102, 110, 154
Burke, Tarana, 1, 2
Bustle, 31
Buzzfeed, 23, 28, 32

childcare responsibilities. *See also* work-family balance
   Desperate Housewives vignette on, 73–74, 80, 86, 88–92
   gender inequalities around, 68, 69, 80, 90–91
   gender stereotypes around, 73–74, 86–90
   generational differences in views on, 86–90
   men attempts at increased, 91–92
   partner expectations and, 86–92
   women aptitude for, beliefs about, 87–90
cisgender heterosexual women
   dating apps and, 102, 105–106
   hookup culture in colleges and, 47, 104–105
   Jersey Shore aspirations and, 51, 63–64
   popular feminism focus on white, 6, 11–12, 68, 155
   second-wave feminism focus on white, 5, 51, 65
   sexual agency and expression views of, 46–47, 63–64, 65
   sexual bargaining experience for, 46
   Tinder use for nonnormative women contrasted with, 111, 117–120, 125
   work-family balance representations focus on, 16–17, 68

class-based issues. *See* socioeconomic class; working-class women
Clinton, Hillary, 18–19, 42
college admissions scandals, 16–17, 84, 165n3
college campuses
   #BlackLivesMatter media posts at, 11
   hookup culture and dating app use and issues on, 17, 18, 47, 102–106, 125
   Jersey Shore focus groups and, 50
   sexual agency and consent issues on, 17, 18, 103, 106–109, 120
   sexual assault on, 17, 120, 124
   Yik Yak thread on abortion and, 7, 8, 9, *10*, 11
Cottom, Tressie McMillan, 92–93

Damon, Matt, 2–3, 4
Dataclysm (Rudder), 111
dating and dating apps, 13. *See also* hookup culture; Tinder
   college students engagement with, 17, 18, 47, 102–106, 125
   emotional connection issues around, 104, 108
   female empowerment claims of, 102, 111–112, 124, 125
   gender inequalities with, 47, 48, 50, 55, 58, 104–105, 113, 122–123, 125
   Grindr, 115–116
   hierarchy of sexual choices and, 159, 165n11
   for LGBTQ+ community, 115–117, 124, 159
   linguistic facility around, 105–106
   media-ready feminism and, 103, 109, 113–115, 117–118, 120, 122–123
   orgasm gap and, 17, 46, 106

popular feminism ethos and, 17–18, 102, 111, 117–118, 120, 124
racial identity relation to, 47–48, 58, 105, 111, 115–120, 124, 125, 157
sexual agency conflicting with realities of, 17–18, 102–103, 105–108, 113–115, 124–126, 154
sexual identity and orientation experience with, 47, 115–118, 124, 159, 166
sexual pressures and consent conflicts with, 59, 102–103, 106–109, 113–115, 120–124, 126, 154, 159, 164n6
Sugar Baby site and, 117
Davis, Angela, 93
Desperate Housewives
breakthrough feminism moments in, 80, 98
childcare at work interview vignette in, 73–74, 80, 86, 88–92
episode selection and background, 73–75
everyday sexism and, 71, 85, 86, 90
feminist scholarship on, 73
generational differences in responses to, 76–86
Lynette likability and relatability for viewers of, 83–86, 97–99, 158
media-ready feminism expressions in, 70–72, 73, 76, 80, 83–85, 88, 90, 91, 96, 98
methods and focus group behind study of, 75–76
partner expectations and, 86–92
patriarchal workplace culture in, 90–91
popularity factors, 72–73
powerful women portrayal in, 74
white affluent women focus in, 72, 93, 99

work-family balance study and, 15–16, 72–99
divorced women, 80–81, 82
double entanglement, 5, 55
double sexual standard. *See* sexual double standard

Ehrenreich, Barbara, 46
Everyday Feminism, 30–31
everyday sexism. *See* sexism, everyday

Facebook
interface compared with Wikipedia, 131, 132
sexual identity option on, 46–47
Tinder and, 111, 119
Farley, Lin, 1, 2
Favaro, Laura, 4, 57, 154
female masculinity, 14, 27–28, 30–31, 37–38, 42, 43
female sexuality
class-based issues around, 47, 48–49, 57–60, 62–64, 157, 164n2
cock-tease or prude labeling and, 53–54, 55
feminist views conflicting with views on, 56–57, 65
Game of Thrones portrayal of extreme, 22, 37, 38, 43–44, 156
hierarchy of sexual choices and, 159, 165n11
Hitchcock blondes and, 48, 164nn2–3
hookup culture and, 17, 45, 46, 50, 55–56, 58–59
misogynistic culture and, 45
orgasm gap and, 17, 46, 106
patriarchal culture impact for, 46–47
racial identity relation to views of, 47–49, 57, 58, 64, 157
reputation factors and fears around, 55–58, 60, 62–63, 64–65, 105, 107, 108, 122, 164n6

female sexuality *(continued)*
    silencing of, 45, 58–59
    virginity and, 43–44, 166n2
feminism. *See also* breakthrough feminism; media-ready feminism; neoliberal feminism; popular feminism; second-wave feminism
    double entanglement of, 5, 55
    glossy, 4, 154
    media-ready feminism contrasted with "actual," 5–6, 11–12
    misogyny relation to extreme, 14
    queer, 24, 28, 42–43
    sexual activity conflicting with views on, 56–57
The Feminist Femline, 28
Feminspire, 27, 28, 32
Friedan, Betty, 139

Game of Thrones
    "Arya" portrayal in, 27–29, 42, 43
    breakthrough feminist moments and contradictions in, 23, 25, 31, 33, 34–35, 39, 42
    "Brienne" portrayal in, 27–29, 42–43
    "Cersei" portrayal in, 31–33, 40, 43, 44
    "Daenerys" as mother figure in, 24
    "Daenerys" downfall at end of, 164n2
    "Daenerys" female power treatment in, 24–27, 28, 30, 31, 34, 37–38, 40–41, 43–44
    "Daenerys" hyperfemininity in, 37–38, 43
    everyday sexism and, 23, 25, 33, 39, 40
    "evil queen" trope in, 31–32
    female masculinity portrayal in, 14, 27–28, 30–31, 37–38, 42, 43
    feminine vulnerability with strength in, 28–29
    gender roles treatment in, 26, 28, 32, 33–34, 39–43
    hyperfemininity portrayals in, 31, 37–38, 40, 42, 44
    hypersexualization of women in, 22, 37, 38, 43–44, 156
    male viewers as target audience for, 33, 34
    male viewers on, 36–37, 41, 42–43
    media outlets reception of, 24–32
    media-ready feminism exemplified in, 22, 23, 25, 33, 35, 37, 39–42, 44, 155–156
    methods behind study of, 23–24
    misogynistic tropes in, 14, 21, 22–23, 24, 25–39, 41–42, 153, 155–156
    mother figure treatment in, 24, 31–32
    patriarchal culture and, 22, 28, 29, 30, 33, 37
    popular feminism tropes in, 14, 22–23, 29, 31, 33–35, 37–38, 41–42, 155–156
    powerful women portrayal and contradictions in, 14, 21, 22, 24–27, 28, 30, 31, 34–35, 37–44, 156
    queer feminism and, 24, 28, 42–43, 156
    "Sansa" portrayal in, 29–32, 37, 40, 41, 43, 44
    sexual violence in, 14, 22, 24, 25, 28–30, 32, 33, 34, 35–39, 43–44, 156
    sexual violence justifications, viewers on, 35–37, 156
Gamergate, 140–141
gay community. *See* LGBTQ+ community; sexual identity and orientation
gender inequalities. *See also* sexual double standard

"bossy" labeling and, 84, 86, 97–98, 158, 166n8
childcare responsibilities and, 68, 69, 80, 90–91
combating, factors behind, 19, 71–72, 91–92, 161–162
generational differences in views on, 84–85, 86–87
with hookup culture and dating apps, 47, 48, 50, 55, 58, 104–105, 113, 122–123, 125
with housework tasks, 67–68, 74
individual focus over collective efforts for combating, 1–2, 7, 12, 15, 67, 68–69, 74, 128, 139, 157
media audiences inability to critique, 72, 139–140, 155
men combating, prejudices experienced for, 91–92
sexual harassment role in, 3–4
Wikipedia and, 18, 127–129, 132, 135–136, 139–151, 153–154, 160
for women of affluence, focus on, 12–13, 16–17
workplace, 79–81
gender roles and stereotypes
childcare competency and, 73–74, 86–90
Game of Thrones treatment of, 26, 28, 32, 33–34, 39–43
hookup culture and, 104–105
in *Jersey Shore*, 52–53
with powerful women, 74, 81
generational differences
Desperate Housewives reception and, 76–86
in gender inequality views, 84–85, 86–87
in partner and childcare expectations, 86–90
socioeconomic class relation to, 92

on work-family balance, 71, 76–86, 96–97
in workplace, 82–83
on workplace discrimination, 80–81, 96
Gill, 4–5, 154, 163n2
glossy feminism, 4, 154
Gossip Girl, 148–149
Grindr, 115–116

Hall, Stuart, 161
Hays, Sharon, 69
HBO Watch, 26
heterosexual. *See* cisgender heterosexual women
Hill, Anita, 2
Hitchcock, Alfred, 48, 164nn2–3
hookup culture
Asian women experience in, 47–48, 105, 111, 118, 125
on college campuses, 17, 18, 47, 102–106, 125
emotional connections and, 46–47, 104, 108, 109
female sexuality and, 17, 45, 46, 50, 55–56, 58–59
gender inequalities in, 47, 48, 50, 55, 58, 104–105, 113, 122–123, 125
gender roles and stereotypes in, 104–105
hierarchy of sexual choices and, 159, 165n11
history and evolution of, 103–109
for LGBTQ+ community, 115–117, 124, 159
media-ready feminism and, 103, 109, 113–115, 117–118, 120, 122–123
#MeToo movement and, 103, 120, 121–122, 125–126
misogyny and, 112, 113

hookup culture *(continued)*
  "obligatory blow job" and, 107, 120, 121, 123, 154
  orgasm gap and, 17, 46, 106
  patriarchal influence over, 47, 125
  racial identity and, 47–48, 58, 105, 111, 115–120, 124, 125, 157
  reputation fears and, 56, 105, 107, 108, 122, 164n6
  sexual agency contradictions with, 17–18, 102–103, 105–108, 113–115, 124–126, 154
  sexual double standards in, 50, 55, 58, 104–105, 122–123
  sexual identity and orientation experience in, 47, 115–118, 124, 159, 166
  sexual pressures and consent conflicts with, 59, 102–103, 106–109, 113–115, 120–124, 126, 154, 159, 164n6
  slut labeling fear in, 56, 105, 165n11
  socioeconomic class view differences on, 62–63
  Tinder use to opt-out of, 112
  women conflictual participation in, 55–56
  women's silence about, 58–59
housework tasks
  gender inequalities with, 67–68, 74
  women aptitude for, views on, 87–88
Huffington Post, 27
Huffman, Felicity, 16–17, 73, 84, 165n3

I Love Lucy, 74, 86, 166n9
intensive motherhood, 69–70, 71, 72, 75, 91, 99

Jersey Shore
  cisgender heterosexual women focus and, 51, 63–64
  "Dirty Pad" episode selection and details, 50–51, 53–56
  everyday sexism illustrations and, 14–15, 51, 59, 62, 64, 65
  gender stereotypes in, 52–53
  media-ready feminism illustrations and contradictions in, 50, 51, 53, 55, 60, 63–65
  methods and focus group demographics in study of, 50–51
  popular feminism and, 57–58, 64, 157
  self-improvement message lack in, 52
  sexual agency contradictions with slut shaming, 54–55, 60, 62, 156–157
  sexual double standard illustrations in, 15, 46, 49–51, 54–55, 58, 60–62, 156–157
  slut compared with prude labeling conflicts in, 53–54, 55
  socioeconomic class factors in, 49, 51–52, 64–65
Johnson-Palomaki, Sarah, 21, 23–24, 164n1

Klinenberg, Eric, 120

Lareau, Annette, 17, 69
Latina women, 16, 37, 79, 86
LGBTQ+ community
  Grindr and, 115–116
  sexual consent and, 124
  Tinder and, 116–117, 159
  Wikipedia edit-a-thons for, 130
Livingly, 28

marriage
  name change with, 147–148
  partner expectations, 86–92
The Mary Sue, 29

Index

media audiences. *See also Desperate Housewives; Game of Thrones; Jersey Shore*
  inability for critiquing gender inequalities and solutions, 72, 139–140, 155
  methodology with, 13
  original intent and content modification by, 9, *10*, 11
  popular and neoliberal feminism reaffirmed by, 12
  understanding interactions of, 4, 154–155, 158–159
media-ready feminism. *See also specific topics*
  abortion postings illustration of, 7, 8, 9, *10*, 11
  breakthrough feminist moments reception with, 4, 12, 15, 16, 154
  Clinton campaign and, 18–19, 42
  dating apps and hookup culture illustrations of, 103, 109, 113–115, 117–118, 120, 122–123
  defining characteristics of, 4–6, 11–12, 51, 163n3
  Desperate Housewives illustrations of, 70–72, 73, 76, 80, 83–85, 88, 90, 91, 96, 98
  domesticating reception of, 9
  everyday and structural sexism interplay with, 5–7, 13–19, 51, 124–125, 153–154, 161–162
  Game of Thrones examples of, 22, 23, 25, 33, 35, 37, 39–42, 44, 155–156
  individual over collective action/change characteristic of, 1–2, 7, 12, 15, 128, 139, 157
  Jersey Shore illustrations and contradictions of, 50, 51, 53, 55, 60, 63–65

popular and neoliberal feminism relation to, 4, 5–6, 11–12, 154
  racial identity and focus of, 12–13
  racism and, 115–120
  sexual consent issues and, 124
  Wikipedia edit-a-thons illustration of, 18, 128, 130, 135–136, 138–141, 151
#MeToo movement
  Ansari sexual conduct allegations and, 18, 121–122, 125–126
  breakthrough feminism aspects of, 3
  everyday sexism and, 2, 3–4, 120
  hookup culture and, 103, 120, 121–122, 125–126
  impacts of, 1–2, 99
  media treatment of, 1, 2, 3–4, 18, 45
  misogyny and, 4
  popular feminism understanding and, 2, 3, 4
  pushback with, 2, 120
  sensationalism with, 3, 45
  sexual consent discourse and, 121–122, 125–126
  sexual harassment awareness with, 1–2, 71, 82, 83
  white affluent women focus in, 1
Milano, Alyssa, 4
misogyny, 7
  extreme feminism imagery relation to, 14
  female sexuality and culture of, 45
  Game of Thrones tropes of, 14, 21, 22–23, 24, 25–39, 41–42, 153, 155–156
  #MeToo movement and, 4
  Tinder use and, 112, 113
Monroe, Marilyn, 48–49, 164n2
motherhood. *See also* childcare responsibilities; work-family balance

motherhood *(continued)*
  African American women obstacles with, 99
  Game of Thrones figures of, 24, 31–32
  intensive, ideology, 69–70, 71, 72, 75, 91, 99
  racial identity and, 72, 99
  socioeconomic inequalities and, 69, 72
  television representations, 69–70
  women bargaining around, 77–78

neoliberal feminism, 1–2
  media audiences reaffirming, 12
  media-ready feminism relation to, 4, 5–6, 11–12, 154
  postfeminist sensibility and, 4–5, 163n2
  work-family balance assumptions in, 15–16, 73

OKCupid, 111
orgasm gap, 17, 46, 106

partner expectations, 86–92
patriarchal culture
  with everyday sexism unchallenged, 154
  female sexuality impacted by, 46–47
  Game of Thrones and, 22, 28, 29, 30, 33, 37
  hookup culture dominated by, 47, 125
  sexual pleasure gaps in, 46, 47
  2016 presidential election and, 19
  Wikipedia and, 18, 129, 144
  workplace, 90–91
popular feminism
  abortion views under, 7, 8, 9
  breakthrough feminist moments impacted by, 12, 14, 153
  dating apps claims and conflicts relation to, 17–18, 102, 111, 117–118, 120, 124
  Game of Thrones tropes of, 14, 22–23, 29, 31, 33–35, 37–38, 41–42, 155–156
  influence of, 165n9
  Jersey Shore and, 57–58, 64, 157
  media audiences reaffirming, 12
  media-ready feminism relation to, 4, 5–6, 11–12, 154
  #MeToo movement and, 2, 3, 4
  packaging and reproduction of, 12
  postfeminist sensibility assumption with, 14
  progressive ideas domestication under, 14
  sexual expression and, 57–58, 59–60
  slut labeling and, 46
  structural change and, 1–2
  white cisgender heterosexual women focus for, 6, 11–12, 68, 155
  work-family balance assumptions of, 15–16, 68–69, 70, 72, 75, 76, 78, 83, 90, 92, 95, 97
Portwood-Stacer, Laura, 19
postfeminist sensibility, 4–5, 14, 163n2
powerful women
  "bossy" labeling and, 84, 86, 97–98, 158, 166n8
  Desperate Housewives illustrations of, 74
  Game of Thrones and stereotypes of, 40–41
  Game of Thrones portrayal and contradictions of, 14, 21, 22, 24–27, 28, 30, 31, 34–35, 37–44, 156
  negative views of, 85–86
  stereotypes and assumptions about, 74, 81

presidential election (2016), 18–19, 42
Press, Andrea L.
  as WOASH founding member, 163n1
  works, 12, 41, 42, 48, 64, 69, 96, 119, 125, 164n2, 166n6, 166n9
prude labeling
  Jersey Shore illustration of slut compared with, 53–54, 55
  sexual double standards and, 45–46, 55

queer community. *See* LGBTQ+ community; sexual identity and orientation
queer feminism, 24, 28, 42–43

race theory, 93, 96
racial identity, 1. *See also* African American women; Asian women; Latina women; white women
  #BlackLivesMatter and, 11
  dating apps and hookup culture relation to, 47–48, 58, 105, 111, 115–120, 124, 125, 157
  female sexuality issues relation to, 47–49, 57, 58, 64, 157
  media-ready feminism and combating discrimination on, 115–120
  media-ready feminism focus relation to, 12–13
  motherhood and, 72, 99
  partner expectations and, 86
  reality television portrayals of, 49
  sexual double standards views and, 58
  slut labeling and, 46, 47–48, 49, 58
  Tinder use and, 111, 117–118, 159
  Wikipedia discrepancies around, 132, 141, 143–145, 149–150, 151, 168n26

work-family balance relation to, 16–17, 68, 69, 72, 78, 79, 80, 86, 91, 92–96, 98–99, 157, 158
workplace discrimination relation to, 93
rape. *See* sexual violence/rape
reality television genre, 49, 54, 164n5. *See also Jersey Shore*
Rottenberg, Catherine, 4, 6, 73, 154, 163nn2–3
Rudder, Christian, 111

Sandberg, Sheryl, 68–69, 84, 93, 166n8
second-wave feminism, 139
  sexual double standards and, 46, 47
  on white cisgender heterosexual women focus of, 5, 51, 65
  work-family balance and, 69, 95–96
sexism, everyday
  Desperate Housewives and, 71, 85, 86, 90
  Game of Thrones and, 23, 25, 33, 39, 40
  inability and language lacking for dealing with, 139–140, 155
  as individual over collective problem, 128
  Jersey Shore and, 14–15, 51, 59, 62, 64, 65
  media confronting structural, 3–4, 161–162
  media-ready feminism impacted by and interplay with, 5–7, 13–19, 51, 124–125, 153–154, 161–162
  #MeToo movement and, 2, 3–4, 120
  patriarchal culture persistence with, 154
  persistent reproduction of, 1, 4, 5, 154, 161–162
  privileged and majority groups ties to, 161–162

sexism, everyday *(continued)*
  sexual assault relation to, 2–3
  sexual double standard illustrations of, 14–15, 51, 59, 62, 64, 65
  socioeconomic class relation to, 60–62, 65, 161–162
  Tinder and, 17–18
  Trump demonstrations of, 14, 19
  2016 presidential election illustrations of, 18–19
  unquestioned nature of, 147, 153–154
  Wikipedia and, 18, 128, 130, 131–132, 135–136, 139–140, 146–147, 151, 160
  work-family balance and, 71, 85, 86, 90
sexual agency/freedom
  breakthrough feminism and, 15
  cisgender heterosexual women views on, 46–47, 63–64, 65
  class differences with, 57–64, 157
  consent issues in relation to, 17, 18, 103, 106–109, 120
  hookup and dating app culture contradictions with, 17–18, 102–103, 105–108, 113–115, 124–126, 154
  regulation of, 63
  reputation factors and fears around, 55–58, 60, 62–63, 64–65, 105, 107, 108, 122, 164n6
  sexual violence and beliefs around, 17
  slut labeling and, 15, 46, 54–55, 60, 62, 156–157
  women's attitudes on male, 59–60
sexual consent
  Ansari incident highlighting issues of, 103, 109, 120–123, 159
  conversation avoidance factors, 124, 125
  hookup culture and issues of, 59, 102–103, 106–109, 113–115, 120–124, 126, 154, 159, 164n6
  implied, issues around, 102, 106, 109, 115, 121–124, 159
  interpretations of, 121–122, 126
  media-ready feminism and issues of, 124
  #MeToo movement and issues of, 121–122, 125–126
  nonnormative sexual orientation relation to issues of, 124, 166
  reputation fears around, 122
  sexual agency relation to issues of, 17, 18, 103, 106–109, 120
  sexual assault and issues of, 123–124, 126
sexual double standard, 13
  everyday sexism illustrations with, 14–15, 51, 59, 62, 64, 65
  in hookup culture, 50, 55, 58, 104–105, 122–123
  Jersey Shore illustrations of, 15, 46, 49–51, 54–55, 58, 60–62, 156–157
  media perpetuation of, 45–46
  orgasm gap and, 46
  prude labeling and, 45–46, 55
  racial identity and views on, 58
  second-wave feminism and, 46, 47
  slut labeling and, 15, 46, 156–157
  socioeconomic class relation to, 46, 51, 58, 59–65, 161
sexual expression. *See* female sexuality; sexual agency/freedom
sexual harassment
  coining of term, 1, 2
  gender inequalities and role of, 3–4
  #MeToo movement impact for, 1–2, 71, 82, 83
  online, and Wikipedia, 136–138, 150–151, 160, 167n11

sexual violence differences from, 4
Time coverage of, 2
WOASH and, 2, 163n1
in workplace, 71, 82–83
sexual identity and orientation. *See also* cisgender heterosexual women; LGBTQ+ community
Facebook options for, 46–47
hookup culture and dating apps experience with, 47, 115–118, 124, 159, 166
sexual consent relation to, 124, 166
sexual violence/rape
abortion debates and, 9, *10*, 11
college students experiences of, 17, 120, 124
everyday sexism relation to, 2–3
in *Game of Thrones*, 14, 22, 24, 25, 28–30, 32, 33, 34, 35–39, 43–44, 156
Game of Thrones viewers justifications for elements of, 35–37, 156
harassment differences from, 4
online simulated, 136
sensational treatment of, 45
sexual agency beliefs and, 17
sexual consent issues relation to, 123–124, 126
Tinder role within culture of, 114–115, 120, 126, 159
Twitter campaign and modifications around, 11
sexuality. *See* female sexuality
slut labeling
class-based issues around, 46, 48–49, 57, 59–60
hookup culture conflict with, 56, 105, 165n11
Jersey Shore study and, 50–51, 53–55, 60, 62, 156–157
popular feminism and, 46

prude labeling conflicts with, 53–54, 55
racial identity and, 46, 47–48, 49, 58
sexual agency and, 15, 46, 54–55, 60, 62, 156–157
sexual double standard and, 15, 46, 156–157
social change
ability to understand steps to, 71–72
breakthrough feminist moments and, 12, 72
individual focus over collective efforts for, 1–2, 7, 12, 15, 67, 68–69, 74, 128, 139, 157
popular feminism and structural, 1–2
transgressive ideologies necessary to create, 19
social media. *See also* Facebook
censorship, 7, 9
#MeToo as catalyst on, 2
story elaboration on, 9, *10*, 11
Wikipedia network relation to, 132–133
Yik Yak illustration of media-ready feminism in, 7, *8*, 9, *10*, 11
socioeconomic class. *See also* working-class women
breakthrough feminism impacted by focus on affluent, 155
Desperate Housewives focus on affluent, 72, 93, 99
everyday sexism relation to, 60–62, 65, 161–162
female sexuality and, 47, 48–49, 57–60, 62–64, 157, 164n2
gender inequality focus relation to, 12–13, 16–17
generational differences relation to, 92

socioeconomic class *(continued)*
  hookup culture views relation to, 62–63
  Jersey Shore focus groups and, 50, 51
  Jersey Shore portrayals of, 49, 51–52, 64–65
  media coverage bias on, 12–13, 16–17, 69
  media-ready feminism focus relation to, 12–13, 64
  #MeToo movement and, 1
  motherhood and, 69, 72
  norm of avoiding explicit language about, 52
  sexual double standard relation to, 46, 51, 58, 59–65, 161
  sexual freedom differences relation to, 57–64, 157
  slut labeling relation to, 46, 48–49, 57, 59–60
  work-family balance relation to, 16–17, 68, 69, 70, 72, 76–77, 78, 79, 83, 91, 92–96, 98–99, 157–158, 161
Spar, Deborah, 96–97
Staal, Lesley, 96–97
Sugar Baby, 117

Thomas, Clarence, 2
Time, 2
Tinder
  billboard, *100*, 101
  college students use of, 103, 109–113, 125
  crude sexual content objections to, 118
  as ego boost, 110–111, 113
  everyday sexism and, 17–18
  female empowerment and, 102, 111–112, 124, 125
  "game" approach and impacts with, 109–112, 114, 120, 125
  gender inequalities around, 113, 125
  LGBTQ+ community and, 116–117, 159
  media-ready feminism and, 103, 109, 113–115, 117–118, 120
  misogyny and, 112, 113
  popular feminism ethos and, 17–18, 102, 111, 117–118, 120, 124
  racial identity and, 111, 117–118, 159
  serious relationships found with, 113
  sexual agency contradictions with, 17–18, 102–103, 113–115, 154
  sexual pressures and consent conflicts with, 59, 102–103, 113–115, 120, 124, 126, 159
  sexual violence culture and, 114–115, 120, 126, 159
  terms of service, 101–102
  for white cisgender heterosexual users compared to nonnormative users, 111, 117–120, 125
transgender. *See* LGBTQ+ community
Tripodi, Francesca (works), 7, 67, 117, 119, 125, 149, 159, 166n2, 166n6, 167n6
Trump, Donald, 14, 19
Twitter, 11

virginity, 43–44, 166n2

Wade, Lisa, 48, 104, 105, 115
Weinstein, Harvey, 2, 123
WhatCulture, 28
white supremacists, 1, 159, 161
white women
  breakthrough feminism impacted by focus on affluent, 155
  Desperate Housewives focus on affluent, 72, 93, 99
  hookup culture use for, 111, 117–120, 124

media coverage bias on, 12–13, 16–17, 69
#MeToo movement focus on affluent, 1
Monroe and sexual stereotypes of, 48–49, 164n2
popular feminism focus on cisgender heterosexual, 6, 11–12, 68, 155
second-wave feminism focus on cisgender heterosexual, 5, 51, 65
Tinder use for minority compared with, 111, 117–120, 159
work-family balance for affluent, 12–13, 16–17, 68, 70, 72, 77–78, 83, 165n3
Wikipedia, 166nn1–2, 168nn23–25
bots role in editing, 135, 167n8
credibility creation, 142
culture of exclusion with, 133–136
deletions and discrimination on, 142–150, 160, 168n26, 168nn21–22
edit-a-thons as illustration of media-ready feminism, 18, 128, 130, 135–136, 138–141, 151
edit-a-thons function and logistics, 127–130, 132–133, 135, 167n7, 167nn9–10
edit-a-thons rise and evolution, 128–130
efforts for combating discrimination and harassment, 150–151, 160
everyday sexism and, 18, 128, 130, 131–132, 135–136, 139–140, 146–147, 151, 160
"Five Pillars," 142–143, 167n15
gender inequalities and discrimination with, 18, 127–129, 132, 135–136, 139–151, 153–154, 160
gendered language and content, 129

interface impacting diversity on, 130–134
LGBTQ+ content, 130
neutral point of view policy and realities on, 143, 145
patriarchal culture with, 18, 129, 144
quality-control standards and justifications, 142–143, 148–149, 150
racial identity and discrepancies around, 132, 141, 143–145, 149–150, 151, 168n26
reach and scope of, 128
sexual harassment and women editors on, 136–138, 150–151, 160, 167n11
social media ties for editors of, 132–133
toxic spaces on, 140–141
username issues for women editors of, 136–142, 160, 167n11
Women Organized Against Sexual Harassment (WOASH), 2, 163n1
Wonder Women (Spar), 97
work-family balance
assertive women and, 84–86, 97–98, 158, 166n8
cultural discourses around, 67–68
Desperate Housewives and study of, 15–16, 72–99
everyday sexism and, 71, 85, 86, 90
generational differences on, 71, 76–86, 96–97
housework tasks and, 67–68
Huffman college admissions scandal and, 16–17
immigrant experience of, 79
as individual over collective issues, 12, 15, 67, 68–69, 74, 157
intensive motherhood ideology and, 69–70, 71, 72, 75, 91, 99

work-family balance *(continued)*
   methods and focus group behind study of, 75–76
   mother-daughter communication about, 78, 79, 80, 94–95, 96, 158
   neoliberal feminism assumptions about, 15–16, 73
   popular feminism assumptions about, 15–16, 68–69, 70, 72, 75, 76, 78, 83, 90, 92, 95, 97
   racial identity and, 16–17, 68, 69, 72, 78, 79, 80, 86, 91, 92–96, 98–99, 157, 158
   second-wave feminism and, 69, 95–96
   socioeconomic class relation to, 16–17, 58, 68, 69, 70, 72, 76–77, 78, 79, 83, 91, 92–96, 98–99, 157–158, 161
   television shows portraying, 69–70
   for white affluent women, 12–13, 16–17, 68, 70, 72, 77–78, 83, 165n3
   women bargaining with, 77–78
Workin' Moms, 70, 86, 99, 165n2
working-class women
   childrearing for, 69
   college sexual experiences and, 47
   Game of Thrones views from, 37
   independence of, 63
   Monroe and sexual stereotypes of, 48–49, 164n2
   sexual double standard for, 46, 51, 60–63
   sexual freedom for, 57–58, 60–61, 62–64, 157
   slut labeling and, 46
   work-family balance for, 69, 70, 78, 91, 98–99
workplace
   Desperate Housewives illustration of patriarchal, 90–91
   discrimination, changes in, 97
   discrimination, generational differences on, 80–81, 96
   discrimination for African American women, 93
   divorced women experience of, 80–81, 82
   generational differences in, 82–83
   sexual harassment in, 71, 82–83
   survival mode for women in, 82
   women competition in, 74, 81–82
   women leadership in, assumptions about, 74, 81

Yik Yak, 7, 8, 9, *10*, 11

www.ingramcontent.com/pod-product-compliance
Lightning Source LLC
Chambersburg PA
CBHW020653230426
43665CB00008B/423